ALONG THE DINGO FENCE

ALONG THE DINGO FENCE

PHILIP HOLDEN

Hodder & Stoughton
SYDNEY AUCKLAND LONDON TORONTO

To Carol Colson

First published in 1991
by Hodder & Stoughton (Australia) Pty Limited
ACN 000 884 855
10–16 South Street, Rydalmere, NSW, 2116.

National Library of Australia Cataloguing-in-Publication entry

Holden, Philip, 1938– .
    Along the dingo fence.
    ISBN 0 340 53600 4.
    1. Country life – Australia, Central. I. Title.
994.2063

Typeset in 11pt Times by G.T. Setters Pty Limited, Kenthurst
Printed in Hong Kong by Colorcraft Ltd.

Contents

Author's Note

The 'Dingo Fence' is the common name given to a 5,309-kilometre dog-proof barrier found within three States of eastern Australia. Each State handles its specific length of fence separately and, in an official capacity, refers to it by a different name. So in Queensland they call it the 'Barrier Fence', in New South Wales the 'Border Fence', and in South Australia the 'Dog Fence'. The length of each section is:

Barrier Fence:	2,500 km
Border Fence:	584 km
Dog Fence:	2,225 km

To make it easier for the reader to follow the sequence of events: the research and fieldwork for this book took place from June to December 1989.

In July 1989, using a hired Toyota Landcruiser, I visited the Border Fence, including Quinyambie station in South Australia. Back in Sydney, the next two months flew by while I researched various aspects relating to the Dingo Fence and also the dingo itself. Much thought, too, was given how to best carry out the rest of the fieldwork.

Once October came around, I set off in my own Subaru four-wheel-drive station wagon and travelled to the Barrier Fence. Ending up on Bulloo Downs station in the south-west of Queensland, I found myself back on the Border Fence, where, as luck would have it, I caught up with several people I'd been unable to meet previously.

And in November 1989, I carried on to South Australia and its Dog Fence and thus rounded off a journey that had embraced three States. A trip from Sydney to Perth, in December 1989, also proved a more than useful exercise.

Without the generous assistance of the following individuals, to whom I extend heartfelt appreciation, this book would never have been published.

So in New South Wales, I thank:

Doug Pearson (Western Lands Commissioner), Allan McMasters, Fran Goodrich, Paddy and Beryl Barlow, Brian Arnould, Brian and Belinda Wren, Bob and Norma Clarke, Allan Littlejohn, Greg and Maxine Beaton, Lenny, Gay, Kenny, and Sharon Dixon, Rod Belville, Lindsay, Isibel, and Roy Russell, Robert Scobie, Paul Jennings, Col Pierce, Geoff Smith, and Terry Hickey.

In Queensland:

Don Webster, Peter Merrell, Jerry Stanley, Cameron Turner, Neville Maunder, Dave Reibelt, Charlie and Peter Russell, Joe, Nancy, Scott and Neville Geiger,

Howard Jensen, Steve Picone, Brian and Gay Tully, Don and June Compagnoni, Ron and Barry Phillips, Bruce Scott, Philip and Adele Hughes, Simon Read, John Bird, Shaun Core, Shirley Clifford, and Libby Stevens (Executive Officer, Maranoa Graziers Association).

Pressing on to South Australia:

Jimmy Staker, Aub Ali, Bill Edwards, Bryan Lock, Donald Byrnes, Louis Davidson, Colin and Keith Greenfield, Ray, Peter, and Bill Wardle, Mick Dobbins, Bill, Hazel, and Malcolm Mitchell, Eric Oldfield, Neville and Pam Barnes, Mick and Audrey Sheehan, and Bryan Nash.

And in Western Australia:

Peter Coyle (Agriculture Protection Board of Western Australia).

For the reader's clarification, the term 'inside the fence' means the protected zone—that is, sheep country, whereas 'outside the fence' means the opposite—in effect, mostly cattle country where dingoes have unlimited free range.

Philip Holden
April 1991

PART ONE

TO SET THE SCENE

1
Arrival Of The Dingo

A warrigal will pick your bones within six moons.

– Aboriginal curse

Quinyambie station
South Australia
July 1989
Early evening.

From amidst scattered timber the tawny-coated dingo watched me intently. It did not appear afraid—wary, more like. In reality it had nothing to fear. All I was armed with was a Nikon F-301 equipped with a 300mm telephoto lens. But of course there was no way the wild dog could have known that.

Again the dingo moved off as before, at a fast trot. And again, it travelled only a short distance before stopping to see what I was up to.

We would keep up this game of follow-the-leader—with the dingo only allowing me to get so close before taking off—for at least 20 minutes before it finally tired of it and at a lope vanished over a sun-burnished sandhill glowing as though on fire.

By this time I had already seen a number of dingoes on this particular property. On this occasion, however, I had deliberately gone out by myself in the hope of actually capturing one on film.

As I tramped towards the Toyota, I reflected with pleasure on the dingo I had just seen. A splendid-looking animal by any yardstick. Like the more recently introduced rabbit, it had appeared entirely at home in this setting. Yet there was a time, admittedly long ago, when there were no dingoes in this country.

After studying the dingo for several years, Professor N.W.G. Macintosh of Sydney University concluded that, 'Its ancestry and affinities remain enigmatic'. Considered its most likely ancestor, is the Indian plains wolf. The dingo is unique to Australia and is grouped, if somewhat loosely, with a number of primitive dogs ranging through northern Africa, south-eastern Asia, and New Guinea.

The dingo most closely resembles the Indian pariah (meaning 'outcast') dog. Indeed, there is a striking similarity between dingo skeletons and those of prehistoric dogs (dating from 3,500 to 4,000 years ago) found in India from Burzahom in Kashmir through to the Indus civilisation city of Harappa.

In biological terms the dingo is a recent arrival to Australia. Thus the Aborigines, who have been here about 50,000 years, did not introduce him (as is commonly thought) to this country. Nevertheless some Aboriginal Dreamtime stories in the east told of the early Sky Gods travelling with a warrigal (or dingo) for company. The dances of the Victoria River people in the Northern Territory, however, depict the dingo's arrival by sea.

Today, the most commonly held belief is that the dingo arrived in Australia by sea from South-East Asia, either as a semi-domesticated companion or an object of trade—perhaps both. The likely period of arrival ranges from 4,000 to 5,000 years ago. In this period extensive voyages took place throughout the Indonesian Archipelago. Undoubtedly these seafarers would have traded with coastal Aborigines in the Northern Territory; they may have even attempted to settle here, losing their dogs.

So precisely when the dingo arrived here is unknown. The lack of dingoes in Tasmania indicates quite clearly that they were not in southern Australia when the last Ice Age ended about 12,000 years ago. Until then the mainland and Tasmania were linked by a causeway, by which, presumably, the Aborigines reached the island. In doing so, they became the first Tasmanians.

The oldest dingo fossil found to date and confirmed as genuine was discovered in Madura Cave on the Nullarbor Plain. It is estimated to be 3,450 years old. Another dingo fossil, this time 3,230 years old, was unearthed in an Aboriginal midden at Wombah on the north coast of New South Wales. But by far the most significant discovery of a dingo fossil was that made by D.J. Mulvaney in 1960 at Fromms Landing on the lower Murray River in South Australia. In near-perfect condition, it was reassembled by the previously mentioned Professor N.W.G. Macintosh, and judged to be that of a male aged about 18 weeks with 'precisely the same proportions as those of present-day dingoes'.

The dingo's vital role in Aboriginal mythology and ritual is well known. But given the unpredictable nature of the dingo, and the fact that it reverts quickly to a wild state, it would seem that whatever hold the Aborigines had on it was tenuous. So either in a wild state or as a semi-domesticated creature living with a nomadic race the dingo spread rapidly throughout Australia.

The impact of the dingo's arrival in this country would eventually prove devastating for two carnivores—the thylacine (Tasmanian tiger) and the Tasmanian devil. Until then they foraged without harassment. But in competition for food neither was a match for the new arrival, which has the strength and fighting prowess to defeat a full-grown alsatian.

Today, the dingo is considered directly responsible for the demise of both these speices on the mainland, the thylacine not less than 2,000 years ago, and the Tasmanian devil about 400 years ago. Dingo-free Tasmania still proved a happy hunting ground for the thylacine in pre-white settlement times. And all went well for it until the white man arrived and brought with him domestic animals. Sheep, for instance. The thylacine discovered it liked the taste of mutton. A bad mistake. Large-scale hunting saw the eventual end of the thylacine, the last one dying in captivity in 1936.

Meanwhile the Aborigines had begun a long association with the dingo. Tribal mythology in South Australia, for instance, linked hordes of starving dingoes with the arrival of famished people from the interior. In Central Australia the dingo appears in tribal lore associated with secret circumcision and subincision rites.

Contrary to popular belief the Aboriginal hunter, with his matchless tracking skills and incredible ability with a number of throwing weapons, had little if any time for the dingo as a hunting companion. The dingo was at best unreliable...and as for actually training one! H. Basedow in his 1925 publication *The Australian Aboriginal* had this to say about the Pitjantjatjara people of Central Australia and their relationship with camp dingoes:

> A native just holds the unruly mob around him for company's sake; he prefers to rely on his own skill and instinct when hunting, and rarely allows his dogs to go with him; in fact, there seems to be little inclination on the part of the dogs to accompany the chase with the master.

In camp, dingoes were generally treated with affection, but their material welfare was of no real consequence which is probably why many joined their wild counterparts. A shortage of food was a problem for tribes living in desert regions. Dogs were fortunate to receive any scraps at all.

The women would feed captured pups at breast, or even carry them wrapped around their waists. But, later, they had no qualms whatsoever about breaking their forelegs. Totally dependent now, camp dogs for life, most of these unfortunate animals were soon in a wretched condition, starving, and flea-ridden. They were in effect living blankets: animated bed-warmers for the feet, ideal to nestle against when temperatures fell to near freezing. The more crippled dogs one had on hand, the warmer one slept.

In camp, dingoes also came in handy to warn of strangers approaching—rival tribesmen, say. During periods of hardship they also figured on the menu. A dog patted affectionately on the head in the afternoon might well be filling the patter's belly a few hours later. Basic survival. The Aborigines hunted wild dingoes of course. Pups were eagerly sought after. Baked pup, done to a turn in red-hot coals, was a particular culinary delight.

May was the time when these particular hunts were carried out. They were discussed and planned for weeks ahead. The areas where the bitches had their dens were carefully noted. Ceremonial observances were carried out, the heliacal rising of the Pleiades group of stars (known as the Kungkarungkara) corresponding with the time of the actual kill.

But not all pups captured were eaten; some, as already mentioned, were suckled by the women until they could fend for themselves. It does appear as though depleted stocks of camp dingoes were replaced each year with those captured in the wild—an annual harvesting, if you like.

In 1890, C. Lumholtz published *Among Cannibals*, an account of four years' travels in Australia and of the camp life of Queensland Aborigines. Of the camp dingo, he wrote:

> It is very useful to the natives, for it has a keen sense and traces every kind of game; it never barks, and hunts less wildly than our dogs, but very rapidly, frequently capturing game on the run. Sometimes it refuses to go any further and its owner then has to carry it on his shoulders, a luxury of which it is very fond.
>
> Its master never strikes, but merely threatens it. He caresses it like a child, eats the fleas off it, and then kisses it on the snout.

To capture 'game on the run' these camp dogs were obviously well fed, far fitter than those found elsewhere. It must be stressed, however, that the main game they hunted was the tree kangaroo, a creature so ponderous on the ground that even a starving camp dog of the desert regions could have caught one before it climbed to safety.

Further evidence of affection held for camp dogs by Queensland Aborigines may be found in the diary of a Major Lockyer who in 1828 visited Stradbroke Island:

> The attachment of these people to their dogs is worthy of notice. I was very anxious to get one of the wild native breed of black colour, a very handsome puppy, which one of the men had in his arms. I offered him a small axe for it; his companions urged him to take it, and he was about to do so, when he looked at the dog and the animal licked his face, which settled the business. He shook his head and determined to keep him.

Interestingly enough, a group of Aborigines reported never to have seen a white man before were found in the Gibson Desert, Western Australia, as recently as 1953. With them were 19 undernourished, skulking dingoes. It was noted that the dogs were fondled but rarely patted. To survive they either scavenged in camp or hunted further afield for very small game, such as mice and lizards. Not only were they not used for hunting; they were chased back to camp should one or more show an inclination to tag along. The only practical use made of them was as warmers on cold nights.

2
Profile Of A Dingo

The dingo is probably the only pure-bred dog in the world—that is, directly descended from a single race of wolf.
                    – The Living World of Animals, 1970

Dingo: *Canis familiaris dingo.* Also known as dog (most common term in the outback), wild dog (used rarely), warrigal (specific, I believe, to South Australia's south-east).

Status: Common-to-plentiful outside the main dingo-proof fence and various vermin fences in Western Australia. Good numbers also found in various parts of the Snowy Mountains and in the high forested country of northern New South Wales. The general view of graziers the author came into contact with in the three States concerned with the dingo fence was that, outside it, they had never been more plentiful.

Physical Description: The dingo is a medium-sized dog. Of 267 dingoes trapped in Victoria, the average length (nose to tail) was 137.2 cm. The male has a shoulder height of 55 cm. He is slightly bigger all round than the female. A good-sized male dingo will weigh around 20 kg. If much heavier than this, it is likely to be a cross-breed.

The most common colouring is yellow or pale sand with white points. A white 'bib' or chest patch is common, so are white feet. Such dingoes typify the species and make up around 86.6 per cent of the entire population.

Dingoes can be white. This is considered rare. More common are black ones with tan markings or points. There are also black dingoes. Some early explorers recorded seeing black native dogs, proving conclusively that this colour, thought by some as un-dingo like, was not a result of interbreeding with domestic dogs. In the high country of Victoria a dingo sometimes has a pleasing reddish-gold coat. Any variations to any of these colourings are almost certainly the result of cross-breeding.

In comparison with domestic dogs, dingoes have a much broader head and larger teeth—particularly the canine teeth. Dingoes are characterised by dense hair (particularly in cold winter weather in, for example, the New England region of northern New South Wales), long muzzles, a bushy, even brush-like tail (invariably with a white tip), erect ears, and strong, non-retractable claws.

Because of its ancestry, the dingo cannot bark. It howls.

Reproduction: Unlike domesticated dogs, dingoes breed but once a year. Normally they do so from late March through to, say, late July. Exceptions occur of course. Gestation takes 63 days, identical to that of domestic dogs. Pups are weaned at two months. They may be abandoned by their parents at about six months or remain in the family group for up to one year. Why such a variation is unclear; there is a possible link with population densities and the availability of food, and there is known to be a high mortality among the four to seven puppies in a litter.

Dingoes are sexually mature at one year.

Diet: The dingo is a top hunter, a flexible opportunist. His motto may well be: If it moves eat it! As a survivor he is, like the equally adaptable feral pig, capable of scraping a living where other animals would perish. This also explains why dingoes are able to survive over such a broad and diverse range of conditions (and climates) in Australia.

Various types of kangaroos, wallaroos and wallabies make up in excess of 50 per cent of the average dingo's intake. Good choice—lean, fat-free meat. It is the red kangaroo which inhabits so much land outside the Dingo Fence that is most often taken as food. This has increased at least tenfold since Europeans opened up the arid interior and brought underground water surging to the surface. Before there had been nothing but varying seasonal rain and, in times of drought, rain might not fall for years. This made vast new areas suitable for red kangaroos. Millions of red kangaroos. The dingo has not been known to object to that.

Europeans also unwittingly made sure of the dingo's survival by introducing that most incredible of animals, the humble rabbit. The spread of this species, and the speed with which it colonised new areas, was awesome. A dingo could survive on rabbit alone—again, lean, fat-free meat. Opportunities to do so in the 1990s are likely to be plentiful.

Make no mistake about it, dingoes are also partial to the animal on the other side of Australia's national emblem: the emu. They are hunted down with enthusiasm. Likewise pigs and wombats. The poor old fox cops it too.

A little-known fact is that in the Maryvale Creek District, some 130 km north of Charters Towers, Queensland, dingoes quite frequently dine on venison. The deer in question are chital, the first species introduced into this country in the early 1880s, and restricted to a number of private properties in this district.

The free-ranging dingo does not object to eating lizards, hares, rodents, grubs, and birds if necessary. Soft fruit may be eaten for dessert. They are supreme scavengers. Look for them along beaches and around rubbish tips. As for domestic animals, we'll look at that later on.

Social Structure: Most field researchers have found dingoes to be rather solitary animals which come together at waterholes and to breed. Again, they may operate in small, tightly-knit family groups. Among these animals will be dominant females and males. They may link up during the day; they may hunt together. Typical year-round activities could read like this:

Above A pure-bred dingo is a handsome animal
Below Among scattered timber on Quinyambie station, South Australia

Above Typical red, sandy dingo
country

Right The wedge-tailed eagle,
Australia's largest bird of prey, rules
supreme in the outback

Below This Australian cattle dog's
dingo heritage is unmistakable

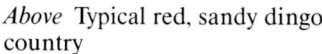

Above Boundary rider Rod Belville looks across the Border Fence to South Australia

Left Boundary rider, Brian Arnould with an original wooden post from the Queensland government's 1890 rabbit fence

Below left Dingo scalps drying in the sun

Below Dingo tracks — and urine stains on the log — indicate a likely place to set a trap

Above HQ of the Wild Dog Destruction Board is in Broken Hill
Below Allan McMasters, Secretary of the Wild Dog Destruction Board

December/January/February
Groups split up within home range. Casual contact continued. Young dogs may assist older ones.

March/April/May
Extensive 'howling' and fighting when groups merge at mating time. Dominance established. 'Lesser' animals, such as young males, may leave.

June/July/August
Pups in den.

September/October/November
Pups weaned. They begin moving around with adults, learning basic hunting skills. Pups on own no later than 12 months. Many of them, especially males, seek territories of their own, sometimes on what might be termed the 'inside' of the Dingo Fence.

Home Territory: This varies. In forested parts of northern New South Wales, the high country of New England, the so-called 'home range' is reckoned at between 25 and 40 square kilometres. In desert country in Western Australia, this may increase from 70 to 125 square kilometres. Whatever its size, the home range has recognisable, distinct topographical features: the edge of an escarpment, a distinct formation of rocks or boulders, a leading ridge in forested terrain, a watering place.

It seems that some dingoes live out their lives in a comparatively restricted area. But whether their territory is large or small, they move around a lot, edgy, checking it out. Are other dingoes around? And what of man, the ultimate enemy? He is to be feared above all else. Most activity takes place in the late evening, overnight, and in the early morning when the food source is up and about.

In a 24-hour period, while hunting and patrolling on regular 'beats', dingoes rest for perhaps nine hours. Which might explain, with its diet, why one never sees an overweight dingo. They are either 'trim' or lean to a point of gauntness.

Enemies In The Wild: Wedge-tailed eagles. They normally hunt in pairs. Adult dingoes are sometimes killed but, more especially, younger animals. We can safely presume that a six-month-old dingo, recently abandoned for a variety of reasons, would make easy pickings for Australia's largest bird of prey.

Saltwater crocodiles. In tropical parts of Western Australia, the Northern Territory and Queensland, they account for a number of dingoes. Which does not mean the unfortunate dingoes are unwary. The saltwater crocodile is a king among predators and strikes swiftly and unexpectedly.

Snakes. A python would have little difficulty in taking a small to even medium-sized dingo. A few dingoes may also die of snake bite.

Goanna lizards. A good-sized lizard would have little trouble accounting for an unwary pup in the open, and an unprotected den, containing pups, would be difficult for these skilled predators to resist.

In Summary: All wildlife has value. Without wildlife the world we know would not exist.

Almost all people who come into contact with dingoes, even graziers who have over the years suffered enormous stock losses, admire them. Rightly so. There is much to admire. As Australia's largest land predators, they play a major role in maintaining the natural, and very delicate, ecosystem. Natural? The dingo has been here long enough to be considered a native.

Organisations like the Australian Native Dog Foundation in eastern Australia, and more general groups such as Friends of the Earth and the World Wildlife Fund consider that dingoes have what is termed 'existence value'. One such value for non-hunting activities is, of course, nature study, often linked with wildlife photography. The dingo in either case is never less than a fascinating subject.

3

With A Generous Measure Of Dingo Blood

The dingo is popularly presented as a savage, ruthless killer with a nature which is essentially predatory, cruel, and cowardly, but I think it is possible to say conclusively that the dingo is, if anything, less savage, less cruel, and less cowardly than most other breeds of dog if faced with the same conditions.
— Professor N.W. G. Macintosh, Challis Professor of Anatomy, University of Sydney

Possibly the first white man to ever set eyes on a dingo was a Portuguese seaman, Diego de Prado. The year was 1601, and, much to his surprise, he observed it foraging for food on a reef at Thursday Island. Fresh food was probably somewhat limited on board, because he apparently shot and then ate the animal. We may presume he built a fire and cooked it first.

Further observations of dingoes were made in 1623 when the Dutch nagivator, Jan Carstensz, reported seeing great numbers of dogs close to Cape Keer-Weer, on the west coast of Cape York peninsula.

The first Englishman to set foot on Australian soil was Captain William Dampier, navigator and buccaneer. In 1688, on a beach at Shark Bay, Western Australia, the tracks of a large dog were observed. Eleven years later, Dampier returned to the same coastline. At what today is Roebuck Bay, he would record that his men had seen 'two or three Beasts like hungry wolves, lean like so many skeletons, being nothing but skin and bone'.

Then in 1770 off Queensland's north-eastern coast (where Cooktown now stands), one of Captain Cook's midshipmen came back after going ashore with the exciting news that he had seen a 'wolf'. As was his way, Cook noted the event in his meticulously kept journal.

One thing we can be quite sure of is that when the first European explorers tracked across Australia's vastness there was not a single habitat that the dingo did not occupy. (While searching for the 'legendary' inland sea in 1828, Charles Sturt recorded seeing dingoes, whose 'emaciated bodies standing between us and the moon were the most wretched objects in the brute creation.')

Merino sheep arrived at Port Jackson with the First Fleet in January 1788. In excess of 100 animals are thought to have survived the passage from Cape Town, South Africa, where, on behalf of his Government, Captain Arthur Phillip had purchased 44 sheep and his officers, or at least some of them, had acquired the rest. The unfortunate animals must have wondered what was happening to them, for, no sooner had they been turned out to feed on wonderful fresh grass, than five of their number were cut down by a lightning bolt. Worse, by 1 May only 29 of the original number survived.

The native dogs, which skulked around in large numbers, were given as the reason for the loss. Possibly this was true. However, Captain Phillip, ever astute, did not rule out the strong possibility that some of his men—crew, not officers—weren't above doing something positive to supplement their meagre daily fare. Nevertheless, rightly or wrongly, the dingo has been taking the blame ever since!

By 1880 about 6,000 sheep could be found around Sydney Town. They were protected from wild dogs during the day by armed shepherds and guarded at night by watchmen, also presumably armed.

In 1813 the formidable barrier that the Blue Mountains presented to opening up the vast land beyond was overcome. Once broken in it would prove ideal country for sheep. Dingoes had managed very nicely there until this time. They would fare even better once the woolly-backed animals arrived in force.

The increasing notoriety of the dingo resulted in 1830 of an Act being instigated for 'abating the nuisance occasioned by the great number of Dogs which are loose in the Streets of the Towns of Sydney Parramatta Liverpool and Windsor in the Colony of New South Wales'. A bounty of two shillings would be paid for the tail. So for the first time the dingo achieved 'outlaw' status.

At this time the Australian Agricultural Company owned a number of properties out on the frontiers of the ever mushrooming pastoral land. Each was under the control of a manager and the flocks ranged from 300 to 500 animals. The dingo problem again necessitated a 24-hour watch being kept. The armed shepherds no doubt delighted in killing dingoes; each one, after all, was worth two shillings to them, perhaps some compensation for what was an isolated existence and an occupation not without dangers. More than one shepherd was speared by Aborigines in emphatic protest against the invasion of their sacred lands.

In 1833 the Dog Act was extended for a further three years. The Dog Act of 1852 took an even harder line than the one that had been in force for 22 years. It was directly aimed at the dingo itself, to 'encourage the destruction of native dogs'.

Among the upper classes of Sydney in the 1830s it was considered quite stylish and modish to have as a pet a native dog. As puppies—fat-bellied, cuddly, playful, responsive—they were delightful. An adult dingo, however, was an entirely different proposition. It was intractable, unresponsive to commands and far from being a well-trained house pet.

It is somewhat ironic, I think, that by this time the Aborigines had largely cast aside the dingo in favour of European breeds. The Aborigines knew what the score was all right. They'd had at least 3,600 years to find out!

Off the leash, the so-called pet dingo, perhaps not overly fond of being called 'Rover' or 'Butch' or any other name his owners might hang on him, proved troublesome. It was a case of 'Kids beware! Horsemen look out!' And as for cats... we'll leave that to what one disillusioned dingo owner of the time had to say:

> He was especially fond of cats: I have known him to eat six in one morning. People thought some new disease must have broken out, cats got so scarce in the suburb where I had him...
>
> I had one vocalist in this line who kept half a terrace vacant for six months, till the landlord bought him in self-defence. It was the pianos made him so bad. Ours was a musical suburb, and no dingo can tolerate that.

The practice of keeping dingoes as pets in Sydney was, naturally enough, rather shortlived.

In this same period, a cattle drover named Timmins was having difficulties with his working dogs of an English breed called Smithfield. They liked to bark—unfortunately too much for the drover's charges en route from Bathurst to Sydney. This soon had the unfortunate result, for Timmins at least, of turning a docile mob of cattle into an unruly one. Also, the dogs, bred for a much cooler climate, were soon reacting badly to the heat.

Maybe on the back of his horse, or perhaps brewing up at his camp fire, the drover considered the possibility of crossing one of his dogs with a dingo. For one thing, a dingo did not bark and with luck that might hold true of the resulting progeny. Again, a dingo, despite falling out of favour with the in-crowd in Sydney Town, was obviously intelligent. It went without saying that they could tolerate heat like a 'native'. So why not? the drover questioned himself. Certainly it was worth trying.

The offspring far exceeded the drover's expectations. They were (wonderfully) silent, eager to obey, and quite fearless, but, somewhat unfortunately, over-zealous heelers (nipping the ankles, hocks, or lower back legs of any beast reluctant to move). Of rather chunky build, a mottled grey in colour, they became known, and deservedly, by the formidable name of 'Timmins' Biters'!

The drover continued to ply his hardy trade back and forth between Bathurst and Sydney. Many of those he encountered along the way were impressed with this entirely new breed of cattledog, which, amazingly, did not bark but more than made up for it by heeling ferociously. There was a steady demand for whatever puppies Timmins' Biters produced.

Much the same thing happened later when a cattleman called Hall, faced with much the same problems as Timmins, crossed his smooth-haired blue merle collies (imported from Scotland in 1840) with a dingo. This particular type of collie was, and is, considered the élite of that particular lineage.

The resulting progeny, born on a station in the Muswellbrook district (Hunter Valley, New South Wales), proved that Hall had not made a mistake with this perhaps unlikely combination. They too were silent, swift and eager to take commands, tireless, and, best of all, worked cattle so well and so instinctively that they may well have been born to it. Which in effect they had been. Not as severe in the heel-nipping department as Timmins' dogs, they became known as 'Hall's Heelers'.

As the fame of Hall's cattledogs spread, the demand for them increased. But like Timmins' breed, Hall's dogs had one big fault. They snapped at the stockmen's horses. Somewhat disconcerting at high speed. This was put down to the 'dingo' blood rather than the other breed used by Hall.

Brothers Jack and Harry Bagworth of Sydney decided to correct this fault by crossing a dalmatian with one of Hall's cattle dogs. No random choice this: in Britain the dalmatian was used to guard stables for the simple reason that, quite apart from being a first-class minder, it genuinely liked horses. The dalmatian's strongly protective nature would be a bonus on the frontier.

So a dalmatian and a Hall's Heeler coupled, successfully. This altered the blue mottles to speckles and, to Jack and Harry Bagworth's deep satisfaction, eliminated any inclination to have a go at a stockhorse. Fortunately, the progeny retained all the desirable features.

The strongly 'protective' nature was particularly appreciated by an itinerant horseman who, perhaps in town to pick up supplies or to find out if a job was going in the district, could leave his horse and packhorse with confidence, safe under the ever-watchful eye of his home-grown cattledog.

Later, the kelpie breed was added giving the dog even more 'gut' instinct when working cattle. Many from this line have reddish coats.

By the 1890s the Australian cattledog was a recognised breed. It is incorrectly called a Queensland blue heeler or Queensland cattledog. In colour it may be grey or red. It is loyal, industrious, friendly to non-threatening strangers, but, in its favour, not as friendly as, for instance, a labrador is. In stock camps, on droving trails, working either cattle or sheep, the breed has won lasting fame. It may in fact be considered the best cattledog in the world.

Way out back, the Australian cattledog is the very best mate of all. In a far-flung land, where perhaps mateship still counts for more than anything else, the real value of the breed cannot be overlooked. Neither can the more than generous drop of dingo blood which in red or tan-coloured animals is unmistakable.

To return to the early 1860s. By now a new and highly-potent weapon had been introduced to deal with dingoes. Strychnine poison.

Soon—by 1863 certainly—large-scale poisoning operations had had an enormous impact on the overall dingo population. Indeed, one could hardly observe a dingo south of the Murrumbidgee. Now, with the number-one predator largely off the scene the delicate balance of nature, evolved over thousands of years, was upset. A lot of the animal populations which until then had, say, been 'manageable' exploded in numbers and spread like a grass fire in high summer. So kangaroos and wallabies increased tenfold. Smaller, lesser known animals such as bilbies, rat-kangaroos, bandicoots, and pademelons became common. Perplexed graziers, until then highly relieved to have got the dingo off their backs, began to wonder what the real answer was when confronted by 'roos in their thousands competing directly (and actually winning) with their sheep for grass. Maybe the dingo had a place in the overall scheme of things?

It was of course only temporarily outclassed. The dingo was soon back. In force.

During the early days of Sydney Town, dingo hunting for sport was popular, one can safely presume, with what we might call the higher classes. It was in fact a pathetic arrangement whereby dingoes, retained in special 'traps' (one was located on George Street), were taken out in sacks or bags on the day of the hunt and liberated when the hunting party, or their dogs, were sighted.

The practice was still carried out in Melbourne in 1871, the year the novelist Anthony Trollope attended the first 'meet' of the season. As many as 250 horsemen, and untold hounds, were on hand for this momentous event, a quarter of which (the horsemen, naturally) were attired as though in the 'Home Country', in traditional red. There may of course have been a few red-coated dogs mixed in there too.

On reflection, and as it proved, it seemed somewhat ambitious of Trollope to participate. He was grossly overweight, at least 108 kilos. Nevertheless he had mounted up, and was looking particularly involved with what was happening, when the Master of Hounds signalled they were off. To keep the hounds hot on the trail, a 'scent' was dragged through the bush in front of them. Who knows, it may have been the carcass of a dead dingo.

For some time Trollope managed to retain his place but he wasn't up with the front runners when the dingo was set free. He did, however, record what happened: 'The animal was taken alive after two miles. So, appearance was maintained of finding game and hunting game to the end.'

On many stations in the 1870s, doggers were employed full-time. Mostly single men, they were paid 15 shillings a week and, as an incentive, a further 5 shillings a tail.

Once the other colonies achieved statehood (until then the laws of New South Wales applied) they brought in their own laws regarding animal control.

In 1886 the settlers of Port Phillip (later Melbourne) were the driving force behind a five shilling bounty being paid out for the head of a 'native dog'. A year later, an advertisement was published in the *South Australian Government Gazette* which offered a reward for 'dingo scalps'.

In Queensland, the Marsupials Destruction Act of 1 January 1881 established Marsupial Boards and Districts with the function of destroying marsupials by payment of a bonus. The Boards' revenue came from an annual levy on relevant stock owners. The dingo was not overlooked in the Act, which remained in force until 31 December 1884. A bonus of 5 shillings applied where it was concerned.

But, soon, a furry little importation would become an even more urgent problem than the dingo was. Rabbits. By the millions. Rampaging unchecked into the far west of New South Wales from the vast desert regions of South Australia.

Somehow they had to be stopped. If not, graziers faced certain ruin.

4

A Land of Fences

Apart from the creation of the Barrier Fences which prevented the initial invasion of rabbits, Board and private fences, and the general unsuitability of much of the country for rabbit survival, Queensland did not suffer the same devastation as other States.
– Queensland Rural Lands Protection Board, 1986

To protect the grazing country of western New South Wales from hordes of rabbits, a fence was erected along the New South Wales-South Australia border. It ran north from the Murray River to Camerons Corner, a distance of 556 kilometres. Work was mostly carried out by immigrant Irish navvies. The fence was completed in August 1890 at a cost of 23,150 pounds, paid in full by the New South Wales Government.

The new rabbit fence was the responsibility of adjoining landholders. It was inspected on a regular basis by a government official who, upon finding damage, would notify the appropriate persons. Facing potential ruin, the landholders responded with enthusiasm: the fence, after all, was the solution to what had seemed an insurmountable problem. However, the fence had been erected several years too late.

In Queensland too the history of vermin fences goes back to the invasion of rabbits from the south in the 1880s. In 1886 the Government of the State began to build a fence westward from a point 25.6 km west of the Warrego River. By 1891 it stretched to within a few kilometres of Haddon Corner in the far north-east of South Australia. In 1903 it was extended to Mungindi, New South Wales.

In the period from the late 1880s to the early 1900s many runholders in South Australia erected their own vermin-proof fences—mostly to protect their stock from wild dogs. Such enclosed areas generally worked well, especially if armed shepherds were on hand. As the runs gradually expanded, the vermin-fences often linked up to form a more effective barrier. Soon they extended well away from the populated areas into the west, north-west, and north. They more or less came under one control when in 1896 the State Government organised the first Vermin Fenced District. By 1908, about 5,000 km of public fencing had been erected to create a number of State Vermin Fenced Districts. In addition there were some 3,800 km of private fencing.

In Western Australia also numerous private vermin-proof fences were erected. Today's State Barrier Fence—maintained by the Agricultural Protection Board against emu infiltration of grazing lands, but also considered a dingo barrier by runholders whose land adjoins it—follows the line of a government rabbit fence of the 1890s.

In the far west of New South Wales as many as 75 per cent of all properties were owned by finance houses in Sydney. One such station was Connulpie Downs, managed by Harold J. Chambers. He wrote in his diary:

17 March 1900:
Dogs are so bad out in the open country, that I had to bring the wethers into Swamp Paddock, so far have caught ten this month.
27 January 1901:
A number of dog losses amongst the two-tooth wethers, they won't come in to water and are scattered all over the paddock...it is impossible to prevent some of them from doing a perish.
30 November 1902:
Ever since July I have had men on fence repairs, shifting sand and attaching foot-netting, in many places putting new fences on top of old ones. Dogs have been very bad of late.
21 April 1902:
...if the dogs get bad I expect they will have to shepherd them again.
...there are two men trapping and poisoning all around the sheep on Naryilco, Dingera and Greece as well as two men looking after the sheep inside the paddock.
19 May 1902:
Yanko: On my return started shepherding again, not only so as to save the lambs but the ewes as well, at first they were unmolested for three weeks. I am quite satisfied that any number of men could not save the sheep for the dogs are not frightened of you, they won't take baits now that they have found the lambs, and have no regular beat so that they may be trapped.
15 June 1902:
Don't renew the Yanko lease, have secured a good eight by ten paddock at Mount Wood watered by Clifton Bore on the east...
Yanko: the dogger has lately caught nineteen dogs, so you can imagine what would have happened had we not got them in hand. They are being shepherded in two mobs, two men in each mob, who go into water alternative days and feed further out the following day.

By 1893 the rabbit fence on the New South Wales-South Australia border was a disaster; it simply hadn't worked. Once the adjoining runholders had reached that conclusion they saw no point in maintaining it.

The Queensland rabbit fence, however, was maintained by seven boundary riders, each man supplied with three horses. They lived in huts at intervals of 30 miles (48 km), the length of fence each man was responsible for.

Meanwhile, a number of vast stations across the border in South Australia—

Anna Creek, Murnpeowie, Cordillo Downs, each shearing up to 100,000 sheep—had suffered sustained pressure from legions of dingoes no amount of trapping, poisoning or shooting could control. Only one option remained. Surrender to the inevitable and turn to cattle instead. Which is precisely what each of these stations did. Soon, graziers in Queensland adjacent to the rabbit fence found themselves facing the same grim situation. Give up sheep for cattle!

Over the border in New South Wales the situation was no less desperate, as can be seen by the following extract from the 1912 Report of the Western Land Board (now The Western Lands Commission).

> Attention may be directed to the Milparinka Pastures Protection Board District, in which it is observed that during the last few years the number of large stock has increased while sheep have decreased. This fact is particularly noticeable in the returns for the years 1910 and 1911, which show an increase of about 6,000 head of large stock and a fairly gradual decrease—seasons being taken into consideration—of the number of sheep since 1907.
>
> This condition has been brought about by the destruction of sheep by wild dogs, which have been flocking into New South Wales from the cattle country and unoccupied lands in South Australia. For years the sheep owners have been complaining of the ravages of these dogs; some of the holdings have in consequence been converted from sheep into cattle properties, and it became apparent that wool growing would have to give place to a less profitable industry, and that in all probability much of the country would be abandoned if remedial measures were not applied.
>
> Realising the seriousness of the position, the Commissioners made representations to the Government, with the result that the advance of a sum of money has been promised for the purpose of erecting 53 miles of dog-proof fence on part of the boundary between South Australia and this State. It is proposed to increase the rentals of all the holdings benefited, in order to recoup the Government the amount advanced, and also to cover the cost of maintenance of the fence when erected. The Commissioners have the assurance of pastoralists who have experienced the benefit derived from the protection afforded by dog-proof fences that the erection of the barrier referred to will have the desired effect.
>
> It may be mentioned that during the last two years about 4,000 dogs have been returned as destroyed in the Milparinka Pastures Protection District, which is on the South Australian boundary, as against about 1,000 each in the Menindee and Wanaaring districts adjoining.

In this same year, Frank Little was the manager of Mount Wood station on the New South Wales side of the rabbit fence and today a historical part of Sturt National Park. The station carried 31,920 sheep and was a prime target for dingoes which, because much of the fence was in disrepair, had little trouble in residing across the border if they so wished.

As a matter of interest, the station also carried 89 cattle, 120 horses, and

51 camels. Nineteen stationhands were employed, plus a blacksmith. One dogger named Riley was on the payroll and he received 30 shillings per annum as, obviously, a retainer.

In April 1913, Little wrote a letter to his employers:

> The dingo question grows more serious each year. You will see that there were 227,000 sheep on the six places immediately across the border in Queensland seven years ago, and today there are none, dingoes being solely responsible for this retrogression.
>
> The rot stopped at the border fence a considerable time, and then Connulpie went [previously mentioned]. Now we are right up against the dingo-infested country. It's time the Western Lands Commission woke up to their responsibilities, for severe national and personal loss will occur if something is not done.

Little, by all accounts, was the driving force behind a number of equally desperate New South Wales graziers who formed themselves into the Border Fence Trust, to convert the rabbit fence into an effective dingo barrier. With the Queensland Government in full support, the members of the Trust, having levied themselves at 9 shillings per 1,000 acres (404 ha) were all set to go. The converted rabbit fence was now a much higher dingo barrier, the cost being 6,500 pounds. In the wake of its completion, local Pastures Protection Board Directors inspected the fence, meeting up along the way with boundary riders Cope, Craig, McCauley, Abbot, Johnston, and Gordon. They reported that the Border Fence was in good repair.

In 1914, the Governments of New South Wales and South Australia shared expenses to convert the now defunct rabbit fence on their borders along similar lines. The 'contract' stipulated that one mile (1.61 km) of fencing per week be undertaken. The contract was met and the fence linked up with the Queensland section at Cameron Corner in 1917.

For many years Len Kelly was the postmaster at Tibooburra. The Border Fence played a significant part in his life.

> Around 1915 my family left Tibooburra to take up a job boundary riding on the Border Fence, which ran north from Forteville to beyond Cooper's Creek. The section 30 miles/[48 KM] was known as Sandy Soak, and in May, 1917, I was brought into the world by Mrs Penrose, a midwife who was accompanied by the Fence overseer, Gordon Williams. They travelled with packhorses and on that trip she'd also delivered Fred Osmond at Stitz Well and Frank Rankin at Bransby. It was eventually found out that I was born in South Australia, but on Queensland territory, owing to the netting having been shifted over some bad sandhills.

On the New South Wales/South Australia Border Fence (while both States contributed on a 50–50 basis for its upkeep, the South Australian Government accepted full responsibility for maintaining it) life could be considered tough. In that red sandhill country still swarming with rabbits, field staff comprised six boundary riders and one overseer. Unlike their counterparts on the Queensland leg of the Border Fence, who lived in good huts and rode horses, each man was supplied with two camels, one to ride and the other to carry essential items such as fencing materials and camping gear. The base camp was a large tent, erected near a bore. Presumably the turnover in manpower was cause for concern.

In Queensland, the original 1885 bounty of 5 shillings per dingo scalp was increased to 10 shillings in 1897. It dropped back to the previous amount in 1905, but leaped to the unheard-of price of one pound (20 shillings) in 1918. This also applied to the New South Wales side of the Border Fence but, possibly, not State-wide. With so many able-bodied men overseas fighting for King and Country, this kind of incentive was obviously necessary in order to keep control of the dingoes.

So a man could get rich trapping dingoes. A boundary rider on the dingo fence, equipped with traps and armed with a rifle, quite often a lever-action Winchester Model 1892, had every incentive to remain with the job.

5

A Battle Without End

The Board fulfils an essential role in the maintenance of the sheep grazing industry in the Western Division of New South Wales. Experience has shown that this area is not generally suited to the grazing of cattle. To succeed with cattle, softer feed and more abundant water supplies are needed than are generally available in a semi-arid region, such as this. Sheep forage more readily than cattle, and being able to withstand the shortages encountered in the Western Division, their presence there is essential to the optimum economic use of the area. Survival of the sheep industry is, however, dependent upon exclusion of the dingo, for experience has also shown that sheep grazing is not a feasible proposition where dingoes are prevalent.

         – Wild Dog Destruction Board, Broken Hill, formed 1957

Until 1919, the Queensland Government, paid by the Border Fence Trust, continued to maintain its section of the dingo fence. But as its own graziers were gaining no benefits whatsoever from it, they were only too pleased to back out of the arrangement. Consequently the Border Fence became the responsibility of the New South Wales Government. Queensland, however, retained as many as 38 separate Dingo Boards, which paid out bonuses for marsupials, dingoes (still one pound) and foxes.

A terrible drought during this period had turned much of the outback into a gigantic dustbowl. All along the Border Fence the water supply began to run out. Boundary riders had no option but to retreat. Fences deteriorated. Dingoes and kangaroos, demented by lack of water and food, eventually came through the neglected fence in untold droves. In sheep country the results were devastating, as can be ascertained from this abridged extract from 'an appeal to Western Land-Holders' by the Chairman of the Wilcannia Pastoral Protection Board, B.H. Williamson, dated 28 October 1920.

> The various sheep holdings west of the Darling have been fighting the dingo for years—acting as a buffer against his advance into the more closely settled portions of the State. But the severe drought just experienced has had the effect of reducing the number of sheep stations who would have fought and would continue fighting. They are now being converted into cattle runs because it is impossible to keep sheep.

The Wild Dog Destruction Act of 1921 applied to the Western Division of New South Wales only, and provided for the constitution of a Wild Dog Destruction Board 'which shall be a body corporate with perpetual succession and common seal and the Western Lands Commissioner shall be a member and Chairman of the "Board". Members representing the three Pastures Protection Boards and the Pastoralists' Association West Darling shall hold office for three years and be eligible for reappointment and meetings shall be held not less than three months'.
Part III of the Act stated that:

> ...it shall be the duty of the owner, etc., of any land, at his own cost, to destroy all wild dogs on such land. Any member of the Board/or authorised person may enter and remain upon any land at any time to ensure that the requirements of the Act are being carried out and, in the event of failure to destroy wild dogs, the Board may enter upon any land and destroy wild dogs, build dog proof fences and charge the cost of the latter to the holder of the land.

Part V of the Act provided that:

> ...any person who carries, drives or passes any wild dog into the Western Division, obtains payments for scalps not destroyed in the Western Division, leaves open any gate in a dog fence, shall be liable to a penalty not exceeding 200 pounds or imprisonment.

The Act provided for the State Government to make an annual grant of 50,000 pounds. Rates would be collected on all rateable land except in a municipality, village, or town.

After the passing of this Act, the Government established a special deposit account with the Treasury called the Wild Dog Destruction Fund, largely made up of rates collected from landholders in the Western Division of New South Wales. Maximum rate payable was one eighth of a penny per acre. For its part, the Government paid a subsidy equal to one quarter of rates collected.

In the late 1920s dingo scalps were worth 15 shillings in New South Wales and Queensland, possibly the same in South Australia, a staggering two pounds in parts of Western Australia, and down to 5 shillings in the cattle country of the Northern Territory where dingoes abounded. Even though the price for bounties was low in the Territory, a man could still make a good living, even more so if he cashed in his tokens elsewhere as frequently happened.

But in the Northern Territory of 1928 trapping dingoes was not without risk. On Coniston station, for instance, it could be downright dangerous. For while working his trap line there, Fred Brooks was speared to death.

The local lawman, Constable George Murray, was badly shaken by this terrible deed, as were other white men in the district. Some Aborigines obviously had very short memories about what happened to those who foolishly went about using white men for target practice. So Murray formed a well-armed 'punitive' party. They overran two camps 50 km apart. The sudden demise of over 60 Aborigines in that area made dingo trapping a comparatively safe occupation from that time on.

There is a lovely piece in Tom Cole's wonderful *Hell West And Crooked.* Cole came to Australia as a 17-year-old in 1923 and the book follows his adventures as a stockman (ringer), horsebreaker, drover and buffalo hunter. Cole might have written this one especially for me.

Cole, more or less between jobs, arrives in Halls Creek, Western Australia, with 20-odd scalps (as best I can deduce the year is 1930). He tells that the local police officer was 'empowered to receive the scalps from any itinerant trapper and pay him two pounds a scalp. At the end of the transaction his duty was to burn them in front of an independent witness. It was freely rumoured that this procedure was not always carried out; it seemed that a few dogs' scalps could generate a cash flow for quite a long time.' Cole 'supposed' that this was a good thing for the local economy.

So with his precious tokens, Cole turns up at the police station. He describes the sergeant as a 'powerful hunk of a man'.

'G'day, Sergeant,' Cole says cautiously. 'I've got some dogs' scalps for you.'

The law swung around in his chair and fastened a beady eye on the bundle under Cole's arm. 'Ah yes, I've been expecting you; you'd be Tom Cole I s'pose.'

Surprised that the sergeant knew who he was, Cole repeated timidly, 'I've got some dog scalps, Sergeant.'

The police officer's reply was classic: 'Of course you've got some bloody dog scalps, I expected you to have some bloody dog scalps. I'm well aware that you've recently come from the Northern Territory, every bloody ringer who arrives from the Territory lands here with a bundle of scalps and they all died this side of the border. Northern Territory dingoes are the most suicidal dogs in the whole of Australia—they all come to WA to die; I've been here for six years and I've never yet heard of a dingo dying in the Territory.'

Tom Cole cashed his 'warrant' for 22 dingo scalps (tossed in a corner of the room where the above incident took place and not burned in front of an independent witness at the end of the transaction) in a local hotel. A man could buy a lot of booze with 44 pounds and Cole apparently did just that, much to his regret next morning when it came time to saddle up.

Dingo scalps were in many parts of the country as good as ready cash, common currency in many an isolated store. The following account of bartering far from the big smoke appears in Ernestine Hill's 1946 publication *Ports of Sunset.*

> ...'miles' of treacle and 'mobs' of onions, blackfella's hats and whitefella's hats, pack saddles and pump oil and eye lotion, the old earth-floored lean-to is packed with the needs of a thousand square miles, but within its walls real money is rarely seen. Little tobacco tins of rough gold from prospectors, dingo scalps, shin-plaster and a couple of eagle-hawk claws are common currency. You can plonk down a few dog-scalps on the counter, and walk off with a shin-plaster and a couple of eagle-hawk claws in change...

The following recommendations are from a Royal Commission's findings into the Dingo and Stock Route Administration in Queensland in 1930.

1. Disband Dog Boards and do not have a rigid policy for all areas of the State.
2. Do not pay bonuses as trafficking is extremely common.
3. There are 20,000 miles of dog fences in Queensland and their effectiveness is questionable.
4. Systematic poisoning should be used.
5. Obligation should be placed on landholders to destroy vermin.
6. A declaration should be made under oath, annually, to ensure that the duty is carried out.

Obviously the powers-that-be took this seriously and, as a result, all 38 Dingo Boards became redundant. For the record, fences erected in Queensland from 1886 through to 1929 were the Government Border Fence of 1,171.2 km, together with Board fences 9,836.8 km long and private fences measuring 36,396 kilometres.

On 1 July 1934, South Australia withdrew from its long-standing arrangement with New South Wales regarding the Border Fence. It was of little if any use where they were concerned. Dingoes did not infiltrate South Australia from the western parts of New South Wales; it worked in reverse. Also, only one cattle station—Quinyambie—existed on the South Australian side of the fence and if they didn't worry about dogs on that huge run then why should they concern themselves in Adelaide? Yes, it made much more sense to concentrate on existing dingo fences in other parts of the State.

So by the late 1930s, thousands of kilometres of iron and wooden posts and wire mesh had been erected in many parts of Australia. They crossed rocky hills, dusty plains, gibber deserts, dry riverbeds that were anything but that in times of heavy rain, and swamps difficult for vehicles to penetrate. Some of these sections were linked together; others were not. What is certain, however, is that during the war years (1939–45), when fencing materials became impossible to find (first priority being given to keeping the 'expected' Japanese invaders out of Sydney and other major coastal centres such as Darwin) most dingo fences fell into sad disrepair. It was very much a case of history repeating itself where the majority of graziers along the fences were concerned. Not even the increased bounty for dingo scalps, back to one pound along the Border Fence, made any difference. The men that counted were gone. Some wouldn't return.

The Agriculture Protection Board of Western Australia carried out the first aerial baiting in that State in 1946 when approximately 80,000 baits were dropped north of Meekatharra. From then on yearly drops were held over large areas in October. The second month of spring in the southern hemisphere was an ideal time in the big West. Normally it was a harsh dry month and water was scarce. Dingoes, parents and fast-growing pups, stayed near obvious water. This was where baits were unloaded from fixed-wing aircraft.

WARNING ☠ NO PUBLIC THOROUGHFARE
FENCE MAINTENANCE TRACK ONLY

Poison baits and traps occur at regular intervals in the vicinity of the fence. Unauthorised persons using this track do so entirely at their own risk.

By order of Chairman, S.A. Dog Fence Board

Above The WA State Barrier Fence was erected and is maintained to keep emus out of grazing land

Left The SA Dog Fence Board spells it out

Below Typical dingo country in WA's Kimberley ranges

Above The Qld Barrier Fence crossing the Maranoa River

Left Charlie and Peter 'Skeeter' Russell making some repairs on the Tambo to Adelaide section

Below Rabbits enjoying the late afternoon sunshine on Bulloo Downs station

Above From Sturt National Park, Paddy Barlow looks towards the tail-end of the Grey Range in Queensland's south-west

Below left A red kangaroo (male) in Sturt National Park, New South Wales

Below right A 'blue-flyer' — female 'red' kangaroo — with joey in her pouch

Above Boundary rider Bob Clarke on the Border Fence between Toona Cottage and Cameron Corner

Below Shirley Clifford at Bulloo Downs station

Also in 1946, the Dog Fence Act came into force across the border in South Australia. This provided for an unbroken line of dog-proof fencing across the northern parts of the State, the idea being that it would fill gaps in the overall fencing scheme and thus link up, unbroken, with the New South Wales Border Fence.

Responsibility for maintaining new and existing fences was that of the landholders abutting the Dog Fence. They would be aided financially (but not with manpower) by a State Government subsidy. Right from the start, that rankled badly with South Australian graziers on the front line!

But erecting new fencing was as difficult as replacing existing netting that had rusted away. A shortage of suitable materials, virtually impossible to obtain since the outbreak of war, would still be felt into the next decade.

The Border Fence in particular—undermined or covered with sand—was in a sorry state indeed by the end of the war. Numerous flash floods in the region in the following years did nothing to improve the situation.

The owner of one station near Milparinka, about 25 km from the South Australian border, knew all about the state the Border Fence was in all right. The so-called dingo-proof fence was a joke, a standing joke, in any hotel bar in the entire Western Division. Those white-collars-and-ties in Sydney wouldn't have a clue!

He had much time to reflect on the condition of the Border Fence as he tried various methods of eliminating dingoes and protecting his flocks. He even tried shepherding them during the day and yarding them at night just as they'd done in the old days. But this resulted in a poor wool yield due, he reckoned, to constant tension amongst the animals. Merinos were not the only ones suffering an acute overdose of stress along the Border Fence.

A plan to erect a dingo-proof barrier around Queensland's grazing land was first voiced in 1948 by a Co-ordinating Board (set up four years previously and the forerunner of the present-day Rural Lands Protection Board). Action was taken in 1954 with the introduction of the Barrier Fences Act. Landholders along the proposed line were duly notified that wire netting would be landed on their properties free of charge providing they established the Barrier Fence to specifications and maintained it thereafter. Apparently most landholders were in favour of this. With good reason. Dingo losses were at this time costing the State around $4 million a year. No figure was put on the personal cost to graziers of waging a war with an enemy you just couldn't defeat. The scheme was financed as follows.

Initial outlay for materials was by way of Treasury loans arranged at various times and at varying interest rates up to a maximum of 5.5 per cent, the last of which will be fully redeemed by 1993.

Rates were levied on the rateable value of all rural lands within the area to be enclosed, such to be collected by Local Authorities and remitted to the Board. Originally it was agreed that such rate would not exceed .83 cents per sheep or sheep equivalent in the protected area. A length of 5,635 km of fencing was involved in Queensland which, with New South Wales and South Australian fences, meant that there was a continuous dog-proof barrier of some 8,320 km.

The breakdown of what was required to complete the 'new' Barrier Fence was detailed.

52 per cent of the fence comprised existing dog-proof fences, 20 per cent provided for the top-netting of existing rabbit fences, 13 per cent upgrading of existing stock-proof fences, with only about 15 per cent of the distance requiring new dog-proof fencing. Six Inspectors were appointed and paid from the Barrier Fences Fund established under that Act. These Inspectors were empowered to inspect the fence and issue orders on landholders if maintenance work was not being carried out.

On 4 April 1957 the Broken Hill newspaper the *Barrier Miner* published the following letter. It was signed 'Far North Grazier'.

The wild dogs are really bad in our area, and it is because the Border Fence is not good at all. It is far from good; in fact it is very bad. We recently had a graziers' inspection committee and it is easy to find stretches of the fence up to 40 yards in length not even in the ground. At other places the mesh was so far out of the ground that the biggest man in our party could get through without apparent effort whatsoever. So much for the fence reported to be in good condition. We pay dog tax and are entitled to government protection. We cannot receive this protection from a moth-eaten fence, especially when it is declared so good that nobody in Sydney would think of doing anything.

It was because of such dissatisfaction expressed by ratepayers close to the Border Fence that in 1957 the responsibility for the Wild Dog Destruction Fund and for fence maintenance was placed in the hands of a Board consisting of representatives drawn from local landholders. The Western Lands Commissioner's involvement was retained by his appointment, *ex officio,* as Board Chairman. The Board's administration was transferred, sensibly, to Broken Hill in the interests of more effective contact with landholders and, of course, a more effective supervision of operations.

The operations of this newly formed Board would be financed by a rate set on all rural landholders in the Western Division—some 32,500 ha of arid and semi-arid land—and further increased with a Government subsidy. It would be known as the Wild Dog Destruction Board.

Meanwhile, work continued on the Barrier Fence in Queensland. At times with very little enthusiasm. The Annual Reports of the Department in control for 1958–59 make that point adamantly clear.

...apathy has been displayed by a few landholders towards the maintenance of the fence and either they have not carried out their maintenance obligation in a satisfactory manner or have only done so under pressure... These few cases are being watched closely, and unless landholders face up to their responsibility, the Co-ordinating Board will have no alternative than to cause the fences to be maintained at the cost of the landholders.

Those doing the 'close-watching' and obviously quite prepared to wave a big stick, if not a stockwhip, were six inspectors stationed around the fence at regular intervals.

Naturally, sheepmen knew only too well who these lazy ones were. Cattlemen. Who else? They were the weak link in the chain. One Longreach grazier rated them cynically, but perhaps realistically, along with brumbies, 'roos, goannas, pigs, foxes and rogue cattle as an equal menace where the fence was concerned. Obviously he was a sheepman.

In 1959–60 the Barrier Fence was completely joined. Now, linked with the Border Fence, which in turn joined forces with the Dog Fence, the three separately run fences spanned an amazing 5,309 kilometres. The fact did not escape the eagle eyes of the *Guinness Book of Records* researchers. They listed it as the longest man-made fence in the world. Indeed, it made the Great Wall of China, admittedly far more substantial, a poor second at 2,415 kilometres. They say that the Great Wall of China will stand for a thousand years. The way things are currently shaping up the Dingo Fence might be there that long, too. But whatever the outcome the barriers have something in common: they were erected as a line of defence against hostile invaders.

The most lethal weapon ever brought into play against dingoes was first experimented with in 1962. The place was rough, broken country near Grafton in northern New South Wales. The men behind it were local graziers who weren't doing it for fun. Teamed together, they hired a fixed-wing aircraft and those who went aloft with the pilot dumped poisoned rabbits along the backs of their properties. The name of the poison was Ten Eighty (hereafter simply 1080). There are no records available to assess how successful this drop was.

This rough, gorge-ridden country in the north of New South Wales offers dingoes a wonderful habitat. They have made the most of it from way back. Have paid the ultimate price too. Way back. The Pastures and Stock Protection Board at Armidale paid out on 15,174 scalps between 1880 and 1902.

A number of Dingo Destruction Boards could, and still can, be found in this part of the State where many of the small towns and stations are at altitudes of 1,000–1,300 metres. Prominent among them in the mid-1960s was the Upper North Coast and Tablelands Dingo Destruction Board, sub-divided into smaller associations, each named after a station or local topographic feature.

Before decimal currency, such Boards were paying out as much as 3 pounds a scalp. Not infrequently a special 'incentive' price was placed on the head of a known 'rogue'. There have been many rogue dingoes in that country, some of them never caught.

In the first six months of 1966, the Upper North Coast Board paid out on 1,300 scalps. In the same period, Aborigines of the Walbiri tribe on Mount Doreen station and at the Yuendumu Mission on the Tanami Track, north-west of Alice Springs, were all for cashing in on dingo scalps too. Which is understandable enough. Steady work is rather difficult to find in that spinifex country. Not so dingoes.

In effect this became an annual event, obviously linked with age-old traditions prized and not allowed to die. The hunt took place each July and perhaps extended well into August. When the big day arrived, as many as 100 Aborigines would head out into the low sandhills into country rarely visited. Because they knew precisely where to go, the hunt tended to be a short-lived affair. On average the excited party would finish with, say, 700 scalps.

The storekeeper on Mount Doreen or any other big run for that matter accepted such tokens without batting an eye. Much the same response had he been handed a wad of pound or dollar notes. Depending on the going rate, the tokens could realise a thousand dollars. You could buy a lot of baccy and cheap plonk and the sore heads to go with it for that much money.

Unlike the white man, the Aborigines hunted for tokens in a different way. Which means that all 700 scalps were those of pups. The bitches were left strictly alone, as they had been in long-ago days, to produce another, similar-sized litter next year.

The taxpayer of course paid indirectly for these and other scalps that were 'harvested' annually. A pointless exercise, since the *status quo* remained the same. No matter. The system had obviously been designed as a 'rip off'. European man had been doing it successfully almost from the time the first payments were offered for the head of a 'dog' running wild in Sydney Town. Who knows? Maybe the very first 'head' paid out on was a ring-in.

The summer of '65 was a tough one in south-west Queensland. Food for those of predatory inclinations was in short supply. Like wild dogs in Africa and timber wolves in the Canadian wilderness dingoes tended to hunt in numbers in that harsh land of Burke and Wills. They could be observed running in packs ten-to-fifteen strong on many stations. Gaunt to a point of emaciation, they were desperate for food—not quite at the cannibal stage but getting mighty close. Wasn't a top time to be a cattle beast, either.

On a drought-plagued run west of Windorah six cows, lacking sufficient strength to free themselves, bogged at a tank overflow. They began to die. Eventually only one remained alive. Presently five starving dingoes arrived on the scene. Who said a dingo's prayers were never answered? Typically, they favoured live meat. When a stationhand arrived on the scene, one side of the cow's rump had been ripped clean away. I would not have enjoyed listening to her horrendous screams. Nor those made over at Durri in Diamantina River country where a live bullock was spotted with as many as 30 dogs tearing him to bloody shreds.

The year 1969 saw South Australia and Queensland lagging behind New South Wales in the bonus payment department. They offered only $2, a third of what the going rate was over the Border Fence.

In South Australia, they estimated (based on the numbers of tokens then being claimed on) that even with a substantial increase it would cost no more than, say, $20,000 to bump up the bonus in line with New South Wales' incentive. Up to six bucks it went.

What the authorities did not expect was the contagious enthusiasm $6 per dingo scalp would generate. By the end of June 1970, a staggering total of 19,382 scalps had been paid out on, the highest figure recorded in that State.

'This isn't on!' some 'white-collar-and-tie' must have cried in anguish. Consequently the payment was dropped as of 1 July that same year. Down to $4 a dog and a miserable $1 per pup. And whereas the bounty would eventually climb in the other States to $10, it had at $4 reached its peak in the south. Presently it would be lowered still further. Down, down to $2. A high-power bullet costs more than that.

Of course arguments for and against bonus payments for dingo scalps have raged for many a year. A bonus system encourages people to make the effort when animals are in good-to-high numbers. Once a population slips below a certain level the whole economics of it must be looked at carefully. In short, effort expended outweighs financial reward. In a situation like that animals are left pretty much alone with inevitable consequences. They build up again, often rather alarmingly. It is a vicious circle not unique to this country. The same thing has happened with coyotes in North America, and with possums in New Zealand, where the price per skin rather than a bounty dictated the number killed, although the latter was tried for a time in the 1950s.

It was in Queensland where most dingoes could be found, and where most scalps were paid out on. Queensland figures are available from 1 July 1932.

Period of Destruction	Dingoes
1932–44	19 734
1945–46	32 408
1946–47	38 142
1947–48	30 817
1948–49	26 767
1949–50	25 821
1950–51	22 411
1951–52	44 941
1952–53	29 965
1953–54	26 380
1954–55	24 035
1955–56	23 395
1956–57	31 394
1957–58	49 908
1958–59	37 283
1959–60	30 596
1960–61	31 521
1961–62	30 084
1962–63	26 529
1963–64	30 037
1964–65	31 981
1965–66	37 096
1966–67	29 241

When one checks the number of tokens claimed on in 1965–66 at a time a massive airborne 1080 campaign was taking place at regular intervals from as far north as Cape York to the New South Wales border one realises the overall dingo kill must have been staggering. But of course we have no way of knowing precisely how many dingoes took a lethal dose. Nor for that matter do we know what native birds and animals fell victim too. Perhaps it is just as well we don't.

Banned today in many countries—all without a dingo problem, of course—1080 is still used with devastating effect to combat the dingo menace. Dingoes have not become immune to it as rabbits have to the myxomatosis virus introduced into Australia with great effect in the early 1950s. Myxomatosis is now judged to be little more than 5 per cent effective in many rabbit-plagued regions.

Many graziers the author met were adamant they would eventually go under if 1080 were taken off the market because they knew of no adequate substitute. Colin Clift is one example. Now in his late 50s, Colin is as hard-backed as an ageing mulga tree. He runs Yandarlo—15,378 ha of top country no great distance south of Tambo on Highway 71 in western Queensland. There, Clift has 14,000 sheep and 500 cattle and ample wildlife, including flocks of plains turkeys. But most of all 'roos. In fact, he had more 'roos, he believes, than the rest of the animals, domestic and wild, lumped together.

Since kangaroos feature quite prominently in this work, and with good reason, perhaps we should take a brief break from one *Canis familiaris dingo* and reflect a little on this animal which is regarded as endangered by many conservationists who claim that all shooting for meat or skins should therefore cease forthwith.

Well, a 'roo is rather difficult to observe on George Street, Sydney. A live 'roo, that is. There are plenty of cuddly stuffed ones there for the tourist market; you can't miss them if you're camped in the Hilton Hotel. Everyone loves dear old Skippy, although he is getting on in years now. But the thought of a thousand 'roos with their heads all down gobbling your precious grass at a rate to put a starving merino to shame soon brings massive disenchantment.

At any rate, on the day I turned up at Yandarlo, I'd left Roma and headed west on the Warrego Highway. The further I went on that lovely Sunday morning in mid-spring the more dead 'roos I saw. Until by the time I'd joined up with the Matilda Highway it was a sad case of one dead 'roo after another. Frequently eagles, hawks and crows were lifting sluggishly into the air because their craws were stuffed chock-a-block with either fairly fresh—they could take their pick—or well matured 'roo meat. Once I spotted a fox racing away from a carcass that was plastered to the bitumen like a black rubber mat. Maybe it was after maggots.

Upon arriving at my destination, on a whim, for once, I was promptly asked to join the Clift family for lunch. They call it outback hospitality; a throwback to a time long since past. It is lovely. And it may not exist as it still does in the outback anywhere else in the world.

Since I didn't expect anyone there to be squeamish, I brought up the number of dead 'roos I had seen, particularly since linking up with the Matilda Highway. Colin laughed without mirth. Right; it wasn't funny. Wiping his mouth with a napkin, he said that I should've seen it early last year (1988). In a mere 90 km stretch, which is spitting distance in south-west Queensland, he had started counting for the sheer hell of it and gave up after one thousand. And, he added, God only knew how many others had been hit, mostly by road trains travelling faster than sound, and had staggered off the road and died in the tall grass or adjacent scrub.

But that's not on Yandarlo, right? No. On Colin Clift's run the situation is even worse. Colin had cultivated good grass. Colin had paid the price for that. On Yandarlo, 'roo shooters operate for most of the year. They are professionals. Spotlighting, or jacklighting, as it's termed in the United States, they work here three or four nights a week, maybe gut 40 or 50 'roos a night. Big 'roos, naturally. These guys, like the Aborigines, know the meaning of the word conserve. They are, with full government approval, allowed to take 7,500 'roos per year off Yandarlo. They do so. But, as Colin Clift says with a philosophical lift of his bony shoulders, that number makes no visible difference. The 'roos continue to drift in from further out west. Right. They get the good word on Yandarlo and make for it as fast as their powerfully developed hindquarters can move them, which in the case of a big red kangaroo is very fast. He can travel long distances at around 48 km per hour—cruising, fifth gear, say. He can, in soaring bounds, top three metres and more and cover as much as nine metres. It wouldn't surprise me one of these days to see such a red kangaroo roped in for the next hop-skip-and-jump event at the Olympic Games. He'd look extremely smart in a green blazer with yellow piping.

But back to the main thread of our story. Colin took on Yandarlo in 1979, a time when the Barrier Fence had again fallen into disrepair. There were numerous places where a dingo could penetrate the fence without so much as scratching itself.

All of this was unfortunate for graziers along that section of the Barrier Fence. Not far to the east and north-east are the Carnarvon Ranges. They are ruled by dingoes. Few if any places would warrant the term 'dingo strongholds' but, like the Warburton Ranges in Western Australia, the wild Carnarvon National Park surely would.

So, periodically, dingoes headed west from their mountain retreat and set up camp in, or close to, sheeplands. On Yandarlo's doorstep, for instance. At night they would invade the property and play harmless games with sheep—something like Russian roulette with all six chambers of a handgun loaded. Because Clift's land did not offer sufficient cover to hide, in the morning the dingoes would nip back smartly through the holes in the Barrier Fence. All in all a dingo's idea of a wonderful life. A normal night's harmless fun added up to 30 or 40 dead greybacks. Colin Clift was most put out.

Prior to taking on Yandarlo, he had leased a station up near Longreach. Few dingoes there. So he had never been in this situation before. The answer might be to do as his fellow graziers did in south-west Queensland. Use 1080.

With enthusiasm, Clift set out twin lines of bait 100 metres apart. The lines were as a matter of fact bisected by the highway. Dingoes often waltz across it. There were maybe 3,000 baits in all.

But to his dismay, it didn't work. Dingoes returned to account for more sheep; not a sick 'un in sight. Nevertheless, Clift persisted. Still no joy. Disgruntled, he thought that 1080 wasn't what it was cracked up to be.

While yarning with a fellow grazier, Clift mentioned his lack of success, admitted worriedly that he didn't know what to do.

'So what did you use for bait?' he was asked. 'Usual thing, I suppose,' Clift replied. 'Such as?' the other man queried. 'Oh, you know: 'roo, goat, wild pig, bit of cow meat. Like I said, the usual thing.' 'Try horsemeat,' he was advised. Horsemeat, the grazier explained, cutting off Clift's understandable protest, was all solid muscle. It held together in the sun much longer than 'roo or sheep meat, which, in some instances, fell apart in a matter of days. Most importantly, dingoes loved the stuff. 'Roo meat after all was old hat.

With nothing but time to lose, Clift experimented with horsemeat as bait. He set out his lines like before, with almost instant success. In the years that followed, and each time dingoes struck, Clift retaliated in the same way. Each time, jackpot! Also pleasing was the fact that the baits proved lethal to foxes, and that resulted in a much better lamb survival rate. (Foxes, showing good taste, are voracious lamb takers.) Again, equally pleasing and perhaps more so, was that it had the same devastating effect on feral cats. No loss this. Like a dingo, but far less excusable, the feral cat kills not only to survive. Like a domestic cat it has the deplorable habit of tormenting its victim until, suddenly weary of the one-sided game, it kills. Weight for weight it is without doubt the most vicious and effective killer of birds and small mammals in the Australian bush. It would be deeply satisfying to be able to state that it is 'endangered'. Unfortunately feral cats must be classed as plentiful and I can't think of one redeeming feature they possess.

6

More Recent Times

The sheepmen next to the fence are not particularly concerned about the fence. The Barrier Fence is not a barrier any more. It is in disrepair and they believe 1080 baiting is far more effective.
– Allan Parker, President, Longreach Branch of the Central and
Northern Graziers Association, 1978

After World War II and until the early 1970s, most of the Barrier Fence was well maintained. But in some instances, pressure had to be firmly applied to landholders, not always cattlemen, who, during the wool depression of that era, lost a great deal of heart and saw little point in maintaining their section of the fence. For these and other reasons there was a gradual deterioration in the longest section of the overall Dingo Fence:

Bad terrain for maintenance of such a fence;
Poor economic conditions;
Change in land use from sheep to cattle of over twenty per cent of landholders on the fence;
Damage by fire and flood;
Some older sections required rebuilding;
The concept placed too high a burden on landholders on the fence;
The successful use of Compound 1080 for dingo control;
Damage by native and feral animals.

By 1975 it was 'estimated' that bringing the whole of the Barrier Fence up to scratch, particularly those regions where in effect it was no longer wanted, would cost $915,000. An estimation is as far as that went!

A Queensland State Government enquiry into animal and vegetable pests in 1976 came up with a number of pertinent points relating to dingoes and the Barrier Fence:

There are as many dogs inside the fence as outside. 1080 is an excellent form of control. However, it may become unavailable (due to environmental pressures or conservation groups bringing pressure to bear to stop its use).
This would leave the fence being the only barrier.
The fence is already there and it would be very costly to abandon it and possibly later want to rebuild it.

The fence is a useful barrier for control of animals in the event of an exotic disease outbreak.

If 1080 had been available in the first place the fence would probably not have been built.

The fence is generally only a 'population distributor'.

RECOMMENDATION

Bonuses should be abolished. The fence should be maintained.

Many landholders, however, were not of the same opinion. They considered the Barrier Fence to be the palest of white elephants.

Severe flooding had a disastrous effect on both the Queensland and South Australian sections of the Border Fence in 1974. Unfortunately the same thing occurred two years later, but, this time, it caused the worst problems along the Queensland border. Here the Bulloo River overflow turned into a huge lake, approximately 24 km wide by 100 km long and extending some 60 km into the Western Division. The Annual Reports of the Wild Dog Destruction Board take up the story:

> The Board became concerned that dogs would move from Queensland along the long fingers of land which stretched across the border towards the sheep raising areas in New South Wales and which would have allowed access to wild dogs as the waters dried up. Dogs were able to gain access through the fences at those points where the fence was lapped by shallow waters in shoreline situations where it could not be kept dog-proof.
>
> Many dogs and dog tracks were seen on the New South Wales side, and approval was given by the Hon. D. Day, Minister for Decentralisation and Primary Industries, for an aerial baiting programme in 'beach' areas, claypans and other sites where dogs could be expected to move, and where baits could not be lost in the metre high grass which clothed the formerly desert landscape.
>
> The specially prepared baits purchased from the Agriculture Protection Board of Western Australia were composed of cubes of butchers' crackle with an injection of 1080 sufficient to kill a dog but insufficient to have any effect on native animals or birds.
>
> The aerial baiting was carried out on 7th September, 1976 in accordance with the guidelines established by the Government following the 1080 Seminar referred to above. The baiting was done with the permission of the lessees, and in co-operation with the Milparinka and Wanaaring Pastures Protection Boards, mostly beyond 30 to 40 kilometres from homesteads. Unfortunately the area was too remote and difficult of access to enable an assessment of results. However, subsequent hard baiting in other areas known to be infected with dogs has resulted in several observed kills and the disappearance of wild dogs from the locality.

The cost of restoring this flood damage was estimated at just under $100,000. The Board were successful in obtaining this amount of money through the

Natural Disasters Flood Relief Vote. By the end of 1977 all but 10 km of the fence had been replaced or repaired in a satisfactory manner. That section still untouched remained under water. It caused constant concern because dingo numbers outside the fence were unusually high. However, a heatwave arrived with the new year and the floodwaters evaporated. Work on the last length of fencing started, and ended, in February.

For the record, 200 dingoes were eliminated inside the Border Fence in 1977 and by the middle of the following year a further 315 had been destroyed.

Also in 1978 a new Board came into existence in Queensland: the Stock Routes and Rural Lands Protection Board. One of its major tasks was 'the preparation of a suitable recommendation to Government for the future maintenance of the Barrier Fence'.

Still in 1978 a working party convened by the Agriculture Protection Board of Western Australia (hereafter referred to as the APB) visited the eastern States to see precisely how each of them ran its own section of the dingo fence, the reason being that they were 'considering' erecting a similar dog-proof fence which would enclose the Eastern Goldfields: that is, the Wiluna-Meekatharra and Gascoyne pastoral districts. In effect, it would stretch from Onslow via Wiluna to a point east of Kalgoorlie. The investigators were to take into account economic considerations and to look for 'proof' that problem dogs actually originated outside the sheep regions.

Some interesting comments regarding this still 'topical' issue in Western Australia were made by Eric Pearson (APB) at the Barrier Fence Administrators' Conference at Thargomindah, Queensland, held on 26 and 27 August 1987.

> There is considerable debate on this question. The arguments are largely a matter of opinion. The truth probably lies between the two extremes. Research on wild dog behaviour has shown that the animals have a home range. Theories of long distance wild dog migration are largely discounted. Given the size of the properties concerned and the distance some dogs are found from the fences, it is highly probable that they are part of a resident population. On the other hand, the failure to clean out the properties over many years suggests the resident population is supplemented by dogs that breach the fence. This could occur in periods when maintenance of the fences falls behind.

The proposed fence wasn't built. However, for the record, a minority report was in favour of an electric fence being built in the area.

From my own research it seems certain that dingoes and wild dogs that cause problems in sheep country in Western Australia do originate in the north. For a moment let me pause to reflect on the first recorded figure for government bonus payments for 'scalps' in Western Australia. This was in 1923 when 6,200 scalps were paid for at 10 shillings each. This amount continued until 1928 when a payment of two pounds came into force, following the creation of the Vermin Act Trust Fund, 1927.

Traditionally dingoes have drifted south in Western Australia from the northern cattle country. They follow the old Canning Stock Route just as they did in the droving days. This leads them to Wiluna, and, further west, Meekatharra.

In the same way, they drift south and west from their strongholds in the Warburton Ranges. This way they reach (again) Wiluna, south towards Rawlinna, pushing on down towards Norseman and well beyond. From those same wild ranges they head east to the Nullarbor Plain. *Canis familiaris dingo* is indeed well distributed in Australia's largest State.

And of course there is always more inclination for animals to head south in times of drought, be they kangaroo, rabbit, emu, or dingo. So in a southward push, to pastures which are hopefully greener, but which isn't always the case, dingoes in the west, and almost certainly those close to sheep country, head south. Some find their way blocked by a high fence. Are we to presume that they then sigh heavily, turn tail, and tramp back dejectedly whence they came?

Of course not. These and many other dingoes either find or make a way through the fence. In Western Australia, they have no fence to contend with. They then become 'problem dogs', for that is the way of a dingo in sheep country.

It is, I think, worth commenting a little on emus in Western Australia. Mass movements occur there in times of drought, generally in a south-west direction. A particularly large number of birds (150,000–200,000) on the State Barrier Fence in 1976. Of this number APB staff wiped out about 90,000 birds. In commenting on this large-scale slaughter, the Board's Chief Executive Officer, A.W. Hogstrom, considered that 'while it would be economically and practically possible to control these mass movements when they occur, the slaughter of 200,000 birds would not be publicly accepted. Letting them die on the fence, on the other hand, raises little reaction.'

It is interesting to note what the cost of dog control activities were in Western Australia just a few years after the overall vote went against a substantial dog-proof fence being built. For the years 1982/1983, and with a 10 per cent contribution by pastoralists, the APB would:

Manufacture 2.4 million factory baits of 1080.
Help pastoralists produce 200,000 fresh meat baits.
Carry out 300 hours of aerial baiting.
Employ 16 doggers.
Pay for 24 contract dogging groups.
Spend $300,000 on dingo research, including $37,000 of sheep industry funds.
Pay bonuses on 3,400 scalps.

The total cost of wild dog control activities in this same period, including immediate supervision but excluding overheads and research, was around $1.17 million.

Little wonder then that there has been strong pressure for many years in the west to build a straight-line dog-proof fence to exclude wild dogs from the pastoral districts where sheep are run. The three basic types of fencing which do exist in Western Australia are:

(1) Encirclement dog-proof fences. Enclosing one or a number of properties, these are found only on the Nullarbor Plain.

(2) Spur dog fence. One dog-proof fence is maintained by the Murchison Region Vermin Council (representing a number of local government authorities). This is linked to the State Barrier Fence near Bonnie Rock and extends in a general northerly direction for 600 kilometres.

(3) The State Barrier Fence. Under the control of the Agriculture Protection Board, this is maintained for the purpose of restricting emu movements. Nonetheless, sheepmen close to it are of the opinion it provides a more than adequate barrier against dingo attack.

At any rate, the *Report Of The Wild Dog Fence Working Party* was published in 1980. Extracts from it, compiled by Simon Whitehouse, reflect the general feeling then about having a Barrier Fence in the region we might loosely term the north of the State.

> Graziers on the fence generally do not want to spend money on fence maintenance. The Warrego Graziers Association does not support the retention of the barrier fence.
>
> The WGA recommended that the graziers in south-east Queensland maintained the fence entirely at their own expense and the rest of the graziers only continued to pay for the loans that were raised for the original construction. The south-west graziers [Cunnamulla] do not want the fence mainly because their own fences are regularly lost due to floods.
>
> Virgil Power, Secretary, Warrego Graziers Association.
>
> The fence in this area is rabbit netting on the bottom plus dog netting above. Generally, the fence is in poor condition. The Association wants to abandon dog fences in the area.
>
> Peter Morris, Secretary, and Allan Parker, President,
> Longreach Branch of the Central and
> Northern Queensland Graziers Association.

So the 1980s had arrived. In the first year of that decade dingoes were reported as 'having once again reached the dreaded level of plague proportions' in the Hawker district of South Australia. On one station, nine dingoes were driven off, leaving behind 200 dead sheep. Five local graziers linked forces to offer as much as $100 for a dingo scalp. Another Hawker grazier, H.J. Spiers, who was also the Chairman of the United Farmers and Stock Owners Dog Fence Committee, blamed what he termed the 'dilapidated state of the Dog Fence' for the build-up of dingoes in the area.

Again there was a 'frightening' increase in dingoes in the Ngarkat Park (south of Lameroo) and other smaller parks and reserves which, collectively, added up to 265,000 ha of mostly wild and unfenced country ideal for dingoes.

To combat the menace, the district councils of Coonalpyn Downs, Pinnaroo, Lameroo, and Tatiara formed the Box Flat Dingo Committee. They hired a dogger, Ken Hancock, the only one south of the Dog Fence. Working a 2½-day-week, Hancock went about the business of killing. But he as well as everyone else in that hard-hit region knew that the problem he, and they, faced was really hopeless. Eradication of the dingo was impossible, particularly when the Ngarkat country linked up with similar terrain in Victoria where it was protected.

Interestingly enough, most of the dingoes Hancock accounted for were black. They were here when the land was first taken up. Locals called them 'warrigals'. Graziers contemplating mutilated sheep had other, less flattering, terms for them. John Ridgway, Chairman of the Lameroo District Council, commented that the only difference between the 'black' dingoes of the south-east and their northern counterparts was in fact the colour: 'They all have powerful shoulders, strong jaws, and the short bushy tail. Some may be crossed but in the main they are the true dingo.'

In the Western Division of New South Wales the effects of the floods of the 1970s were long-term. The Board, in an attempt to rid the grazing lands of dingoes, had in 1980 three doggers on its payroll, one alongside the South Australian fence and the other two on the Queensland stretch. They were kept busy.

During the summer of 1979–80 heatwave conditions made life almost unbearable for fence workers. By September 1980 a severe drought was being experienced in both South Australia's northern sections and over all of south-west Queensland. During September and October rabbits began arriving on the South Australian side of the fence. The Board reported that '20–30 cm of soil were fretted away on the sandhills on the South Australian side of the fence as a result of the constant traffic by hundreds of thousands of rabbits. Rabbits died by the millions but the fence was made vulnerable by rabbits burrowing under the netting. Fortunately, dog numbers were low on the South Australian side at the time.'

By November life on the Border Fence was grim. No surface water remained; house tanks at the various cottages were running dangerously low. High winds—a searingly hot blast that made it difficult to breathe—constantly shifted the sand about which meant that long sections of the fence were undermined or drifted over. Some gut-busting work was necessary. Very simply, a host of various animals, all heading south, and all frantic for water, had arrived along the Queensland section of the Border Fence. Among them, in huge numbers, were 'roos, emus, brumbies, wild pigs, and, of course, dingoes which, while not going short of a feed, were equally desperate for water. In particular, enormous pressure was put on the fence in the vicinity of both Adelaide Gate and Bindara where water remained in the house tanks and the frantic animals could smell it, but not get at it.

This was the situation in November when Supervisor, Paddy Barlow, worked with his field staff and landholders on 1080 hand-baiting campaigns on stations on both sides of the Border Fence. Dingoes got through of course. Nothing would stop them taking advantage of holes made by other animals.

A total of 642 dingoes were killed in the Western Division that year. Later, the Board reported:

Since 1981, the field staff of the Board have observed a steady decline in the dog population which is attributed to more effective fence maintenance and the eradication measures undertaken within the Western Division. Bounties paid in recent years were 250 in 1984, 199 in 1985 and 327 in 1986.

By the early 1980s dingoes in their thousands were reported to be breaching the virtually 'defunct' Barrier Fence in those regions where it was no longer maintained. With stock losses reaching alarming heights, sheepmen in central southern Queensland angrily and collectively lobbied the Queensland State Government to protect their flocks. Failing that, the sheep industry as they knew it was ultimately doomed. The Government took heed. Through its Rural Protection Board, they agreed to fund the reconstruction and realignment of the Barrier Fence. The following stipulations were to apply:

(1) The Government would meet the cost of $2.735 million on the up-grading and realignment of the main barrier and check fences in the south-east of the State. This proposal was based on the shortened barrier fence line.
(2) Existing Precepts on Local Authorities were to be collected for the current financial year, which included all of those Authorities within the original barrier fence concept.
(3) The existing loans would be referred to Treasury for consideration and new Precepts, to commence in the 83/84 financial year, would be collected based on the latest available stock figures from the Australian Bureau of Statistics, with the first year's Precepts for all areas to be set at 5 cents per protected animal with an inflation factor to be added each year depending on actual costs.
(4) The Government to bear the balance of the annual maintenance cost estimated to be $193,000 plus escalation over the next five years.

Annual Reports of the Rural Protection Board inform us precisely what would be entailed:

The reconstruction and realignment to be carried out over a three-year period will commence at Moombidary, on the New South Wales border, and will include the reconstruction of the Fence from Moombidary to Hammond Downs including the realignment through the Bulloo Channels and new fencing where required between Hammond Downs and the western boundary of the Booringa Shire. Repairs and further minor realignments will take place between the western boundary of the Booringa Shire through the Bungil, Bendemere, Murilla, Chinchilla, Jondaryan and Wambo Shires. Further repairs and reconstruction will be undertaken in the Shires of Tara, Inglewood, Glengallan and Waggamba, possibly a spur in the Stanthorpe Shire and top netting of the Darling Downs Moreton Rabbit Board Fence where required.

Work began on the fence in July 1982. At a cost of about $3.6 million it was finished in 1985. Basically it contained the sheep country of central southern

Queensland, supporting an estimated seven million sheep. Linked with the Border Fence near Hungerford, it ran north to Hammond Downs station at Windorah, then east towards Adavale, swinging north-east to Tambo, carrying on south-east to Mt Maria station, to end at Jandowae, north of Dalby.

Despite the much shorter length of the Barrier Fence, the Dingo Fence, collectively speaking, still remains the longest man-made fence in the world.

PART TWO

NEW SOUTH WALES – THE BORDER FENCE

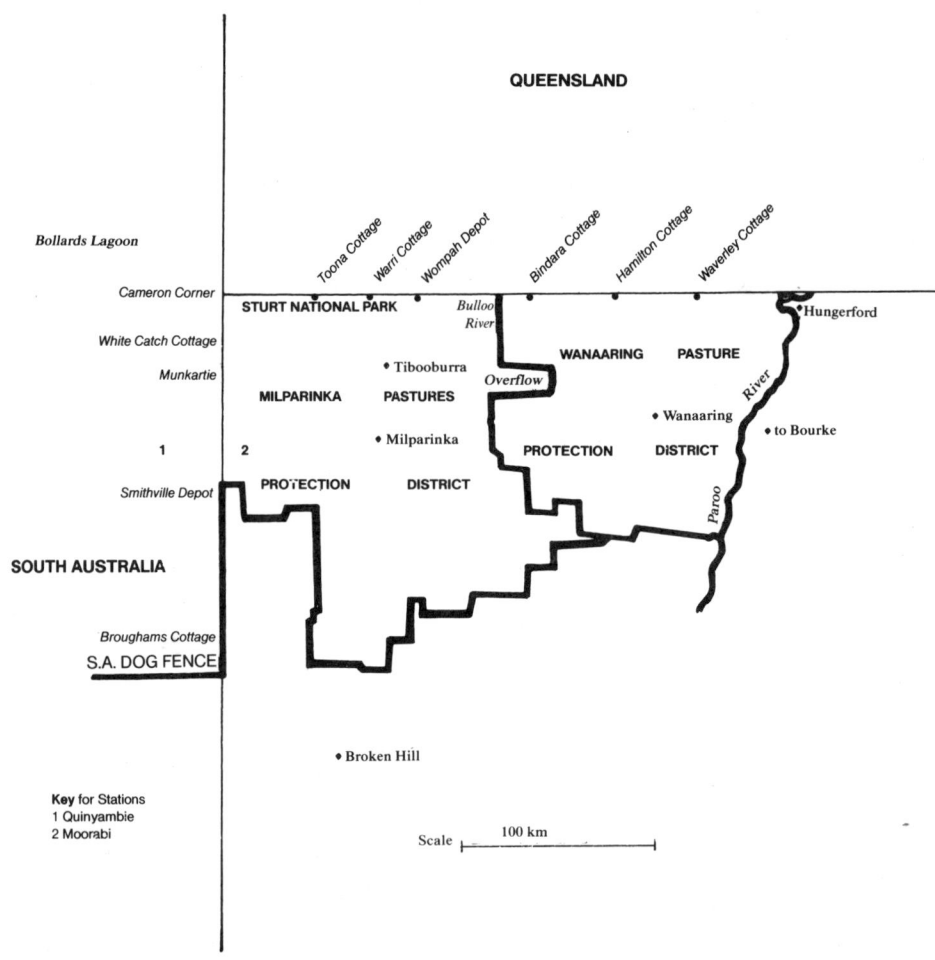

MAP 1   THE NEW SOUTH WALES BORDER FENCE

7

To The Border Fence

And the station owners say they can get no sleep
Instead they're chasing dingoes that are killing sheep.
They brag about the holes they find, where the dogs just gallop through.
Then go to the Sydney heads, and half of it's not true
                                    – a verse from 'The Border Fence Song',
                                                      author unknown

Sturt National Park
Western New South Wales
Early July 1989
Early morning, too
Several red kangaroos, ears pricked and standing rigidly to attention like smart guardsmen on duty at Buckingham Palace, watched with keen interest as a dusty Toyota Landcruiser of early '80s vintage barrelled into their sight along a rough dirt track.

A big buck towered over the others. He reared up, uncoiling, on powerful back legs, the better to see. The other three, with their short front legs tucked hard against their chests in a semi-defensive manner, did not move. Neither did the big fellow now. Positioned on a low, rocky ridge they were profiled dramatically by the sun slanting across the burnished Mitchell grass.

Typically, the grey-coated doe broke first. Almost immediately the smaller versions, cut from the same bolt of cloth, followed suit. Lowering himself almost ponderously, the buck sort of hunched himself up, lunged forward, and moved smoothly into the form of locomotion, hopping, that is unique to his Australia-wide family.

East, towards the sun-hazed ridges, more 'roos were on show; feeding, running, or forming statue-like silhouettes on the skyline. It might have been Australia in pre-European times.

Still more 'roos stayed right next to the track as the four-wheel-drive wagon jolted into view. Heads up, they displayed no inclination to run until, through the open passenger's window, I was close enough to make eye contact. That was not to their liking. But one large buck remained, to stand his ground. Obviously he knew, what every other red kangaroo in Sturt National Park— estimated to number 102,000 in early 1989—should have been acutely aware of, that within the park's far-flung boundaries was 'sanctified' ground where they were concerned. All they had to be afraid of were wedge-tailed eagles and the odd dingo.

'Eagle,' Paddy Barlow said soon after. Sure enough, a handsome wedge-tailed eagle was perched nonchalantly on the knobbly limb of a low mulga tree. The hunting was better than good here. Rabbits abounded.

There are, I should think, projects in most authors' working lives that they dearly want to tackle. Circumstances more than anything else dictate whether or not they get the opportunity. One of mine was a book about the dingo fence. The idea had lurked about in the back of my mind, like a spectre, ever since I had seen a very small section of South Australia's Dog Fence (where it crossed the Eyre Highway) while en route to Perth in 1974.

The very notion that an unbroken length of fencing went through three States, was maintained by men to keep out killer dogs, fascinated me. Whatever I read about 'the fence' after that was devoured avidly, the facts stored away. Maybe one day, I told myself. Much later the opportunity to tackle it arose. While planning how best to undertake the considerable fieldwork, I happened to pick up a magazine some months out of date (*Time*, 12 September 1988). Flicking through the pages with little interest, I was confronted by this riveting headline: 'Australia: Along the Dingo Fence'.

Briefly, the piece told that one Paddy Barlow, aged 59, was after 12 years service retiring as Supervisor of the New South Wales Border Fence. Apart from facts such as that this was the longest man-made fence in the world, the article concentrated mostly on Paddy. It included his thoughts on outback life while on the Border Fence.

> Ninety-nine per cent of my time I'm just on my own. But when you're out here, you're not lonely. When you go to the city and there's 50,000 people and no one will talk to you, that's when you're lonely. I wouldn't give you two bob for the city.

Such sentiments, I feel certain, have been echoed by many a bushman cast adrift in the big smoke. Paddy also made some observations on the dingo.

> The dingo is a smart, sneaky fellow. But if he was good for anything, our grandfathers would've found out about it. He's been tried as a guard dog and a Seeing Eye dog but he won't work as either. The dingo's only use has been in crossbreeding to produce a type of cattle dog...
>
> There is a sheep industry inside the fence; outside there is none. Some dingoes will go to any extreme to penetrate the barrier, while others take one look at the fence and walk away. The wild ones usually try to dig under. When we catch them, we pull their claws out to stop them from digging.

Even before I had read that last line, a familiar gut reaction was hard at work. This was the man to contact first.

The article stated that Paddy Barlow lived in Broken Hill with his wife, Beryl. No trouble to find his telephone number then. Even less of a problem, once I had it, to dial the correct digits.

Paddy's wife answered. A friendly sort. No, Paddy was not home. Paddy was at the pub. Paddy was always at the pub this time of the evening. Try later, she suggested. Six-thirty.

Next time I tried the number, a distinctly 'twangy' Australian voice came on the other end of the line. The man himself. In good humour. Those few drinks with his mates, I expect. He mostly listened to what I had to say without butting in; that is, apart from a soft, kookaburra-like chuckle from time to time. Must have been the beer, all right? Or maybe he was like that most of the time? But better to cackle like a happy little kookaburra than growl like a testy bear.

'. . .and all going well I should be up there early in July,' I finished.

'That sounds okay,' Paddy drawled easily. The media, whatever form it took, was old news where he was concerned. Bad news, mostly. 'I'm going fishing with a mate of mine who works on the fence end of June, so that'll tie in nicely.' We chatted a few more minutes and then, to my surprise, he said, 'Listen, I could show you around some of the fence if you like. . .' Like? 'Hell! That's fantastic!'

He laughed quietly. 'Normally we could get right around it, no big deal. But that heavy rain we had recently stuffed things up over towards Hungerford.' He paused. 'Floods cause us a lot of problems. . .' In his mind Paddy was still working on the fence, hence the 'us'.

I asked him how long he thought it would take and he replied the best part of a week. I digested that quickly. Maybe that wouldn't sit too well with his wife? I put that to him. 'She'll be glad to see the back of me. Reckons I get under her feet too much since I retired. Probably do, too.' No humour in the voice now.

I started to thank Paddy for his wonderful offer but he broke in. 'No worries. Just give us a call when you'll be here and I'll organise a wagon and meet your flight.' Just like that.

At the time, I thought that Alan Sinclair Barlow, better known throughout the Corner Country as Paddy Barlow, was out of the goodness of his Irish heart doing me a real big favour. The reality was it worked both ways. You see, Paddy could never get back quickly enough to his beloved fence. It had been his life. Yes, back to Tibooburra, the gateway to the Border Fence; back to see his mates at Smithville Depot, Lenny and Gay Dixon and their two young 'uns, both of whom worked on the fence too. I had presented him with a golden opportunity.

Broken Hill in early July was cold. Bitterly so, an icy wind whipping down the main street. Bleak, you'd call it. The locals reckoned it was typical. Just as baking heat was in summer. Very little in between, either. Best head north, then. To Tibooburra. Tibooburra. . .?

Good question. How does a 337 km drive via the Silver City Highway to New South Wales' most remote settlement sound to you? Like outback? Good, you'd be dead right.

The term 'Highway' is used rather loosely in this context. Almost all of it is dirt. The surface is like corrugated cement in high summer. Rain, and not too much of it, turns it into a shocking mess. There are creeks and rivers to ford. 'Roos and emus and the odd fox and countless rabbits watch as you go by. Above, birds of prey—wedge-tailed eagles, brown hawks, and kestrels—follow the ever-present air current.

It was a slow trip. Rain meant that the big Tonka-toy-like graders were at work. Rain was the reason why several mud-covered vehicles, lacking four-wheel-drive, had been abandoned by their owners.

Midway to Tibooburra is Packsaddle. There is a pub at Packsaddle. Packsaddle *is* the pub. We had a light lunch at Packsaddle—in the pub, naturally.

It was mid-afternoon when we arrived at our destination. Tibooburra?

Well, for openers the population, admittedly a floating one, is around 150. It exists almost solely because of the grazing industry. Take the Border Fence away and eventually there would be no Tibooburra. To some that might not seem too much of a loss. To long-time residents, however, Tibooburra is paradise. About as far as you can get from the city.

Tibooburra was founded in 1883. Its Aboriginal name means 'The Granites', so it comes as no real surprise to discover that it is encircled with big boulders, some as smooth as marble. In places there are heaps of them, one on top of the other as though an Aboriginal giant of prodigious strength deliberately stacked them that way. In truth, not legend, they are the remnants of immense volcanic action long before the dingo arrived on these shores, way back before the Dreamtime. Way, way back.

They say gold was the reason why the settlement came into being. By 1890 as many as 20,000 adventurous souls had flocked there, some of the prospectors mounted on camels.

So what about today? There is a church here, the Church of the Corner, catering for all denominations; a post office; two general stores; a hospital and the Flying Doctor Service. You might note that the staff of the Flying Doctor Service are not as good-looking or as well groomed as their TV counterparts. Fortunately, they are a great deal more skilled than most actors when it comes to fixing a broken leg or to diagnosis of a sudden illness. Also, there is a National Parks office here; a couple of garages, although whether or not they would have the 'right' spare parts is a different question. A lawman? Certainly. This one has an area the size of Wales to look after. Fortunately he's not restricted to a horse.

And most importantly there are two hotels: the Tibooburra Hotel, founded in 1890; and the Family Hotel, erected two years before that. Without them, Tibooburra would curl up and die.

So, yes, not too many folk have been to this tiny place. It's also a fact that even fewer have heard of it. Fair enough. What goes on in Tibooburra doesn't make headlines on Channel Nine too often. But that might work both ways. For instance, a great many taxpayers in New South Wales aren't aware of the contribution their taxes make towards the upkeep of the Border Fence via the State Government's $100,000 annual allocation.

For the record, the rest of the required funds are raised by land rates. Some 1,100 graziers in the State pay annual rates of 2.35 cents per hectare. Around $752,000 is raised that way. It's worth noting that upwards of seven million sheep graze in comparative peace south of the Border Fence—reckoned the most vital link in the overall structure—with a wool clip worth about $160 millon annually.

Also, Tibooburra shares the dubious distinction of being New South Wales' hottest settlement. Few if any would dispute that in summer. Temperatures soar. Mid-30s is a pleasant day. Often it lingers in the high 40s for weeks on end. It may top 50 degrees. When winds sweep in from the desert, like the fiery breath of an angry dragon, people have been known to go mad or commit suicide. Fence workers start at daybreak. Finish before noon.

Wildlife? Even the creepy-crawlies are smart enough to use a suntan preparation—lizard brown, I think it's called. Foxes moult alarmingly (after all, their ancestors came from Europe). 'Roos stretch out in whatever shade they can find, fanning themselves with pawfuls of grass. Sheep, panting madly, huddle together under trees and bushes. Are you sure it's not shearing time? Cattle stand placidly in dried-up dams and pretend they are knee-deep in water. Doesn't help much. Rabbits fare better. They retreat to cool underground motels.

Dingoes? Well, those south of the Border Fence—in Sturt National Park—are in real bad trouble. Outlaw country. Those to its north, in cattle country where game (with the exception of rabbits) is scarce, plot ways of breaching the fence.

But it wasn't summer now. Winter. A wonderful day as Paddy drove into Tibooburra and parked outside the house of his replacement, Greg Beaton. No, he was not at home. Out on the 'fence' somewhere. No worries, Paddy said. We'd most likely catch up with him tomorrow on our way to Smithville Depot.

From there we drove the short distance to the Tibooburra Hotel where Paddy was greeted by everyone like an old mate. And presently, holding me firmly by the elbow, he showed me where the house bar was. It was 4.30. A bit early, still. . .

'What's it to be?' Paddy look around and saw a couple of people he knew. Introduced me to Brian and Belinda Wren. Somewhere in there I said, 'Fosters'. I didn't have to repeat it.

'G'day,' Brian said, smiling easily. He wore a tan-coloured Akubra with a dark sweat stain around the hat band. He was a mailman: letters, stores, whatever. One of his regular, four-day jaunts took him out through Wompah Gate to south-west Queensland. Often, he said, dogs followed him for miles. They 'had a thing' about vehicle tracks. 'You wanna see dogs, you come for a trip with me. I'll show you dogs. Heaps of the bastards.'

Later on, some of the locals arrived, in from the stations. Most wore big hats, too. They also had check shirts, dirty moleskins, and elastic-sided boots to go with them.

There was even a collection of hats arranged on the wall of the main house bar. Hats with holes in them. With torn crowns. With grease, sweat, and red dust stains. Hats by Akubra, Thomas Cook, Stetson; hats with character donated by stationhands, ringers, 'roo shooters, maybe even a boundary rider in from the fence.

So, yes, it was the kind of setting where you might expect to find a film crew today. No trouble to picture a director lining up Jack Thompson at the bar, beer in hand. Shooting a scene for a sequel to one of his best movies, *Sunday Too Far Away*. This one called, perhaps, *Monday Too Bloody Soon*.

The ex-Supervisor of the Border Fence was still going strong when I chickened out at about 10.30. I had no trouble finding my room. It was at the top of the stairs.

So there we were next morning, Paddy and I, heading out in a rented Toyota through the magnificent array of wildlife you can observe almost any day in that harsh, special part of New South Wales called the Corner Country, with its high, broken-capped, mesa-like formations providing excellent cover for shy wallaroos. They called this type of terrain 'jump-up' country on account of the way the hills appear to leap up from the rolling downs.

'All this land,' Paddy said, firing yet another tailor-made smoke, 'used to be Olive Downs. Famous station in its day, went right back to the early 1880s. The Kidman family eventually got hold of it, or held most of the shares, anyway. It became a part of the Park in 1973.'

We crunched to the top of a stony rise. Suddenly emus were directly in front of us, four large ostrich-like birds striding it out as if they were going somewhere in a tearing hurry. Paddy cursed as he stabbed a foot on the brake to avoid hitting the last one in the backside.

'Stupid bastards!' he muttered. The emus must have heard him because they suddenly darted off the track. 'Real menace on the fence at times, you know.' Paddy shook his head. 'Plenty of them around this year too by all accounts. You get years like that. Same thing with 'roos and rabbits and everything else out here.' He suddenly tapped my arm significantly and, with a tiny smile, pointed straight ahead.

There before my delighted eyes was a strung-out line of high wire and iron post. The Dingo Fence!

At a big gateway, Paddy stopped. He turned to me with both forearms resting lightly across the steering wheel, a rather whimsical smile on his sun-ravaged features.

'One thing about being the driver...'

'I know, I get to open all the gates.'

The heavy gate swung open; the Toyota lurched through. With the gate half-closed, I paused to gaze north at a stony part of Queensland's south-west. Harsh country, designed to break a settler's heart, or to snap his wife's mind. Deservedly it was called Heartbreak Corner.

'C'mon!' Paddy bawled. 'The fence doesn't need fixin'!'

Heading west now, on a track running alongside the fence. The country remained desolate. Almost no wildlife. Better further on, Paddy said. Where the sandhills were. Heaps of wildlife there; this type of Godforsaken country had never done a thing for him. Suddenly, he squinted ahead. A pair of sunglasses or even a hat would have helped, but, as I'd already discovered, he favoured neither.

'Someone's coming.'

Sure enough, a vehicle was in sight, a fraction blurred because of the distance and haze. But real all the same. An engine thudding under a bonnet; a driver most likely wondering who the hell we were.

'One of the boys, I expect.' Paddy meant a boundary rider. Of which there are 12 on the Border Fence. All up, the Broken Hill Wild Dog Board has a field force of 21. Apart from those that ride the boundary, there are two fence overseers, one at Smithville and the other at Wompah, one leading hand, and five plant operators.

Paddy was still acting like an owl in dazzling sunshine. 'Might not know this bloke.'

'What's his name?'

'Blowed if I know!'

The vehicle was much closer now, hugging the fence, moving slowly. I knew it was a Suzuki because I'd been told that the Board had a fleet of them: lightweight four-wheel-drives, ideal in sand because, rather than sinking like heavier vehicles, they go over the top of it. Also, they are easy to maintain, cheap to run and, like most things from Japan, extremely reliable.

The two wagons stopped just short of each other. Not quite 'roo bar to 'roo bar. A tall character slouched outside. He wore see-through sunglasses, an Akubra with the brim tugged low over his eyes, blue jeans, a green jacket.

'G'day.' He stuck out a meaty paw and said his name was Brian Arnould.

After introductions (and he'd heard of Paddy all right) the ex-Supervisor jerked a thumb in an easterly direction.

'You're at Warri?' He meant Warri Cottage.

'Yeah.'

'How long you been there?'

'Over three months.'

'Married?'

'Yeah.'

'Always helps.' Paddy smiled coyly, like an Irish leprechaun. 'Keep "Mum" happy and everything's okay in the kitchen.' I was rather surprised that he didn't say 'bed'.

Brian nodded.

Paddy said, 'How's it going?'

'The job?'

'Yeah.'

'No worries.'

'Beaton okay?' Paddy was extremely interested to see how his successor was shaping up. The general verdict was very well.

'All right so far.'

Paddy tried a different tack. 'Any dogs about?'

'Few. . .' Brian was expressionless.

Paddy nodded. 'Usually is along this stretch.'

'Set a trap yesterday,' Brian said. He left that opening hanging there like a wet towel in dire need of another peg to support its weight.

'Any luck?' That was me proving I was the master of short sentences, too.

Brian shook his head, pulled a disgusted face. 'Naw! Bastard was there, but. Saw where he pissed on a log.'

'They get smart!' Paddy said, nodding his head up and down like the original wise old man. He then turned to me and indicated the fence. I was told that the bottom part was the old rabbit fence. 'Not many places where you can see it now,' Paddy continued. Brian did the right thing and posed while I photographed it. Suddenly Paddy checked his wristwatch. 'Holy cow! Is that the time? We'll be pushed at this rate to get there by dark.'

'Goin' through to Smithville?'

'Uh-huh.'

'Greg's over that way.'

'See you later, mate,' Paddy said.

'See ya.' Brian lifted a hand in salute. Home to mum soon. Nothing quite like it. On the Border Fence.

The conversation had hardly been stimulating. But it was enough. You could always make up for it later. With your mates, in the pub. A choice of two. In Tibooburra.

The landscape remained uninviting. The Border Fence stretched away to the horizon. Men patrolled it on horseback once, I reminded myself. Men leading packhorses loaded down with supplies, tents, and fencing materials. Once.

With no prompting, Paddy kept up a running commentary about the 'fence' and those he had come into contact with while working on it. One of six brothers and four sisters, Paddy was born in 1929 on the Veldt, a 21,085 ha station in the Milparinka district. In his early 20s he became the manager of Brindiwilpa, some 45,731 hectares. This was in 1951, two years after floods had devastated sections of the Border Fence.

'There were no sheep on the place,' Paddy recalled. 'You could only run cattle. My God, there were some dogs there then; the station was infested with the bastards!'

Frequent flooding over much of the 1950s continued to cause havoc with the Border Fence. Profitable sheep raising was impossible for about 112 km on both sides of the Queensland and South Australia borders.

But in 1959, when morale on the fence was possibly at an all-time low, the Board took on Brian Neill as Supervisor, not an enviable position. Neill, however, proved a man of strong personality, humour, and, most importantly, the type to inspire loyalty. If only the elements would give him a fair crack of the whip.

Surprisingly they did. Within a year, Neill's workforce had done wonders.

The Border Fence was in great shape again. Neill's sterling efforts did not go unrecognised. From that time on, he had the graziers in the palm of his hand.

With untold enthusiasm, Neill would continue in that capacity. He was there at the helm in 1974 and again two years later when floods tore the heart out of much of the Border Fence along both the Queensland and South Australian sections.

But by early 1976 Neill, undermined by poor health, was ready to call it quits. He remained longer than he ought. His resignation, which the Board accepted with regret, was to take place on 4 November 1976. On the very eve of his retirement, Lawrence Brian Neill, MBE, died.

There are no flags on the Border Fence. But had there been, they would have been lowered to half-mast.

So for the first time in 18 years the Supervisor's job was up for grabs. It would, the Board realised, be difficult to fill Neill's boots adequately. In an Annual Report they announced Neill's successor.

APPOINTMENT OF SUPERVISOR—MR. A.S. BARLOW

Mr. A. S. Barlow, formerly representing the Milparinka Pastures Protection Board district on the Board, was appointed as Supervisor following interviews of several able contenders from a large field of applicants. The Board considered that Mr. Barlow's long experience in the area and proven managerial capacity, as well as his knowledge of the wild dog and its habits and habitats, fitted him best for the position. Mr. Barlow commenced duties with the Board on 29th November, 1976.

At no time would those who voted for Paddy Barlow have cause to regret their choice. Nor, for that matter, would those directly under him on the Border Fence wish someone else had been appointed to the position. Not even those who, when given a job, were sent out to Bindara Cottage, about which Paddy said in 1984:

We tend to test new people at Bindara Depot—a regular salt mine which is the most isolated and bleak of them all. If they can survive a year in that awful place we reckon they'll stay with us for years.

And it was to Bindara that Arthur and Shirley Clifford and their three-year-old daughter, Tammy, went in the mid-1980s.

Arthur Clifford, 50, was a bushman from way back. Bindara held no secret fears for him, particularly with his wife and daughter with him. Mostly, he had worked on stations in the far west of the State. In his spare time, to bring in extra money, he trapped dingoes. Initially for something to do, Shirley had tagged along. The whole process of dogging—of matching wits with an intelligent animal—appealed to her greatly. Given time, she too became proficient in the art of setting traps, of using the right lures. Out at the cottage called Bindara, she continued dogging. Made sense that she did. Apart from collecting $10 for each scalp, the Board, recognising her worth, paid her a yearly bonus of $5,000 to keep up the good work.

So everything was pretty 'sweet' for the Cliffords. Arthur went about his job of maintaining the fence in his own vehicle (as yet the Board did not provide these) and Shirley continued dogging in her four-wheel-drive Suzuki.

Then one Christmas, Arthur, now 52, complained of severe chest pains. A heart attack followed a few days later. From Tibooburra, Clifford was taken by the Flying Doctor Service to Broken Hill Hospital.

Shirley: 'Paddy was there; he was wonderful to me and Tammy. Arthur seemed to be getting better but then he developed bleeding ulcers, which we never knew he had. The chest pains came back, but much worse. They rushed him to Adelaide but it was too late; he was gone.'

The deep shock of losing her husband was compounded by the fact that she and her daughter were effectively without a home anymore. 'We were in a terrible position; I really didn't know what to do for the best. But Paddy was there again just when I needed him the most. He put it to the Board if I could live at Adelaide Gate until I sorted myself out.' (Adelaide Gate Cottage was no longer in use, the boundary riders on either side of it, one of whom had been Arthur Clifford, had shared the old Adelaide Gate run between them.)

After due deliberation, the Board agreed with Paddy's request, which allowed Shirley to live at Adelaide Gate rent-free but not to receive the $5,000 a year bonus.

So Shirley Clifford, in her mid-40s, went to live 32 km west of Bindara. A testing period. At times, she seriously wondered if she would get through it. Her only companion was her daughter who was then not quite of school age. Her only contact with the outside world Geoff Smith, the Overseer at Wompah Depot. He called her every morning to see if everything was all right. Once a week he came out with mail and supplies. That is, if the Bulloo hadn't overflowed.

In the 18 months she lived there, the Bulloo River broke its banks several times. No one could get in; no one could get out. Food was never a problem; she had made sure of that. The real fear was that either she or Tammy would get sick. But fortunately that never happened.

In 1987 Shirley was offered a job on Bulloo Downs station just across the border in south-west Queensland. Living at an out-station on that huge run once owned by Sid Kidman, she would look after the bores, cleaning out dead rabbits, etc., checking on windmills, casting an eye on the cattle, just being there. Also, she trapped dingoes. Ten dollars always came in real handy for a gutsy woman on her own.

Presently sandhills and ground-hugging growth began to break up the hard rocky land. Rabbits, so many rabbits. Most sandhills were riddled with burrows, so there were eagles too. Same old scenario, the hunter and the hunted, the chain reaction.

Seeing an eagle at close range led Paddy to say that he'd seen them attacking 'roos. Not small ones, either. Airborne attack with beak and claws, drawing blood with every hit, until the bloodied, bemused 'roo could take no more.

The feast would begin soon after. Basic. The very bottom line. Along the New South Wales Border Fence.

Low-slung Toona Cottage was set amidst shade trees. An appealing spot where the main colour was the rich redness of the earth. Birdlife was prolific; you would not require an alarm clock there. Rabbits could at times be seen from the doorway. Rabbit stew? Why not. Meat doesn't come much leaner. Animals aren't any cleaner in their habits.

No one was home at Toona; Paddy reckoned we'd meet them, a married couple, out on the fence. Several tame-looking emus watched us depart. Almost certainly they were pets of whoever was out there.

The Toyota ground through loose red sand in the far north-west corner of Sturt National Park. The sun blazed like a fireball in a sky of deepest blue. Rabbits in their thousands: impossible to count them. At regular intervals eagles and hawks and the odd kestrel were perched on the fence. They and their offspring had it made here. Some wattle trees were alive with birds: galahs, cockatoos, brightly-garbed parrots. 'Roos and wallabies, kicking up sand, scampered away. An infrequent fox, glancing furtively over its shoulder, was resplendent in its reddish coat which in such a setting provided ideal camouflage. I was in a constant heady state of entrancement.

Now a small four-wheel-drive was coming towards us. The middle-aged couple we met were Bob and Norma Clarke. They had been at Toona since February that year. They loved the life. Toona was a beautiful spot. Yes, the emus were pets of sorts. Yeah, Bob said, Greg was okay; a darn good bloke, in fact. Paddy digested that like something he was unsure of. Said, 'Hmmmmm...'

In the cabin I noticed a rifle, a .222 Sportco fitted with a 'scope. Bob was not opposed to downing a dog. They were, he reckoned, 'pretty thick' on the stations along this stretch.

Paddy turned on the ignition. A gutsy roar followed.

'Seemed happy enough,' I commented.

'Why shouldn't they be, eh? Kids off their hands. Best cottage on the fence. Wouldn't mind living there myself...no worries.'

'What about Beryl?'

'Naw, she's happy enough in Broken Hill. Suppose I am too, come to that.' He paused. 'Bob's the right age for this lark. No good for young jokers. Can't hack it. Have to get to town too often; on the grog, women. That's why the Board likes married men. More stable. Bushmen make the best bet of all. Can't really put a city bloke out here, y'know. Too much can go wrong: floods, bushfires, dust storms, accidents. City bloke's no use in a situation like that. He's flat out simply surviving!'

Cameron Corner, where three States meet, is named after the surveyor, John Cameron. Unable to find a suitable rock with which to mark this spot, he used a fence post instead. The date was 18 September 1880. There are camping facilities here now, like a wooden table and room to pitch a tent. We drove out through the fence and parked in the shade of trees. A brew would go down well. Uncorking a flask, Paddy, with a dark scowl, said that bloody tourists flocked there in the holiday season. Christmas and New Year was like a three-ring circus. He gestured broadly. 'I mean, what's here in summer, for Pete's sake?'

Good question. Worth considering. I gazed about me with my usual keen-eyed interest. Rabbits. (What? Them again!) Heaps of rabbits. They may have resided in South Australia, New South Wales (providing they could wriggle under the netting buried 30 cm underground) or in Queensland. Perhaps those living in South Australia went to Queensland for their holidays and vice versa, swapping burrows sort of thing?

Paddy, hands on hips, seemed to be still waiting for an answer. So what else *was* here? Red sand. An enormous amount of it. A track winding off in a sort of nor-westerly direction. Innamincka was at the end of it, about 260 km away. And the fence, of course. Mustn't forget that.

I drained my mug. Wiped the back of a hand across my mouth. Slowly refilled my mug. Even more slowly worked a teabag back and forth. I looked up at Paddy. He was still wearing the kind of dirty look graziers reserve for the sight of a dingo getting stuck into their sheep.

'Heaps,' I said at last.

'Hmph!' the ex-Supervisor went.

The mid-afternoon sun slanted across the bonnet of the Landcruiser as we followed the Border Fence south. Somehow it infused this magnificent desert setting with a special quality all of its own. For it was one red sandhill after another now as the fence snaked in and out of hollows, stretched out across wide flats, or topped fair-sized hills.

In all there are 400 sandhills along the entire length of the Border Fence. They represent a continuing maintenance problem in dry weather as the fence is alternately undermined or drifted up by sand. Impressed beyond belief, I was reminded strongly of what the explorer, Sturt, wrote of this far western part of the State: 'Here on every side are stupendous and almost insurmountable sand-ridges of fiery red.'

Beyond the fence, to the west, was of course South Australia. Specifically Quinyambie station, owned by the Sid Kidman group. They run around 13,000 head of cattle here, mixed breeds. They have the space, all 12,119 square kilometres of it.

With a throwaway motion, Paddy gestured out the window. 'More dogs there than you can shake a stick at. Great breeding country. Never seen as many rabbits as I have on that place. Millions of them. In a really bad drought they instinctively head south in search of water. The fence buggers things up for them of course. They give up and die then. Happens every five years or so here. Sixty-nine was a bad one. Rabbits were piled up along the fence three-to-four feet deep. Christ! The stink!'

Presently, White Catch Cottage came into view. A few shade trees would have brought some measure of relief from the summer sun to the old, rather broken-down dwelling that was due to be replaced soon.

'Bloke named Allan Littlejohn is the boundary rider here,' Paddy informed me, slowly. 'Which reminds me: he's from your part of the world too.'

'That right? Where?'

'Blowed if I know.' Paddy shrugged. 'In the South Island, I think.' He applied the brake.

'On his own, is he?'

'Naw! He has a woman. Jennifer Jones is her name. She's a nurse in Tibooburra—works at the hospital there. Stays out here at the weekends. Good sort, too. Allan's okay too. . . for a Kiwi!' He had parked next to what I took was the Toyota's equally dusty brother.

'Good,' Paddy said, moving away from the vehicle, 'we're in luck. Lenny and Greg are here.'

The men in question—overseer and supervisor—had been carrying out maintenace work on a Caterpillar DSB bulldozer, a highly-versatile machine mostly used in tandem for quick repair work with a giant-sized Caterpillar IT28.

'How's it going, Lenny?' Paddy was lighting another smoke.

'No worries, Paddy,' Lenny Dixon replied with a smile. He started to wipe dirty hands on an equally dirty rag. 'We've just about done here.' The burly, 43-year-old stood around 176 cm. He was wearing a blue check shirt and a light coloured Akubra hat like Tom Burlinson wore in *The Man From Snowy River.*

Greg came over as I was being introduced to Lenny. He too wore a big hat, a black Stetson, a high-crowned affair like they favour on cattle runs in the Kimberley region of Western Australia. In his 49th year, Greg stood a lean 182 cm, wore a brown check shirt, carried a folding knife in a pouch at his waist belt, and had the slightly worried look of a stockman who can't find his horse in the night paddock. The job, he later explained to me at Tibooburra, was not without its difficulties. He might, I thought, have echoed Paddy's words there. But these were early days where Greg was concerned; he was still finding his feet in an occupation different from any he had tackled before. There was one common denominator, however. The dingo.

8

Trouble-Shooter in the West

If you trap a dog, the bitch'll hang around for anything up to two weeks.
Which gives you ample time in which to get it. But should you trap the
bitch first, the dog'll only stick around for one night afterwards. If you
don't get it then—forget it!
– Greg Beaton, Tibooburra, talking about trapping dingoes in Western
Australia in the late 1970s

Before taking on his present position, Greg Beaton had spent his entire working
life on sheep and cattle stations, doing stock work or as a dogger employed
by the Western Australian Government. It seemed to me after talking with
him and his wife, Maxine, at the new Supervisor's house in Tibooburra, that
he had earned the right to wear that big black Stetson.

Over the past eight years, Greg and his family (two young sons) had ranged
over a great deal of the outback. In the Northern Territory and in Queensland
he had been employed as a head stockman. He had gained experience to handle
that demanding role in his home State of Western Australia, where his father,
Don, had managed various sheep and cattle stations.

In time, Greg too had become a manager of a station, Glifford Creek, 402 km
inland from Carnarvon, deep in the Gascoyne River Basin. It was top sheep
country if you could raise them. The Lyons River ran through the middle of
the station.

It was 1972 when Greg arrived there, in his early 30s, rail-lean, unmarried.
To make the station a paying proposition would, he knew, demand a herculean
effort. Indeed, he had wondered if he was doing the right thing. On paper
it seemed a no-win situation. The problem was that the owners, with great
persistency, were still trying to make a go of running sheep on the place. They
had put 54,000 sheep on the place over 14 years, yet when Greg turned up
he was informed that stock numbers stood at about 5,000 sheep and 25,000
cattle. Incredibly, they had no return at all for their outlay. The dingoes had
seen to that.

For the next two years, Greg and his men waged an all-out war on dingoes.
Traps mainly. You carried a rifle with you at all times. And poison. It was
dropped in large quantities once a year. Normally, a number of dingo-infested
runs linked forces and were assisted with a government subsidy.

Baits were made of meat, often kangaroo meat. Each small cube contained

Above The Border Fence between Warrie and Toona cottages with New South Wales on the left, Queensland on the right

Below The Fence runs on to the sandy country on the horizon and eventually to Cameron Corner

CAMERONS CORNER.

IN 1882–83 SURVEYOR JOHN CAMERON WAS IN CHARGE OF THE TEAM THAT COMPLETED THE FIRST BOUNDARY SURVEY BETWEEN N.S.W. AND QLD. HE PLANNED TO BUILD A CAIRN HERE BUT A SHORTAGE OF STONE FORCED HIM TO ERECT A PEG INSTEAD. THIS PEG IS NOW ON DISPLAY IN TIBOOBURRA.

Above White Catch gatehouse on the NSW-SA stretch of the Border Fence is typical boundary rider accommodation

Left There are about 400 sandhills like these along the Border Fence

Below In the winter of 1989, Allan Littlejohn was based at White Catch

Right Smithville cottage is the home of the Dixon family, Kenny, Tess, Gay, Sharon and Lenny Dixon (holding his grandson Leonard)

Below Back to the setting sun, the author's shadow stretches out towards Smithville — mainten— ance centre for the South Austra— lian section of the Border Fence

Top In south-west Queensland drought is common

Above A plains turkey striding along the Fence

Left Greg Beaton favours a Stetson rather than an Akubra hat

half-a-grain of alkaloid strychnine. One-third of a grain was considered a lethal dosage.

Greg: 'But no matter what you came up with there was no way you could control their numbers. At the end of two years all the sheep were gone. Oh, we might have had 50 or so left. We sold them and that was the end of sheep on Glifford Creek.'

It wasn't until the introduction of 1080 poison in the mid-1970s that there was any great decrease in the numbers of dingoes in Western Australia.

Married to Maxine now, but with no children as yet, Greg looked for a new occupation. Nearly four years at Glifford Creek had been enough. He found what he was looking for with the Agricultural Protection Board in Carnarvon. The job they offered was as a dogger. True the pay wasn't up to much: $150 a week. Worse, you had to supply everything. But it meant an outdoor life and he knew nothing but that. Also, he would match his wits against a cunning and clever predator that had forced considerably more than one station in the West to change from sheep to cattle.

For a year the Beatons, with a caravan as their base-camp, went from one station to another. To make their income stretch even further, they camped out in their swags whenever they could, living off the land.

Greg: 'Wild duck, 'roo, goat, pig. You name it, we ate it!'

Maxine: 'We even tried donkey once.'

'And it was bloody horrible!' Greg finished.

With a year of straight-out dogging behind them, Greg's worth was noticed. He was offered a somewhat different role. Trouble-shooter. This meant that he covered a much wider area than before. At far-flung stations, losing lots of sheep and no-one knowing how to stop it, he would advise and demonstrate how best to deal with the common enemy.

Greg: 'Lots of men who are damn good station managers have no real idea what dogging entails. Only a few of them, for instance, know there's more to setting a trap than chucking it in the ground. It has to be set and adjusted correctly. You've gotta know where to put it too. I mean, set it in the wrong place and you're likely to catch anything but the bloody dog!'

There had been a great call on Greg's services from early winter through to late spring. 'That's when the dogs are more active,' Greg said. 'They kill a lot more then. It's also the time when there's a fair bit going on at a station— mustering, shearing, lambing. So it's soon obvious if any killing's going on.' He broke off, and then at my request elaborated. 'Once a dog and bitch team up they hunt hard. Kill far more than they need to. It's all a big game really. Maybe the dog likes to show off a bit, too. This goes on until the bitch is too heavy with pup to hunt any more. So she remains in the den while he does all the hunting. He gorges himself before going back to the den and then, outside it, regurgitates the lot.

'Once the pups are born and can see, they are curious enough to follow their mother when the dog comes back with food. Soon they start to pick at it. This might go on for, say, six to seven weeks. The pups are getting big now.

Need a lot to eat. It's too much for the dog to cope with and so the bitch gets into the act again.

'Next thing you know the bitch has the pups out with her; educating them to hunt and kill. Often it's ewes with lambs.'

Greg concluded by saying that it wouldn't be unusual for a dog and bitch over a three-month period to kill as many as 300 sheep between them.

It was one such notorious pair of dingoes, on a big station north of the Gascoyne River, that Greg Beaton was called on to deal with by the owner. Later, in October when I caught up with him and his wife at Tibooburra, Greg related what happened.

On an overcast and windy August morning, just after dawn, Greg Beaton arrived in a four-wheel-drive Suzuki in the area where recently a large number of sheep had been killed. Water was scarce. One windmill provided the only water for miles around. Any dogs working the immediate area, Greg knew, would certainly drink there.

Greg clambered out of the rugged little wagon. Quickly, he found fresh signs consistent with a good-sized dingo. For eyes as practised as his, it was similar to reading bold headlines in a daily newspaper. Even so, skilled as he was, there was no way of knowing from a paw mark if it was a dog or bitch. Where a dog cocked its back leg on a bush was something else: a dead giveaway. Still, because of the season, he was pretty sure it would be a male animal. Ten-to-one the bitch would remain closer to here, where she could keep a watchful eye on the den. Another thing, the surrounding terrain was flat and mostly featureless. No commanding spots to speak of where a dog might, while resting, watch for possible signs of danger.

Slowly, Greg started to circle the windmill. Birds were still watering. A big red 'roo watched him from a short distance away; not even the growling sound of the Suzuki had scared it off.

Presently, Greg found a distinct pad. The tracks of a dingo were there, clear-cut, leading away. The thing was to get onto them early, before the ravaging effects of sun and wind dried them out. He raised thoughtful brown eyes and stared into the distance: rough, broken country. A likely place, he mused inwardly. He could of course have set traps here, near the pad, and possibly caught the dog overnight. But the station manager had been insistent. He wanted both dog and bitch destroyed, and all the pups too. It was what being a trouble-shooter was all about. Even if killing such appealing youngsters as dingo pups was distasteful to the likes of Greg Beaton, you went with the flow and did what they paid you for. He was nothing if not conscientious.

Shanks's pony, then. Same old style, one foot in front of the other, eyes mostly scanning the ground, reading signs like the print in a book.

From his vehicle he selected one of two weapons, a .270 Winchester rifle. It was fitted with a 'scope sight, a 3×9 Tasco. The calibre was suited to his line of work: a far-reaching cartridge of extremely flat target, good to about 400 metres. Moreover it hit hard at the other end. No way was he over-gunned for dogs!

He started off, the trail simple to follow, the rifle a solid but reassuring weight on his shoulder. He tugged the brim of his black Stetson to a lower angle over his eyes, the better to see into the glare of the rising sun.

In a direct line, the dingo's spoor took him towards the mesa-like country nudging the not-so-distant skyline. The sun had retreated behind a heavy cloud barrier and he might not see it again that day. If anything the wind was stronger, a cold blast from the south.

Greg Beaton knew that he might be in for a long day. Dawn 'till dusk would not surprise him. Previously, he had followed tracks from a dingo's regular watering place, in stinking hot conditions for anything up to 13 km and still failed to see an animal with pricked ears and a long bushy tail at the end of it. He'd even tracked the same dog a dozen or more times and still been right out of luck. Other times he'd spotted a dog not too far from where it had watered, meandering along in its own territory, drawn to an old kill, where it left its droppings on a regular basis.

Within an hour or so, he reached a low escarpment. Careful not to skyline himself, he edged warily in a semi-crouched position over the broken rim and then sat down, the .270 lying across his lap, his hand resting lightly on its wooden stock.

He was overlooking a rather narrow valley, shaped like a scooped-out hollow. A watercourse zigzagged through its middle. Low bushes and mulga offered shade. On the far skyline, a long rifleshot away, were spiralling, turret-like rocks. The overall nature of the terrain was hard, as hard as granite. Tracks close to hand, less than an hour old he estimated, revealed where the dingo had started downslope.

Without difficulty, Greg could visualise puppies playing among the small rocks scattered about the valley bottom. The young of a dingo were exactly the same as the offspring of any breed of dog. And as his eyes swept back and forth, he knew with a hunter's gut reaction that this was the place where the den would be. Question was could he actually locate it? At a half crouch, he too started downslope.

But even before the ground levelled out, a flash of movement told him he'd just about caught up with the dog he was tracking. Less than a hundred metres away a dingo was leaping a narrow channel which, in times of rain, fed the watercourse.

With practised ease, Greg slammed the butt of his rifle with the flat of his hand and the weapon, spinning on the axis of his shoulder, was tracking after the dog as if it had a mind all of its own.

Normally there was no way he would attempt a running shot. Better to wait and hope that the animal might pause to check its backtrail, which on the skyline they often did. Better to shoot then. But this was the kind of running shot that wasn't too difficult for a skilled rifleman: the one when the target is heading directly away.

Breathing easily, Greg swung the muzzle past the dog as if he were using a sweet-handling shotgun and the name of the game was pheasant. A split-second later the dog appeared in the outer circle of the slope and, a milli-second before the cross-hairs were centred on the spinal column high on its neck, he touched the hair-trigger. The .270 roared, the muzzle lifting in violent recoil.

No mistake. The dingo was hit hard. It lurched, staggered, and then, still caught up in its own momentum, covered a few more metres before pitching headlong into the watercourse. Dead, Greg knew. Instantly, he worked the bolt, replacing the spent cartridge with a shiny replacement. Motionless, then, except for the continual shift of his eyes, he waited. One dog usually meant two.

Five patient minutes became ten. Still vigilant, he decided to leave the dog where it was for now, to first check out the turret-like rocks topping the skyline. For some reason they now drew his attention like a magnet. Cautiously, he approached the higher ground, scrambling up the last steep stretch of it. All rimrock here, hard as iron. The main thrust rose above him like a cave-ridden tower perhaps 60 metres high. A dozen dogs could find likely dens here, he thought.

With some difficulty, he started to climb. Flaky rock broke away under his feet. Heart hammering, he was doubly careful of his next foothold. Suddenly he was confronted by a recess, a sort of flat ledge was how he would have described it. He hauled himself upon it and his eyes were drawn to a roundish hole. Elbowing closer, he peered into it. Like a chimney or chute, it opened out maybe seven metres below into a pool of light, a chamber-like room obviously linked with the outside by a cave or narrow entrance of sorts.

And it was here that Greg Beaton, with a sharp intake of breath, saw a fat puppy move across the line of his vision. Got you! he thought triumphantly.

With haste, he returned to his vehicle, nearly 5 km from the den. With careful driving, he was able to cover about half that distance back before stopping. Then with a 12-gauge shotgun tucked in the crook of his arm, he retraced his previous steps. The 5-shot pump-action Remington would be ideal for what he intended.

Now that the den was pinpointed, finding the actual entrance to it proved simple enough. It was more of an inward sloping chute than a cave. He could hear the pups inside.

From his daypack, he took out a tin of milk powder and sprinkled it generously upon the ledge directly in front of the entrance to the den. Then he retreated a short distance. The weapon was fully loaded, safety catch off. Presently a pup emerged, drawn by the strange, tantalising smell.

Seven would fall victim to the often-worked ruse before Greg was convinced no more were left alive. He scalped the puppies. Concrete proof for the station owner. Next, he dumped them in a heap and covered the bodies with rocks. He didn't want crows pecking at the carcasses, walking over the two traps he'd set just off the ledge, alongside a pad. No lure was used. He didn't require any.

Shortly afterwards, he reached his first kill. A dog, like he had thought. It was a ginger-red colour with a white collar. That indicated domestic dog breeding. Nothing new in this country. Oftentimes dingoes mated with station bitches. The other way round, too. The offspring of such a pairing was often more vicious than a pure-bred dingo. He dragged the dead animal away from where it had fallen and it too was covered with rocks.

At his vehicle, Greg made camp. August nights were often cold in the north-west, bitterly so on occasions. To combat that, he pitched his tent and crawled into his swag early. It had been a full and rewarding day and he felt the natural satisfaction of a job well done. With luck, he would have the bitch tonight. All over. But he'd been too long in the game, seen too many setbacks, to count on anything.

A pale streaky dawning saw the rangy West Australian already well on his way. He approached the immediate area of the den with stealth. Upon reaching the ledge near where the traps were set a momentary flicker of disappointment crossed his face. One of the traps had been dug around, the plate revealed, jaws gaping. She had done that with a feather touch.

You cunning devil, he thought with a lift of his bony shoulders. Fortunately this was the bitch and not the dog he'd shot yesterday. Just as well. Kill the bitch first and the dog had to be taken the next night. After that it was gone, fast, clear out of its territory. On the other hand the bitch—perhaps her feelings of loyalty and commitment went deeper—would remain in the vicinity for as long as two weeks, Greg would have said if asked to put a specific time to it. In this particular instance, the loss of her pups as well would make it a virtual certainty that she would stay in the valley. Time was on his side then.

While he really considered it a futile gesture, Greg nevertheless left the traps where they were. With both concealed again, he began to think how best to catch the bitch. That thought was a constant pressure as he made his way out and then drove to the station headquarters.

The manager, a fair but hard man, expressed disappointment when Greg admitted the bitch was still alive. Give me time and she won't be, said Greg, his confidently spoken words belying his inner apprehensions.

Mollified, the station owner smiled and asked Greg if he fancied a cup of tea? You never said 'no' to that offer in the outback and Greg wasn't about to set a whole new trend.

Two days later, Greg returned to the traps. In the meantime, crows had somehow spotted a small patch of fur in the heap of rocks and pecked at what little of the carcasses they could reach. In doing so they had danced all over his traps—disturbing the ground but not activating them.

Other clear-cut evidence told him the bitch had been back too. He saw where she had lain down, facing the traps, perhaps studying the ground. She had, he saw, been no closer than two metres from either one. She knew, all right. No way was he about to end it here. Not in a month of Sundays. Not that she would linger that long.

Pressing work elsewhere of the same nature was quickly and successfully attended to. So it was a full week before he returned to the valley. When he did, it was a fine warm day, spring was in the air. But Greg's mood was not light-hearted. He faced a severe test of his ability. Had he been a gambling man, he would have placed all his hard-earned dollars on the bitch coming out on top. It hadn't once crossed his mind that she would be gone. Instinctively he knew that wasn't so.

Several painstaking hours elapsed before Greg, his khaki shirt soaked with sweat, struck paydirt. He found where she had been lying on a well-used 'roo pad. A good place to ambush one, he realised. But more than that it offered the bitch a commanding view of much of the valley, importantly, a clear one of the entrance to the den. He realised that she might have been watching him cut down her young, setting traps. He smiled wryly. Was that round one or round two to her?

Thoughtfully, he dragged the back of a hand across his stubbly jawline. No, he wouldn't set a trap here. Too simple. Somehow, he had to do better than that. But how?

Greg Beaton moved on, needing another link in the chain. He found it where the dog had been hit and where, before plunging limply into the watercourse, it had bled. Sign of the bitch was heavy here, as it was on the 'roo pad above. Certainly she would use the same route to move from one to another.

A plan began to unfold in his mind. Quickly he found the pad she had been using to come here. Next, he dug up the 10-day-old carcass of the dog. (Dingoes did not play by the rules. Neither did man when taking retaliatory measures.) Using two long sticks—he couldn't have touched the damn thing in a million years—he dragged it to where he would set his traps.

With the utmost care, the traps were set, placed back to back, say 25–30 cm apart, and chained together but not pegged in the ground. Catch a toenail in a pegged one and she was most likely history. But this way, with two traps chained together, gave him a more than even chance of pulling it off. Providing she came back.

To each trap jaw he applied hessian, wrapping it around tightly, like a bandage. Strychnine, in either powder form or crystals, adhered well to the rough material, held in place with wire. The idea being that once a dingo was trapped and the initial blinding panic was over, it turned its attention to the jaws that held it prisoner. In tearing frantically at the hessian, the dingo, all going to plan, took the odious brew directly into its mouth. The poison started its evil reaction almost instantaneously, but didn't always kill. But either way, the dingo invariably went berserk, often breaking its teeth, certainly biting through its tongue.

With the traps covered with smoothed earth, Greg played his master card. Delicately, ignoring the horrendous smell, he dragged the maggot-crawling remains of the dingo back and forth over the ground. To his enormous satisfaction, he had hardly disturbed it at all. Immediately, he returned the carcass to its previous burial ground. He reasoned this was the best he could do. If this didn't trap the bitch, most likely nothing would.

Two days later. Dawn was no longer a pink blush when Greg Beaton arrived yet again on the escarpment overlooking what by now was very familiar territory. Determined not to rush things, he angled downhill. Even so, it was extremely difficult not to hurry. One question hammered repeatedly at his mind: had it worked?

With a burst of elation, he saw that the traps had gone. The ground where they had been might have exploded from powerful inner forces. But other animals could have caused this, he knew. A 'roo, for instance. But the possibility of that sped from his questioning mind when he saw the bitch's spoor. Yes, he'd got her all right. She could, and possibly would, travel some distance. He would find her dead or alive. Near water, too. The burning effects of the poison would make sure of that.

Downstream, he found the bitch. She had travelled perhaps five kilometres. As he approached, he saw she was small with long crinkly white hair. Not uncommon in this country. She stared at him with a mixture of fear and apprehension. Mostly apprehension. She actually cowered when he raised his rifle.

For Greg Beaton one more trouble-shooting chore was over. One hundred per cent success. Oddly, he felt no upswing in his mood, no elation. Rather, he felt a little depressed. Certainly the kill had been an anti-climax.

Thoughtfully, he considered the still body. She had been undoubtedly intelligent, loyal to her mate. But a job was a job, wasn't it? He sighed heavily. And you did what they paid you for, right?

Presently his reverie was over. In a practical fashion he reached for the knife at his waist belt.

9

Smithville Depot

Once you get the red dirt on your boots you'll always want to come back.
> – Allan Littlejohn, boundary rider,
> New South Wales Border Fence

The slim, bent figure beside the Border Fence was Allan Littlejohn. Long-handled shovel in hand, he was just about to fill in a hole a few kilometres south of White Catch Cottage when Paddy, topping a rise, suddenly spotted him.

With an evil chuckle, Paddy immediately swung off the track and barrelled along the fence as though he hadn't the slightest intention of stopping.

Littlejohn stood there, mouth gaping. Roadhogs aren't common out there. Especially those that seemed hellbent on running you down. It was only when Paddy applied the brakes suddenly, and Allan recognised the driver, that a warm smile replaced the thunderous expression on his tanned, bearded face. The two men greeted each other warmly.

'Fox, Allan?' Paddy asked, indicating the hole.

Allan nodded. 'Yeah, Paddy. Fox!' He leaned on his shovel and pulled a disgruntled face. 'They're pretty bloody active at present.' He jerked a thumb at the hole. 'Have to fill up holes like that—and on the other side of the fence too—every bloody day.' A chunky cattledog cross came bounding up to the New Zealander. Wanted to be patted; Wink was not disappointed.

Paddy grinned. 'So what's new, mate?'

'Not foxes,' Allan grimaced. 'That's for sure!'

Apparently a fox often gets an inclination to dig a hole because it is curious to see what it's like on the other side of the fence. More activity of this kind takes place during mating time. It would appear that a fox might identify its ideal partner by sight and smell—nose to nose, as it were—on the other side of the fence. An intolerable situation. So on one side of the fence the dog starts to dig with enthusiasm and on the other side the bitch with no less eagerness. Eventually both holes are linked. The inevitable coupling takes place.

There used to be two boundary riders' cottages between White Catch and Smithville Depot—Munkartie and Hawker Gate. The last men to live there are gone too. One of those boundary riders, Clarry Illies, lived at Hawker Gate for a time during the war years and kept a diary:

19/1/43:
Left Smithville for Hawker Gate and carted water for boring plant.
25/1/43:
Dressing pine posts for rebuilding sandhills, cleaning out soakage.
26/2/43:
Cleaned buckbush off sandhill and put in six yards of foot-netting on the 83-mile.
8/3/43:
Mending dog traps and setting them for dingo on NSW side.
24/4/43:
Looking for dog trap with kangaroo in it.
25/6/43:
Repaired buggy, put in new spring and screwed up the body, followed dingo in trap for one and a half miles. Saw sheep through gate and set traps for dingoes on NSW side.
6/9/43:
Carted wood and water and looked for goats but couldn't find them, raked and burnt buckbush off sandhill on 92-mile, met boundary rider Morris.
2/1/44:
Took over in charge, unloaded chaff and put on windmill gear, got to Tilcha, loaded 200 gallons of water for Munkartie.
12/2/44:
Shovelled down big sandhill on the 77-mile and topped-up sandhill on the 78-mile.
8/3/44:
Carting wood and water, getting camp gear ready to camp out. Finished building motor buggy, patrol one mile of fence to give it a trail...

Smithville came into sight as the sun was low on the horizon and the red sandhills surrounding it glowed as though on fire and birds were calling raucously from the shade trees and the obligatory windmill stood out in sharp profile against the still deep blue of the sky.

'Here we are,' Paddy said, drawing to a halt outside the biggest dwelling there. 'What you could say is a long way up the dirt track from Broken Hill.' Not wrong. It was a slow, 264-km drive over a mainly rough track from the nearest town of any importance.

It is true there is not much to interest a tourist here. Most of the ten-strong population—the others are too young to cast a vote—will tell you that suits them fine.

So Smithville Depot consists of four houses dating from the mid-1930s. They are ringed by high corrugated-iron sheeting which is ugly. But looks don't count here. It is there for protection should blinding sand or dust storms sweep in from the west. There are a few outbuildings that have seen much better times. A couple of caravans provide makeshift accommodation. There is also a large vehicle shed-cum-workshop. Everything is neat and orderly inside it, if dusty.

This tiny settlement exists for one reason: it is the nerve-centre for the 225-km section of the Border Fence running south from Cameron Corner to the intersection of South Australia's Dog Fence, which, at that point, heads west, separating Quinyambie (outside the fence) and Mulyungarie stations. The responsibility for keeping this stretch of fencing in tip-top order rests, not always easily, on the broad shoulders of Lenny Dixon.

Lured to the far west of New South Wales by a rather colourful article depicting life on the Border Fence, Lenny Dixon first came to Smithville from Sydney in the winter of 1966. His wife, Gay, was 18 years old. She was also pregnant. He has never once regretted the move and, after a long period of adjustment, neither does Gay.

Kenny Dixon is 21, his sister, Sharon, a year younger. They grew up in a harsh land where self-reliance is a way of life. Like many bush kids they soon displayed an easy familiarity with firearms. Both are fine hunters. They are healthy and clear-skinned—good advertisements for their upbringing and environment.

Naturally mechanically-minded, Kenny operates the previously mentioned Caterpillar IT28. At the time of my next visit (a week later on my own) to Smithville Depot Kenny was servicing one of the Suzuki four-wheel-drive vehicles used by all the boundary riders, including his sister.

A typical day in winter for Kenny's father, Lenny, starts at 7.30 when, after a solid breakfast, he contacts by radio transceiver Allan Littlejohn and a boundary rider to the south of Smithville, Rod Belville. On this particular morning, Lenny's mood, like that of many Australians to whom cricket is a religion, is hugely expansive. The bloody useless Poms are once again getting thrashed in a Test match. So all's right in Lenny's world. Thanks to an ABC satellite TV dish—provided recently by the Board—he had been able to watch with untold glee a number of the Englishmen's wickets fall before retiring to bed around midnight.

First thing, Lenny rings Allan Littlejohn. Tells him he'll be up later with supplies. Stores and other essential commodities required to keep Smithville Depot operational are delivered once a week by Robert Scobie, out of Broken Hill.

Rod Belville lives at Broughams Cottage, 81 km away. He confirms with Lenny that he will be bringing up his vehicle for its regular service.

'Wife and kids coming?' Lenny asks.

'Yeah,' is the reply.

'Good. Gay'll be pleased to see them.'

Rod Belville and his wife, Karen, have lived on the Border Fence for four years. They have three children, all boys. The eldest of the three is four. A loner, Belville enjoys his work on the fence. ' 'Long as you do your job properly,' Belville says, 'they leave you pretty much alone.' That suits him fine. He takes a deep drag on his smoke and stares off into the faraway distance like bushmen the world over are apt to do. After a long time, he adds, 'Lenny's a bloody good boss.'

In particular, Belville delights in the varied wildlife he encounters almost every day of his life. He too is having trouble with foxes—'worse than ever' he reckons—and puts it down to the fact that a good market for winter skins no longer exists so there is not the heavy hunting they were subjected to a few years ago. A top skin in 1986 could realise $35.

Belville is fortunate, and is wise enough to know it, that his wife finds the life rewarding and wouldn't want to live anywhere else. Just her and her four men. But Karen will be even more contented shortly. A brand-new, three-bedroomed, fully air-conditioned cottage complete with a satellite TV dish will replace the iron-roofed dwelling (murder in summer) that has stood there for so long.

At eight o'clock, Lenny picks up a packed lunch, clamps his hat firmly on his head, and walks outside. There is red dirt on his boots, the sun is shining and the song of a multitude of crimson rosellas fills the air. He breathes deeply. The air sparkles like French champagne. He smiles and sighs deeply. It is a relaxed sound. He realises he is that rare animal, a contented man.

It will be warm later on, he tells me. About 25 degrees. A far cry, this, from mid-summer when, for weeks on end, temperatures range around the 40-degree mark and may climb as high as 47 to 49 degrees. 'You'd wish you were almost anywhere but here then,' Gay says meaningfully. At such a time even Lenny is apt to agree with her.

At the vehicle shed, Lenny allocates work for the day. Sharon has already left. As always, she is armed with a .22 Hornet rifle, held in a special rack behind the driver's seat. Wearing snug-fitting jeans and a blue baseball cap tilted at a rakish angle, she will head south today and cover around 30 kilometres. She will perhaps fix a tear in the fence caused by a big 'roo. Certainly she too will have foxholes to attend to. Tomorrow she will take off in the other direction to cover the rest of her responsibility. This is the procedure every five working days on the entire length of the Border Fence. For this reason alone, it is by far the best maintained section of the entire length of the three separately operated stretches of the Dingo Fence.

As already said, a $10 bounty applies in both New South Wales and Queensland but not in South Australia where the two bucks per scalp was no incentive at all. South Australian dingoes, therefore, were overjoyed to hear the price had fallen markedly. And more than one Queensland dingo, after reading about it in the *Dingo Times,* had packed a swag and headed south where with luck a more relaxed lifestyle could be enjoyed. But despite the lack of financial incentive, the scalps of at least 30 dingoes shot on Quinyambie are drying in the sun at Smithville. Hot-shot Sharon accounted for more than her fair share of them.

5 pm. Smithville Depot. Kenny Dixon, last to leave the workshop, is strolling towards the small cottage he lives in with his wife, Tess, 21, and their 15-month-old son, Leonard. So now three generations of the Dixon family live on the Border Fence.

On my own, I looked closely at the carcass of a yellowish dingo Lenny had shot on his return from taking supplies up to White Catch Cottage. With the evening starting to close in, I was reminded of a story Lenny had told me earlier. A month back, he and his son had driven to White Catch to deal with a troublesome bore. They had spotted a dingo bitch on Quinyambie and Lenny had shot it.

On their return, they had expected to see the usual crows or eagles feeding on the carcass. Only one bird had been there, an eagle. It was crouched low on the ground about 20 metres from the dead animal. The reason it was not on the kill, gorging itself, was because a male dingo was lying alongside the dead bitch with his head on her chest. So distraught was the dog that he didn't even bother to raise his head when they drove towards him. A bullet from Kenny's rifle ended his misery.

'You know,' Lenny Dixon admitted, 'I felt bad about that one for days afterwards, bloody upsetting really. Makes you realise what they feel for each other, doesn't it?'

A footnote. In presenting his paper at the Australian Dog-Fence Administrators' Conference at Arkaroola, South Australia, in November 1983, the Western Lands Commissioner, R.W. Condon, had this to say about that section of the Border Fence which is the direct responsibility of Lenny Dixon:

> If the fence were allowed to fall into disrepair it is estimated that it would take only 10 to 20 years for dingoes to become established throughout all areas of the Western Division. It is also considered that although the fence may have cost $507,000 in 1981, it is worth an estimated $15 million annually in lamb crops and another $5 million in better wool yields in the absence of the dingo.
>
> Some idea of the ability of the dingo to penetrate into areas which have been free can be gauged by the shooting of one on the Darling River near Tilpa and the sighting of another recently on the southern side of the Darling near Louth and others in the Wilcannia and Menindee districts in 1983 and 400 km south of the Queensland border. Unless they were brought in illegally, they would have come through the holes in the Queensland fence in 1976.

10

When The Border Fence Went Down

He's a menace, a cruel killer. If they just killed for a feed it would be
all right. But they tear off back legs, rip out throats. When the dogs've
been in you're shooting fly-blown sheep for weeks afterwards.
– Lindsay Russell, Broken Hill, talking about dingoes on Moorabi station
after they came through the Border Fence in 1974

Quinyambie station
South Australia
July 1989
Mid-morning
'Hey! There's one!' snapped Lenny Dixon. He brought the Toyota to a sudden
spine-jarring halt on a sandy track snaking across a saltbush flat. The engine
ticked over; to stop it suddenly would almost certainly cause the dingo he had
observed to run. 'Won't see a better looking dog than that,' he said, shaking
his head.

Ears cocked, the white-chested dingo watched us intently. He did not appear
afraid, curious more like. Typical of dingoes found in desert regions, he was
mostly a pale beige-yellow in colour. A washed-out shade—sun-faded, I suppose
you could say.

'No mixed blood there,' Lenny muttered quietly. 'A real pure-bred dog and
no mistake.'

The dingo, I noted, was particularly well developed through the chest and
shoulders, like a well-built middleweight boxer, all the power up top and the
rest lean and trimmed-down. His head was chunky, his ears still pricked, his
tail shortish, like a brush. He remained motionless. Nevertheless, I sensed that
any second he would run.

'Easy shot,' Lenny remarked. And there was every reason for him to reach
for his rifle, a Ruger M-77 in .22/250 calibre, a supreme long-range weapon,
about the ideal cartridge for dingoes. It had been 'blooded' many times.

'It is with that.' I indicated the rifle.

But on this late morning my companion made no move to take a life and
I was more than thankful for that. Suddenly the dingo wheeled. Off at a lope,
stretching out but still holding back. He could keep that action up for long
periods. Especially when hunting: the pungent smell of prey was alive on the

wind's tell-tale breath. Now, altering his course, he headed towards mulga-dotted sandhills barely smudging the western skyline.

'Better get a spurt on,' Lenny said. The dingo, now a brownish speck amidst spinifex grass, was already forgotten. He struck a match and lit another cigarette. He and Paddy made a good pair! The Toyota went into its act. 'Should see a few more before the day's done,' Lenny said.

And on this massive cattle run set in the lower stretches of the vast Strzelecki Desert we did see more dingoes. Six, in fact, four your traditional brown shade and one black version. But that was hardly surprising. According to the head stockman there, Jimmy Staker, it was 'nothin' to see 30 or as many as 40 dogs a day when they were mustering.' Mid-afternoon. Lenny's business on the station was done. The sun was flashing off the bonnet of the Toyota. Smithville was a couple of hours away, maybe longer. Lenny broke a friendly silence. 'Stand a brew?'

'Thought you'd never ask!'

One thing about the outback, it is almost always easy to find dry fuel. It was so today. Soon water was bubbling merrily in a smoke-blackened quart pot; the tin mugs came with it, a bushman's set. We drank it like a pair of drovers too. Black.

The sun was hot and this was mid-winter. The flies were bearable, just. Nonetheless I wouldn't have wanted to be anywhere else right then. I had after all seen seven dingoes that day.

'How common are black dingoes here, Lenny?'

'Common enough,' he replied. His Akubra was tilted low over his eyes, the better to shade his face.

'Seven, eh?' I mused thoughtfully.

'Uh-huh.' He sipped his tea, pulled a face. Still too hot.

'Makes you wonder just how many there are here, doesn't it?'

'Thousands,' Lenny said emphatically. 'There's thousands of them here... If it wasn't for that fence...' He let the words hang there, didn't need to elaborate. He then said that the station dropped 1080 from time to time. Which did knock them back a bit. But no matter what you did, there was no way you could ever stop them drifting down from the even drier regions in hard times, down from around Innamincka and the Simpson Desert country. 'Yeah,' he finished, 'there'll always be a ton of dogs here.'

'Just as well too.'

'Eh...?'

'I mean, you'd be looking for new employment if there were no dingoes here, right?'

'Good point,' he conceded with a dry-as-bones chuckle. He was still amused as he began to refill his mug. Pausing, he tipped back the brim of his hat and gave me a level look. 'Why d'you suppose I didn't barrel that dog this morning, eh?' Touché! I too refilled my mug.

'Hey,' exclaimed Lenny, slapping a meaty thigh, 'I've just remembered!'

'What?'

'Gay packed lunch for us.'

'Afternoon tea, you mean!' I snorted, suddenly ravenous.

'Whatever,' Lenny said, starting to the Toyota.

Gay's mutton sandwiches, while basic fare, were a treat and I said as much to Lenny.

'Can't beat a good bit of mutton,' he said, chewing enthusiastically. 'Pretty popular around here'—he waved a hand carelessly—'if given the chance.'

I had to laugh. Then, suddenly, wondered what it would be like for sheepmen in New South Wales if for some reason this fence were put out of action? It was a sobering thought and one I put voice to. Lenny listened to what I had to say and then said that, yeah, it had come down some years before.

'When?'

'Not that long ago,' he replied. '1974 to be exact.'

January and February of that year saw unprecedented rains and subsequent flooding bring disaster to much of the Western Division of New South Wales and southern Queensland. One station in the Tibooburra district recorded a staggering 48.26 cm of rain in just 24 hours. Tibooburra itself received twice its January average rainfall (36.57 cm). Homesteads were extensively damaged. Sheep losses were numbered in their many thousands. At Wompah Gate Depot a sudden flash flood in February destroyed two cottages and personal property was lost to the swirling waters. Many parts of the Border Fence went down. Along the South Australian border, for instance.

'So what happened?' I asked Lenny as he chucked the dregs of the tea on the fire. The fire spluttered and flames lost interest in living.

'Happened?' he echoed. 'Lots happened. But go see Lindsay Russell when you go back to Broken Hill. He'll tell you exactly what happened.'

Lindsay Russell was born in Broken Hill in 1912. When I visited him he was in poor health. His gracious wife, Isibel, asked me not to take up too much of his time and I said that I wouldn't. But when Lindsay started to recall the old days his eyes took on new life and his voice was stronger and with his wife's blessing I would stay several hours.

In his early days, Lindsay was a drover and shearer. The Corner Country was familiar turf. When the Government offered land to ex-servicemen in the aftermath of World War II, he snapped up four blocks.

The station would be called Moorabi—73,655 ha right on the Border Fence. Forty-eight km of the fence, both north and south of Smithville Depot, was in effect the station's western boundary.

Once sheep were established in the district, a full-time dogger was employed on the run. Generally speaking, the fence was in good shape then and what dingoes did get through the wire were quickly hunted down.

'Used to get real bad droughts then,' Lindsay recalled. 'Doesn't happen the same now. Sand storms were common. Go for days. It was so bad sometimes you could hardly see your hand in front of your face. One time it was so bad the fence was completely covered over with sand.' Lindsay paused, remembering. 'That was in 1946, I think.' In a quiet voice, Isibel confirmed it.

'Dogs crossed it of course but not too many before it was fixed. Lost a few sheep, but'—he shrugged a bony shoulder—'no more than we usually did.'

An even more severe drought came with the summer of 1955–56. While Lindsay's hardy sheep somehow managed to scratch a living of sorts from the dusty, sunbaked earth, some of his cattle began to die.

But all was not lost. Talk from down the bushman's line said there was plenty of good feed out beyond Cameron Corner. Moreover, it had been raining there recently. Hard. Maybe 15 cm had fallen. And Lindsay knew this country from his droving days. It was Crown Land. Anyone with enough savvy could take advantage of it.

So with his teenage son, Roy, and a good 'blackfeller', they started the trek north. Stockwhips cracked like rifleshots; cattle bellowed, reluctant in their weakened state to move. But move they did, all 1,200 head of mostly Hereford stock.

On reaching Cameron Corner, they entered South Australia and pushed on to the vicinity of Bollards Lagoon, about 112 km from Moorabi. There they found what they were looking for.

The general, rabbit-infested country of Bollards Lagoon, to the east of the Strzelecki Track and south of Innamincka, is known for the numbers of dingoes that inhabit it. Naturally enough, they were there in large numbers in the summer of 1955–56.

'They used to run sheep out there in the old days,' Lindsay recalled. 'Had woolsheds and fences and everything.' The 'old days' referred to here are the depression days of the 1920s and 1930s. 'But in the end the dogs beat them and they rolled up the wire and sold it and mostly went into cattle. Still see the odd woolshed out there if you know where to look.'

Lindsay Russell would keep his cattle out there—six months in all—until substantial rains fell on Moorabi and the land came back to life.

'Dingoes, you ask? My word they were thick out there. We saw lots every day, they followed the cattle most of the time. They'd pull down calves and if any cows got stuck in bogs they'd chew them up alive.

'One day we were sitting in the tent 'cause it was cold and raining and bugger me if a dog didn't sneak in and sit next to the fire.

'Then one evening a brumby stallion got in with the horses and we shot him. Next morning all that was left was his head. Dingoes? Don't ask me about dingoes!'

But Lindsay Russell's most bitter experiences with dingoes were yet to come.

The torrential rains of 1974 had a devastating effect on people in the Corner Country. Smithville Depot, for instance, was isolated for months. South of there resembled a great lake. There was no way the fence could be fixed. Food was air-dropped out of Broken Hill. About a third of Moorabi's boundary fence—the Border Fence—was eliminated. Dingoes started killing there very quickly.

'You'd see them every day, out mustering,' Lindsay recalled. 'Took the best part of a year to get the fence right again. By then they were on the place in droves.'

Above A caravan on a remote NSW sheep station is home-away-from-home for 'roo shooter Col Pierce and his dog Sheba

Right The author and Lenny Dixon enjoy a 'brew-up' on Quinyambie station

Below This Caterpillar IT 28 is used for repairs, maintenance or to clear windblown sand from the Fence

Above Don Webster, Executive Director (left) and Peter Merrell, Manager, Animals Pest Board, Roma

Top The Maranoa Graziers Association (Qld) has its HQ here at Roma

Left Cameron Turner's store does good business

Above The hard man at Roma —
Jerry Stanley, Barrier Fence
Project Officer

Above right Bruce Scott, President,
Maranoa Graziers Association

Right Ron Phillips of Currawong
station inspects a hollow-log
dingo den

Left A Queensland bottle tree, the Barrier Fence and the Russells' heavily laden Mitsubishi south-west of Tambo, October 1989

Below A kookaburra hopelessly trapped in wire netting, Currawong station

Bottom With a determined dingo raiding his sheep, Barry Phillips of Barlin station is adding an 'electric' wire to his section of the Fence

On average some 2,500–3,000 lambs were born on the station. In 1975 and for the next five years thereafter (by which time the dingoes were virtually gone) not a single lamb reached three years of age. Even today, Lindsay Russell can still express bitterness at what happened when the New South Wales Border Fence went down.

'People in town used to say to me, "What the hell d'you need a dingo fence for?" and I'd say that without it there'd be no sheep industry in New South Wales. Never convince them, you know.'

But was Moorabi an isolated case? Hardly. Same thing took place on Winnathee station, to the north of Moorabi, where a similar length of the Border Fence was down for about 18 months. The 71,227 ha run, owned by Bob and Joyce Scobie, had been taken on in 1948.

In 1975 they marked 1,900 lambs. At shearing time they counted 130. It would take a similar length of time here too before the Scobies knew they had won. In that time 176 dingoes, with a $20 bounty paid by Bob, were killed by stationhands and boundary riders.

On Waka station, near Tibooburra, they lost 3,870 lambs in the aftermath of the rains, representing a loss in income of nearly $13,000 a year.

Prior to 1974, scalps presented for payment in the Western Division numbered less than 30 a year. But with an influx of dingoes from South Australia, the Board decided to increase the bounty from $6 to $10. In their words: 'The increase will serve not only to redress the position caused by loss of value due to inflation—it will provide a further incentive to doggers and others to ensure the destruction of those dingoes that have gained entry into the Western Division.'

11

Always Two Sides To A Coin

Kangaroos are a real problem, which appear to be getting worse all the time. Whereas they can be controlled by shooting where the fence crosses grazing land, some 30 per cent of our fence borders the Sturt National Park and the 'roos here are completely protected and are, at times, on the fence in very big numbers.
– Paddy Barlow, speaking at the Barrier Fence Administrators Conference, Thargomindah, Queensland, 1987

Ever since high fences were first erected to exclude dingoes and, in Western Australia, emus from sheep country or grazing lands, kangaroos have posed a never-ending problem. In particular, this applies to the largest of the kangaroo family, the red, or plains, kangaroo.

The red kangaroo was of course here first. Which was never a consideration for Europeans. Only the far-ranging Aborigines knew how to live in harmony with the land, never taking anything of value from it. Even the grass and scrub fires they created in the dry interior were in the long-term beneficial where wild game were concerned inasmuch as they allowed new growth to flourish.

So the semi-nomadic kangaroos suddenly found a strange new barrier blocking migratory paths they had used for generations. *What was this?* Worse, the high fences barred access to water. Fatal in times of drought. And drought-stressed animals will naturally always attempt to get to water whether through a fence, or over it, or under it. Whatever is necessary.

It is not unusual for a full-grown kangaroo (which may stand in excess of 182 cm and weigh in the vicinity of 66 kg) in attempting to clear a fence (and remember that the Border Fence stands 1.83 m) to mistime its leap and, as a result, a front or back leg is somehow lodged and immediately trapped between two wires. The sudden downward pull of its weight on the trapped limb is considerable and only serves to compound the situation: it tightens the wire around the leg and makes the angle more acute so there is no way of freeing it. And the more the unfortunate animal struggles, the more hopeless it all becomes. No escape from what is now a vice-like grip. Death is the only release.

The sun burns down. The 'roo has ceased to struggle.

Death may come in the form of dingoes padding restlessly along the fence as they too seek a way to the far side. That is perhaps the best scenario. At least death should come quickly. Or it may come in a completely different fashion. A trapped and therefore helpless 'roo is soon spotted from the air, an easy prey for an eagle, hawk or crow. This will be a terrible death. Pecked alive. Eyeballs torn from bloody sockets. Failing that, death will inevitably come from starvation, or, more likely, thirst. But whatever the outcome, it is no way for one of God's creatures to die. During the period I spent on the Dingo Fence, I saw the carcasses of kangaroos that had died in this unfortunate manner in all three States.

When a red kangaroo hits the Dingo Fence at high speed, and this may be at 48 km/h, it is with considerable force. Should the netting be aged, as much of it is in South Australia and Queensland, then there is no way the flimsy material will check him and it will part as did the Red Sea before the raised hands of Moses.

It is worth noting that dingoes—a dog and bitch, say—are smart enough to know how to utilise the fence when hunting 'roos. Once they have a suitable target picked out, they then drive it towards the fence where it forms a sharp corner or T-shaped wing. So on two sides the fence blocks the 'roo's escape and the other escape routes are of course covered, too. This is when a 'roo, out of its mind with fear, will often smash into the fence. A good-sized animal will go right through aged netting. Dingoes do not mind that. They now have access to sheep country. Probably nail the 'roo, too!

On the other hand, should the fence be in tip-top condition, something like the following is much more likely to happen.

Quinyambie station, with Paddy Barlow. Before us, a mob of red kangaroos broke from lightly scattered timber. A big buck was there, the rest were considerably smaller, mostly females, blue-grey in colour. Pretty rather than handsome like the buck. Because of its coloration, the term 'blue flyer' is commonly used for the female of the species.

And they were flying now through the Mitchell grass, a grand sight through the none-too-clean window of the Toyota. All smooth style and well-practised grace, with something always held in reserve in case a sudden uplift of speed is needed—pacing themselves, never burning out.

Altering their course, the 'roos, a sleek doe leading, crossed the red track some 50 metres in front of the vehicle. The big buck's muscles rippled as with a spectacular leap he sailed over the track.

My God, how I came to love the magnificent wildlife of the equally magnificent Australian outback. What a priceless gift it is. Just as long as one is realistic about it. Animals in reasonable numbers is the key term. Better for the country. Better for their survival.

Ahead, I could see the Border Fence. Still the 'roos barrelled along tirelessly. They could keep that gait up for hours—from one isolated waterhole to the next—and then on again until they put the drought-ruined country behind them and found adequate pastures, or a fence that stood as tall as the tallest of them.

'Dog Fence,' Paddy said, gesturing. So for the first time I saw South

Australia's Dog Fence where it linked up with the Border Fence. I thought the moment quite significant.

At this point the big buck, instead of following the others which had just swung away to the west, headed off by himself in an easterly direction. In the New South Wales direction rather than deeper into Quinyambie's vastness. Under the circumstances it did not appear a sensible choice.

And as he bounded flat-stack towards the Border Fence it occurred to me that he might not be able to actually see it, that his eyes, like the lens of a telephoto camera, were focused distantly and that the closer ground was deliberately blurred. You question that? Well, birds of many kinds fly into the fence. Pilots of light aircraft and helicopters frequently fail to see wire stretched out across gullies. All with devastating results.

So only at the last split-second did the 'roo seem to realise that, hey, there was something high in front of it. Which all too likely accounted for a badly mistimed leap. It hit the fence at about three-quarters of its height. Hit the guitar-string-taut wire so hard that I winced. In effect, he might have hit a high diver's springboard: he performed a complete head-over-tail somersault and landed, facing away from the fence, nimbly on his big paddle-like feet. At a gathering of gymnasts that 'roo would have earned a generous round of applause. The judges might have scored him 8.75 out of 10. Jokes apart, I expect he both bruised and cut himself. Nevertheless, he bounded away smoothly, in the direction the others had taken, so any damage was, I suspect, superficial. And maybe he was an old hand at crashing into the Border Fence. Numerous 'roos were.

The man who'd seen it all before shook his head and commented wryly: 'Happens all the time on the Fence. Sometimes when you're driving along it they'll stay right in front of you. Every so often they'll crash sideways into the fence. Often they'll get caught up in the skirting. It's as though they were somehow drawn to it. Never understand it, you know. I mean, they only have to break in the other direction...don't they?' Again he shook his head. 'Emus are even worse than 'roos. Gawd, they're dumb bastards!'

Later, we returned to New South Wales. Moorabi station. 'Roo country. Thousands of them.

At night on this track, which eventually takes you back to Smithville, you travel at your peril. 'Roos are up and about after daylong siestas. On a cool night they may lie on the track, which still somehow retains the sun's heat. Avoiding them in such circumstances would, I suppose, be something like driving through an over-loaded minefield. Meaning you have no real idea of where and when the next explosion is going to come from. In the Western Division of New South Wales red kangaroos may be described as 'abundant'. They are far from being 'endangered'.

The following segment, taken from the 1980 Annual Report of the Wild Dog Destruction Board, is interesting inasmuch as the same situation applies nine years later.

Kangaroos

The good seasons since 1973 and the closure of the American market to imports of kangaroo products has favoured the kangaroo and numbers have continued to increase.

Field Officers of the Western Lands Commission provide monthly reports on kangaroo populations in their areas and these are forwarded on to the National Parks and Wildlife Service to assist that body in its kangaroo management programme. These reports repeatedly referred to kangaroos in plague proportions in areas which received the benefit of scattered storms during the drought of 1977 and early 1978. Lessees who were hoping to take advantage of the forage response to such falls were frustrated to see the green pick removed and the paddocks fouled by hordes of invading kangaroos.

Last year I reported the results of the aerial survey carried out by the National Parks and Wildlife Service and University of Sydney which revealed a kangaroo population for the Western Division of about 3 million, or about 1 kangaroo for every 2 sheep of normal carrying capacity. This means that the average property in the Western Division is carrying about 2,000 kangaroos. With this in mind, it is not difficult to see that if one property receives a helpful fall of rain and the kangaroos from the ten surrounding properties move on to it, the property would be carrying 20,000 kangaroos. If the lessee was carrying that number of sheep the Commission would consider the properly to be grossly over-stocked and would be asking the lessee to reduce numbers drastically.

Fortunately, the good rain in the winter of 1978 has caused the kangaroo population to distribute itself more evenly but, unfortunately, this is expected to lead to further population increases.

In 1989 an there were estimated 102,000 red kangaroos inhabiting the 344,097 hectares of Sturt National Park. Paul Jennings, the 41-year-old Superintendent of the National Parks and Wildlife Service, Tibooburra district, considers there are similar numbers to this on properties adjoining the park.

In articulate fashion, Paul Jennings explained that the New South Wales Government has a culling programme for red kangaroos. It is based on damage mitigation and naturally applies to other types of kangaroos, too. So a grazier who has a 'roo problem can apply for a permit to kill a certain number. A problem is defined as direct competition with stock for feed and water and damage to fencing. Usually the three reasons go together.

Interestingly enough, a 1989 CSIRO survey on kangaroos, involving questionnaires being sent to 600 graziers with a 'roo problem, estimated damage reduced livestock carrying capacity by at least 10 per cent and was responsible for between 30 to 70 per cent of fencing costs. All up, the survey considered the kangaroo was costing farmers and graziers about $113 million annually.

But Sue Arnold, of Australians for Animals, was quoted in an article in the *Sydney Morning Herald* in late 1989 ('Bloodying our national symbol', by

Paul Bailey) as saying that the said survey had no scientific basis and 'was merely representative of the opinion of some landowners... The situation we have now, is that the poor old kangaroo and the emu, which are our national symbols, are covered in blood. These animals are being exploited in the grossest fashion.'

Ms Arnold may not have travelled along the Dingo Fence or spoken to graziers faced with overwhelming numbers of kangaroos. Unless culled, the 'roos would simply drive them off the land. She should of course follow the inside, rather than the outside, of it.

I guess it's the same old story, isn't it? All depends what side of the fence you're standing on. The cattleman and the sheepman, the fence between. Never ever going to bridge it. Always two sides to a coin, right? Heads you win, tails you lose.

12

'Roo Shooter On Moorabi Station

Better than being a bloody mechanic in Mildura, mate!
– Col Pierce, when asked by the author what was it like being a
professional kangaroo shooter

In the Tibooburra district an allocation of 100,000 kangaroos was made for 1989 (by October half this number had been taken). Since recreational hunting of kangaroos is outlawed, hunting may be done only by the holder of a current kangaroo trapper's licence. They are issued to holders of occupiers' licences— landowners or occupiers—or a person who has the endorsement of the local kangaroo wholesaler responsible for that particular area.

According to Paul Jennings, there were 11 professional 'roo shooters 'on their books'. Four of them operated out of Tibooburra and the rest elsewhere. They received from 26 to 28 cents per kilo, and a skin fetched around $8.50. For the record, an average 'roo might tip the scales at 40 kilos (dressed out weight).

A few facts and figures for you to digest about the kangaroo industry as it applied to 1989, the year in question. The commercial kangaroo industry operated all year round. About 3,500 men held an appropriate licence. The export of hides and skins involved 17 countries. The bulk went to Italy and Japan. Meat for human consumption went (in order of quantity) to Japan, Papua New Guinea, Norway, the United States, and West Germany. Pet meat was sold in eight countries. In the three Australian States the Dingo Fence ran through, at least 1.45 million kangaroos would be killed. Possibly the number would be exceeded in 1990. Collectively, the kangaroo industry was worth about $12 million annually. As a former President of the United States, Jimmy Carter, might say: 'That sure as hell ain't peanuts, boy!'

One of the kangaroo shooters operating in the Tibooburra district is Col Pierce. Specifically he kills lovable kangaroos, but not cuddly koalas. Never has he 'bloodied' an emu!

Col Pierce kills at night, from a four-wheel-drive vehicle. He uses a powerful, 12-volt spotlight. That is not fair. It is not meant to be fair. He is not shooting for kicks. It is his livelihood. Col Pierce is very proficient at it.

Col Pierce kills quickly and effectively. It takes one 50-grain, soft-point projectile fired from a .222 calibre rifle at around 3525 fps (handloaded rather than factory loads). Invariably he aims for the head. Only rarely will he miss.

He is of course sitting in the cabin of his Land Rover, with a craftily designed rest to support the forearm of his rifle. A head shot means there is no damage to the skin. This is important. It is also ethical to head shoot an animal if possible. Col Pierce is an ethical hunter.

A head-shot animal is dead or as good as, before it hits the red earth, which should go without saying. It is killed in the most humane way yet devised by man. Suddenly, in its own environment. So not for it the slow and painful death by 1080 poison. Nor the trauma of live game capture.

So, yes, Col Pierce kills kangaroos because that is a necessary aspect of outback life. True, he is there for the lifestyle. That is his privilege. Most of us strive to find an occupation we enjoy but very few, sad to say, ever achieve it.

Also, Col Pierce is a caring, and, dare I say it, compassionate man. It is a paradox that many hunters are. So, yes, he is far removed from the uncaring, callous, blood-and-guts characters depicted by some as working in such a profession.

There have been many men like Col Pierce in the Australian outback. The one I happened to catch up with was camped in a caravan tucked away in the tinder-dry scrub somewhere on Moorabi station in the winter of 1989.

Noon. We were sitting in the somewhat cramped interior of Col's caravan. Although we had met only an hour before, when I had turned up unexpectedly, we were enjoying each other's company. Kindred spirits, I expect. While we yarned, Col was meticulously handloading cartridges for the forthcoming night's foray: the loading press was attached by a clamp to a formica table.

'One more done,' Col said, about to pop the bullet into the tiny slot of a narrow cardboard box holding 50 such compartments. But when I held out my hand, palm upturned, he dropped it into it.

'More coffee?'

'Sure,' I replied.

The case of the bullet I rolled around in the palm of my hand was dull and pitted. Used a number of times, I expect. The projectile was, however, pristine bright, a well-polished gold nugget. It would be used but once. There is very little if anything you can do with a misspent, flattened lump of lead apart from digging it out of a kill with a knife and commenting intelligently on how well it expanded and other such mumbo-jumbo foreign to normal people.

'So you saw old Lindsay in town...'

'Uh-huh.' I nodded thanks when he put a full cup of the black, bitter stuff in front of me.

'How was he?' There was genuine concern in his voice.

'Not good.' I liked the cool feel of the .222 bullet, I knew what it was capable of in the hands of a skilled shot.

'Bastard gettin' old.' Col shook his head.

'Worse if you're sick with it.'

'Not wrong,' Col agreed. 'He's a damn good bloke. His wife's a great sort too. Real lady, you know. They've got plenty of friends in this country, I'll tell you that much.'

'Lenny and Gay speak well of them.' I thought about Gay telling me that every Christmas without fail Mrs Russell would visit Smithville and bring presents for all the kids. Never forgot one of them. She had done so until sickness had made it necessary for her ailing husband to move to town. I mentioned it to Col.

'Yeah, they were like that. Always see you right for a feed. Great people.' He paused as he carefully measured out powder. 'Roy's okay too. You meet him?' I nodded yes and Col went on, 'He could've told you a few home truths about dogs. My word he could!'

'His dad didn't do too badly.'

'No, I expect not. Must make a point of seeing him soon...'

I was still playing around with the cartridge in my hand. Felt like old times; maybe the best of times. Then, tiring of it, I put it in the box. Almost full now.

'Lethal devils, aren't they?' I said.

' 'Roos don't walk away from a triple-two.'

'Neither do deer.'

'Put down pigs too.'

'You tried it on dingoes?'

'Yeah, no worries. Got a dog last year with it. Just before Christmas. It had been killing sheep for about five months. Made Roy's day.' Col smiled at the memory. He glanced across at me. 'Rangers use it in the Park.'

'So I was told.' Park Board staff had by October 1989 taken 31 dingoes in Sturt National Park, including a bitch with nine pups. As Paul Jennings had said: 'Just imagine the consequences had we missed out on her.'

'Coffee okay?'

'Wet and black, if that's what you mean.'

Col grinned. 'Something like that. There! That's enough to see me through tonight.' He stood up abruptly: a tall and tanned 52-year-old of husky physique. He had come out to hunt professionally on Moorabi in 1977. Had owned a service station in Mildura before then. Yes, he and his long-time mate, Bruce Pedder, had changed their favourite hobby into a largely stress-free occupation.

A kind of off-white whippet appeared in the partly-open doorway. She looked expectantly at Col who, catching her eye, shook his head and said, 'Outside, Sheba.' With an expression of acute disappointment she retreated.

'Good dog, that,' Col said. 'She's been out here as long as I have. Be lost without her.' He chuckled. 'Reckon we could both find our way around this place blindfolded.' He ran splayed fingers through his hair and, giving me a direct look, asked, 'You heard about old Bruce, I expect?' I had. Col's 62-year-old friend had dropped dead of a heart attack one morning after putting rabbits in a chiller.

'Must've been rough.'

'Bloody hard all right. We was mates a long time. Miss him at times, old Bruce. Terrific bloke. Not been the same since he went, you know. Couldn't make another mate like that. Not possible.' He shrugged his broad shoulders. 'Prefer to be on my own now. Better that way.'

The 'roo shooter and his dog, I thought. Mates in the bush. She would never let him down. Dogs don't. Only people do that. We all let someone down very badly in our lives. Don't mean to. Just happens.

'So that's the .222 is it?' I said, indicating a Sako rifle propped out of the way in a corner. Top make, Sako. We go back a long way together.

'Yeah, that's it.' Col handed it to me with the bolt open.

'Solid,' I said.

'Meant to be.'

'Right.' This was a heavy barrelled model, fitted with a 6× Pecar 'scope that had taken a few knocks. Being a steel-tubed job, it could take that. Too heavy to carry afield, unless you believed in self-punishment, it was a target hunter's dream. Probably put five shots through the same hole at 100 metres. Or almost.

Cra-ack! Down went yet another head-shot 'roo. Perfect skin. Name of the game.

'Heavy barrel makes all the difference,' Col said as I handed the Sako to him. 'Can't get that pinpoint accuracy with a lighter tube. Doesn't heat up as quickly, either. That's important if you get onto a few together.' Since Col was allotted 1,000 'roos a year on Moorabi, I expect there were times when more than one set of glowing eyes was illuminated in the dazzling rays of the light.

But it wasn't always 'roos he was after. Rabbits last night. Taken with a .22 decked out with a 6× Burris' scope. Ended up with 150 pairs; a lucrative caper young Kenny Dixon was also good at. His sister knew all about it too. He had taken the rabbits onto Quinyambie station, where, at a going rate of $1.70 a pair, they became the property of one Aub Ali, a professional rabbit shooter and contractor operating out of the old Quinyambie station homestead.

We went outside into the sun. Lovely day. Sheba came up for a pat and got one. Col smiled. He looked relaxed in a way few, if any, city folk are.

'Pity the bottom has dropped out of the market for fox skins,' he remarked with regret. 'Good money while it lasted. They've really built up here in the last couple of years.'

'Foxes don't mind.'

Col laughed. 'No, I guess they don't. Probably come back again. Most things do.'

On a normal night Col worked around ten hours. He went home every three weeks and stayed there a week to ten days. How did his wife cope with that? She was used to it, was the answer. 'Problem's going to be when she's got me home full-time again. May have to stay out here forever.'

'You and Sheba.'

'Yeah, something like that,' was the reply of a man who had taken a calculated gamble a dozen years back and found the kind of lifestyle in the bush that most of those who avidly devour outdoor magazines can only dream wistfully about.

But like I've already said: there have been many men like Col Pierce in the wonderful Australian outback where winter skies are mostly blue and the smells of wattle and mulga replace smog-filled air choked with petrol fumes. I guess Col Pierce would have agreed with Allan Littlejohn that once you get the red dirt on your boots you'll always come back.

PART THREE

QUEENSLAND –
THE BARRIER FENCE

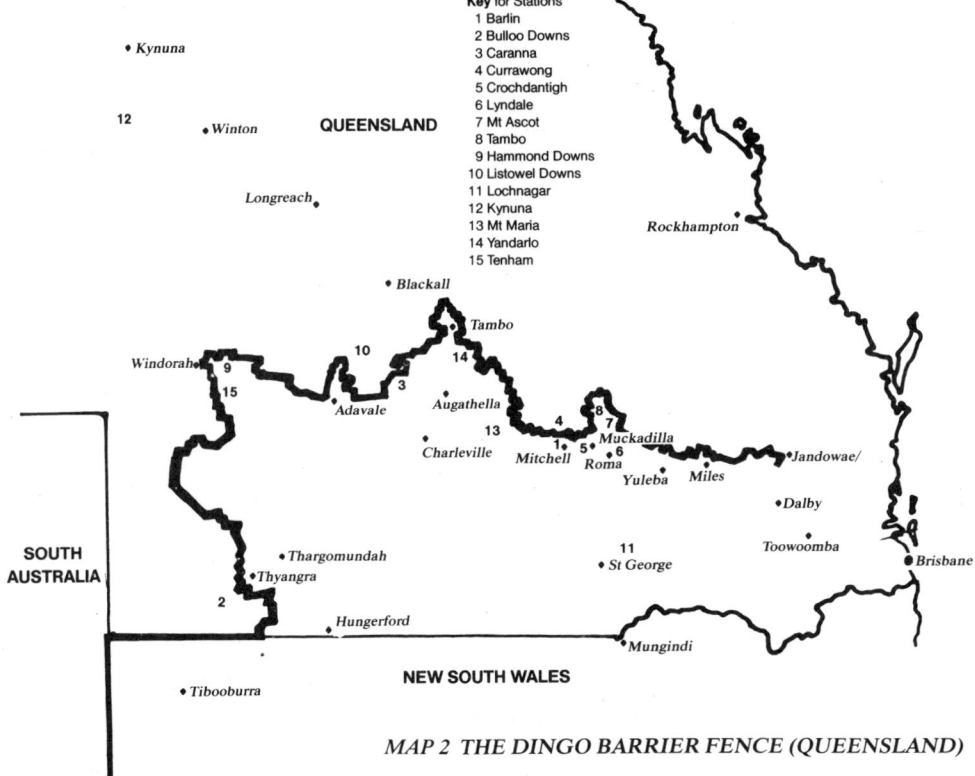

Key for Stations
1 Barlin
2 Bulloo Downs
3 Caranna
4 Currawong
5 Crochdantigh
6 Lyndale
7 Mt Ascot
8 Tambo
9 Hammond Downs
10 Listowel Downs
11 Lochnagar
12 Kynuna
13 Mt Maria
14 Yandarlo
15 Tenham

• Kynuna

12   • Winton   QUEENSLAND

Longreach •

Rockhampton

• Blackall

Tambo

Windorah • 9
10   14
15   3   Augathella
    Adavale
            13   4   8   7
        Charleville   1   5 • • 6   Muckadilla
                Mitchell Roma   • Jandowae/
                        Yuleba   Miles

                                • Dalby

SOUTH   • Toowoomba
AUSTRALIA   • Thargomundah
        • Thyangra   11   • Brisbane
    2   • St George

        • Hungerford

                    • Mungindi

NEW SOUTH WALES

• Tibooburra

MAP 2 THE DINGO BARRIER FENCE (QUEENSLAND)

13

Hard Man At Roma

The Barrier Fence, I suppose, would be 90 per cent dog-proof; I couldn't
vouch for more than that. I am pleased with the work the boys have done.
I just reckon I need two or three more years to lift it to top-class standard.
We're on target!
– Jerry Stanley, Barrier Fence Project Officer, Roma, October 1989

The headquarters of the Rural Lands Protection Board can be found on the corner of George and Elizabeth Streets, Brisbane. To be more precise, on the first floor of the Family Services Building.

On a Friday morning in early October, Queensland's biggest city was humid; the temperature was expected to reach 30 degrees. Nothing new there.

A gangling 49-year-old, Don Webster, was the Executive Director in charge of all facets of the Barrier Fence. He sported a neatly-trimmed moustache and a nice open smile.

Together with Peter Merrell (Manager, Animal Pests Branch), and Jerry Stanley (Barrier Fence Project Officer), Don had recently undertaken an inspection of Queensland's 2,500 km section of the Dingo Fence. Don considered it was in excellent shape for the most part. True, some of the netting was old and needed replacing but given time that would be done.

At that point, a dark-haired, fit-looking type in his mid-30s entered the office. I was introduced to Peter Merrell. He too was full of suggestions about how best I should carry out the Queensland leg of my field research.

Sipping coffee, Don said, 'I've been in touch with Jerry, so he's in the picture.' He slipped a piece of paper across his desk on which was written an address and a telephone number, both relating to Roma. 'Better give him a call first. He'll be able to spare you a day or so—most likely take you out on the job with him. Fair enough?' He broke off at that stage to stare thoughtfully into his near-empty cup. Looking up, he said, 'Stay on Jerry's right side and he'll do just about anything for you.'

Peter grinned. 'By that, Don means he's got a short fuse, if you know what I mean.'

'Not only that,' Don went on, 'but the press have been rather hard on various aspects of the Barrier Fence. Expense, etc. Some of it was far from accurate. Jerry takes all that to heart. And once something's been published'—he spread his hands wide—'you know what it's like.'

'Gospel,' I offered.

'Exactly.'

'So it's made him, well, rather wary of reporters.'

'So what is his role, Don?'

'Jerry reports to either me or Peter here. Having said that, he really runs the fence the way he sees fit. We don't bother him because we don't have to. He has the right to hire and fire men. It's not a job for a desk-bound bureaucrat; far from it. It needed a Jerry Stanley to get it done and to keep it running smoothly. He's a hard man but fair; the blokes know exactly where they stand with him. The amount of work he got through when the fence was being rebuilt was incredible. No matter how much credit for it he might be given it'll never be enough.' He gave me a slow penetrating look. 'Just be straight with him and he'll be exactly that way with you.'

Couldn't ask for more than that.

Monday. I was mulling over what Don Webster had said as the signposts started to hammer the point home that Roma—480 km from the big smoke— was getting awfully close. Bad press, huh? Well, one Paddy Barlow knew how tough reporters could make it for you when they didn't get their facts straight or hurried a story too much because they had a deadline to meet.

Roma. Population 8,000. Centre of a vast grazing area. Five o'clock. No rush hour traffic to worry about here. I made camp in the Motel Carnarvon. It had a swimming pool. Tea and coffee making facilities. I made a coffee and then, sitting on the edge of the bed with it, rang Jerry Stanley.

He had just arrived home, he said. We chatted away, and he said, yes, he was going to take me out to the fence in the morning and, yes, he had worked out a list for me of people it would pay me to approach. I suggested a beer later on, to break the ice even more type of thing. Later meant after a shower and a meal; I hadn't eaten since breakfast.

'What's wrong with now?' Jerry said.

Turned out that Jerry's home was but a short drive from my motel; but then, so was everything else in Roma. The man himself greeted me at the door. He was a big, hulking character sporting a Mexican-bandit moustache. Still in his work clothes. Like me, he was in dire need of a shower. He gave me a bear-like paw to shake, introduced me to his wife, Marie, and started for the door.

'See you later, love,' he called. Outside, he said, 'Pub's only a stride away.'

It was too. On the intersection of the street he resided on and the main drag.

'Handy,' I said.

'Yeah, isn't it?'

I can't recall the name of the hotel. I do remember that it had batwing doors like in western movies, the usual town drunks propping up the bar in case it fell down, and an attractive young woman serving drinks. There was no sawdust on the floor. Things have improved a little in Roma in recent years—not as many bar-room brawls!

'What're you having?' Jerry thumped a handful of loose change on the bar.

'Victoria Bitter, thanks.'

'And one off the tap for me,' Jerry said to the blond who knew him.

Jerry proved to be amusing company, with tall tales—but more than likely true—of when he was working in Western Australia, up in the Kimberleys on cattle stations. Presently a mate who'd worked with him in the far west sidled in through the batwing doors so silkily he might have been a wary Billy the Kid half-expecting Pat Garrat to be breasting the bar. This was the 'Ringer', a slim, gregarious type who had lived a full and exciting life.

Later. How many beers? Who's counting! For a reason I can't bring to mind (and we can say the beer was to blame for that), the Ringer had got on to the subject of Mel Gibson, the actor, whom he'd met somewhere.

'Must be the best-looking bloke you'll ever see,' the Ringer said, hitting the bar with the flat of his hand for further emphasis.

'That right?' Jerry said, his disinterested manner suggesting he couldn't care less what Mel Gibson looked like.

'Bloody oath! You should see the way the women perve on him. Unreal.' The Ringer chugged on a rum chaser.

Also at the bar were two Telecom workers, up from Brisbane for the week. One in particular had already shot the Ringer a few hostile glances. Now as the Ringer continued to rave on about Mel Gibson's great looks, he started to snicker behind a partly-raised hand.

'He's a bloody good bloke too,' the Ringer carried on. 'Not up himself like you'd expect. Great body on him too.' That was it for the man from Telecom.

'What are you, mate?' he demanded in belligerent tones. 'Some sort of poofter?'

A heavy silence followed those words. Fighting talk, this. Billy the Kid might just reach for his Colt. The Ringer froze with a bottle of beer midway between his mouth and belly. He put down the bottle with heavy emphasis. Suddenly he snorted, 'Poofter! Listen, mate,' and he stabbed a finger at the man from Telecom's chest, 'I've had more women than you've had hot feeds!' He glared hotly at Telecom.

'Has to,' Jerry said matter-of-factly.

'Hmph!' went the man from Telecom, and wisely dropped the subject. Reckon the Ringer could have had him, too. But only for breakfast.

Later still. . .'Bar's closed, boys.' I turned to the batwing doors. How come there was four of them now?

'You all right, mate?' That was Jerry.

'Yeah, great.'

'Good.' Jerry slapped me hard on the shoulder. A mistake. Only a sudden grab for the bartop saved me from hitting the deck.

'He's pissed,' Jerry said to the Ringer.

'Ain't the only one, mate,' the Ringer admitted.

Out through the batwing doors I went, lurching. The cool night air did not help in the least.

'Listen,' Jerry said, an arm partly around my shoulder, 'we're going on to a mate's place. Wanna come?'

'No way,' I said sensibly.

'Okay, please yourself. Sure you can find your way back?'

'Back?'

'To your motel.'

'Oh. . .yeah. . .sure.'

And somehow I did.

At a pre-arranged time I turned up at Jerry's place. Eight o'clock sharp. Freshly shaven, eyes like bright brown buttons, he bounded outside. He'd gotten home around three o'clock, he said. No worries. At his age, 32, you can just barely get away with that.

'How're you feeling?' Jerry swung into the driver's seat of a well-appointed Toyota Landcruiser.

'Like I've just been dug up.'

Jerry roared and slapped a bare, meaty thigh. 'By Christ—you were tanked outa your skull last night.'

'Tell me about it,' I moaned as though I were in physical pain. Correction: I was in physical pain.

'Don't worry, mate. I was shot too.' He engaged the reverse gear. 'Doesn't show on me like it does on you but. Reckon I get more practice, eh?' Reckon he did.

Jerry laughed again; I was pleased someone was getting a charge out of last night's disaster. 'Don't worry, mate. You'll be back into it tonight. Ringer'll be there too.'

'No chance!' I said flatly. For some unknown reason this caused the Project Officer to laugh again. Great sport getting an author drunk. Might have made up somewhat for all those unkind things journalists had dared to write about the Barrier Fence.

The hard man at Roma was still vastly amused as we roared out on Highway 54 towards Wallumbilla. But as I would discover, the night's heavy drinking was not a mistake, proving something good can come out of almost anything. Because in the process we had become mates, free and easy with each other. Because that's what mates do all the time in south-west Queensland.

Get drunk together!

Mid-morning on the Barrier Fence. Heading west. Toyota churning up the dust. A well-maintained track ran alongside the fence which, I noted, was not as high as the Border Fence, maybe 1.5 metres. Fresh tyre marks, according to Jerry Stanley, meant that patrolmen Neville Maunder and Dave Reibelt were on the job. Not too far away, either.

'Should've seen this stretch before we put it right,' Jerry said. 'Talk about bad! Hell, you couldn't drive along here. The scrub and timber were that thick. God knows how many chain saws we wrecked.' He shook his head. The recent past all too vivid. 'Wouldn't want—hell, couldn't—go through all that again.'

A big yellowish goanna with dark mottled patches was suddenly in sight. Looking for a way through the fence. I don't know what the attraction was. That side looked exactly the same as this side. Strange.

Aware of us now, it suddenly reared up on its hind legs and sprinted hard.

It was about 1.3 metres in length. Specifically this was a Gould's sand goanna, a type common in desert regions.

'Plenty of those along here,' Jerry informed me. 'Don't cause much trouble, though. Not like porcupines.' Had I heard him right. Porcupines? 'Yeah, they'd be the number-one problem animal on this eastern flank between here and, say, the Maranoa River.' The Toyota lurched down a steep rocky incline to a narrow dry wash. In heavy rain this would be bad news. Certainly the fenceline would suffer, most likely be washed away. Jerry confirmed it was so.

Soon after, on level ground again, a dead porcupine was observed on the side of the track. The carcass was untouched by carrion eaters—Gould's sand goannas, for instance. Nor had rigor mortis set in. Time of death not so long ago, then.

Jerry turned it over with the toe of his boot. 'Wonder what happened to it?' The last thing he sounded was concerned.

'Looks like it was shot to me.' Brilliant observation. There was a bullet hole in it.

But Jerry shook his head in the negative. 'Uh-uh,' he said. 'Couldn't have been. They're a protected species.'

'Must've walked into the path of a bullet aimed for something else,' I suggested.

'Possible,' Jerry conceded with a faint smile which was all but lost under that handlebar moustache.

'But unlikely. They don't move that fast.'

'They do when they're digging.'

Back in the Toyota, Jerry flicked on a UHF radio and spoke into the mouthpiece. During the past year, all Barrier Fence vehicles and the Roma base had been equipped with them. It made liaison between Barrier Fence staff and landholders a simple matter instead of the difficult thing it had often been before. Again, it was a priceless asset in case of an emergency. Brave patrolmen faced everything from scrub fires or sudden flood to the possibility of snakebite. It was a definite case of, be careful out there.

Again Jerry failed to make contact with Neville Maunder. 'Not in his vehicle,' Jerry muttered to himself, 'that's for sure'. Then he tried again. This time communication was made. Neville in a deep, slow voice explained they were on Stacy Valentine's run—Kurrajong—laying netting across a washout.

'It'll take us about an hour to get there,' Jerry said. 'Wait for us, okay?'

The Project Officer worked through the low gears. 'Good blokes, those two. In fact, we've got a top crew at the present time. Makes my job so much easier.' By the way he spoke, I gathered that wasn't always the case. He nodded as a couple of grey 'roos bounded off through low scrub on the safe side of the Barrier Fence. Maybe the sixth or seventh sand goanna was checking out the fence. There had to be something interesting over there. 'There's an awful big turnover in manpower out west at times. Tough country out there. Tough conditions. Too bloody tough for most blokes. Course they don't realise that till they get out there.

'You get a real dickhead now and then. No intention of working hard; reckons it's just going to be a holiday. Some holiday! But you soon catch up with the likes of them. Holes in the fence might not say anything but they sure as hell tell a loud story.

'Got rid of a bloke like that not too long ago. Must've thought I came down in the last shower!' He took a deep breath.

'Thing is, I tell them how it's gonna be right at the start. That means they do it my way. My way is simple. You work. So they either do their — job or,' he went on heavily, 'it's down the road real quick. No ifs, buts, or maybes about it.' Jerry was all fired-up. The Barrier Fence had become a passion where he was concerned. But just as suddenly as he had flared up, he shrugged and visibly relaxed. 'Like I said, I've got a bloody good team now and I'm thankful for it, too.'

Another pair of 'roos, mother and young, weaved away through the low growth. Simultaneously a bustard or plains turkey was striding it out in grand, high-stepping style. The Barrier Fence sure has a way of attracting all types of wildlife.

Jerry's attention, momentarily diverted because of the 'roos, was back on the track. If asked to, he could probably drive it blindfolded. Not that I was about to pop the question.

'What were 'roos like in New South?' he asked.

'Bad.'

'Lousy up here with them at present. You could take 2,000 off most places and not notice they were gone.' He frowned. 'They give us heaps at times. You get a couple of big bucks on either side of the fence that take a dislike to each other. You know what they do? They sit down on their tails right on the fence and start to kick at each other. Must rip their feet to pieces. They'll take out 30, 40 feet of netting. You come along later and find it down. The whole lot's covered with blood and hair.' Three more examples of problems caused by animals came out with machine-gun precision.

Emus: 'Saw at least 2,000 in one mob last year out west. They run on the apron wire. Tear it up something terrible.'

Pigs: 'Don't care what sort of fence it is—even electric. If a pig wants to get through, it will.'

Bulls: 'Now and then you might get a couple sparring with each other. They'll soon punch holes in the wire.'

'An eventful life,' I offered.

'Ain't bloody boring. That's for real.'

No, I didn't imagine it was. Tedious, maybe. Boring, never.

Almost to the hour, Jerry pulled in alongside an open-backed Toyota chock-a-block with netting wire, tools, a chain saw, and even a bull mastiff cross called Blazer. Strong looking dog; looked as if it hunted pigs for a living. Maybe they got Blazer hard at it on the chain saw?

The first thing I thought when I saw Neville Maunder and Dave Reibelt was that here were a pair of real bushies. Akubras. Shorts. Suntans. Real happy with their lot. Lucky men.

After introductions, Jerry said, 'Dead porcupine back there.' His face was expressionless.

'Yeah,' Neville drawled.

'Pity.'

'Isn't it,' Neville agreed.

'One thing...'

'Shoot.'

'Won't be making any more holes.'

'Never thought of that, Jerry.

All but Blazer laughed. Death on the Dingo Fence. Happens all the time from one end of it to the other. Maybe happens every minute, like a murder in the United States. Inevitable, like sunrise.

There was, I'd already noted, a 'scoped rifle in the cabin. Calibre .22 Magnum, a deceptively hard-hitting little number. Carried purely for self-defence. You kept it close at hand at all times. Had it within easy reach when you fixed a hole in the fence. Otherwise how were you expected to defend yourself should an angry rabbit or stroppy wallaby suddenly take to you?

Hunkered down with a smoke, Jerry nodded at me and said that he'd mentioned how much trouble porcupines caused. He left that dangling there, knowing that Neville would expand on the subject. The 39-year-old married man with seven years on the job obliged. 'Yeah—they'd be our main problem...right, Dave...?' Dave, single and two years shy of 30, nodded as solemnly as a judge about to hand down a life sentence on some poor unfortunate. 'They're pretty much like a fox, you know,' went on Neville. 'They'll dig at least a foot down to get to a likely partner or mate on the other side.'

Dave looked up. 'March and April's the worst.'

'Bloody oath! That's when the pressure's really on the fence. You're flat out fixin' holes then, all right, sometimes you come to a stretch and you'd reckon somebody had been along there with a rotary hoe; all churned up. The buggers just keep digging until they find a weak spot. No stopping them then. Right, Dave?'

'Yeah...,' Dave said seriously.

'You can put a 60-kilo rock on a hole they've dug or on skirting wire like that over there,' Neville pointed at the quick repair job they'd carried out, 'and he'll just tip it off, no worries. The sheer traction and power they've got is amazing.'

Jerry straightened. Ground out the butt of his smoke. 'And once they cut out the 'roos take over.'

Neville raised his eyes to the sky. ' 'Roos! Don't talk to me about 'roos, mate!'

About a year before kangaroos had started building up on two stations to the south-west: Caranna and Lambert. Feed was scarce there. More 'roos flooded in. The situation did not improve. Stopping the 'roos from heading north to better grazing was the Barrier Fence. In particular places untold numbers of them began to gather on the fence, putting it under enormous pressure. Word of this came down the bushline, to Roma. Jerry conducted an airborne survey. They were right. Things were definitely crook. At least 6,000 'roos had gathered on just one part of the Barrier Fence. How many there were on both stations was anyone's guess.

Neville (working that beat then) knew all about it from grass roots level. 'It was nothing to have a thousand of them barrelling along the fence in front of you. In maybe 20 km you'd see half-a-dozen on the outside of the fence but there'd be 5,000 keeping you company on the inside of it. Couldn't avoid hitting them.'

'They had 'roo shooters on both places,' Jerry picked up the thread, 'and they were shooting heaps. But it made no difference. The more they shot, the more there were.'

'Heard about it, you know,' Neville said, 'but until then I'd never really believed the stories about how many 'roos there could be in a situation like that. You remember those old photos of rabbit plagues? Well, it was just like that on Caranna.'

'It was too far to carcass shoot out there,' Neville continued, 'so they just left the skinned carcasses in heaps. Pigs soon got stuck into them.'

'When Neville says "heaps", we're taking out three or four hundred in a pile.'

The solution to this predicament was to open five panels of the Barrier Fence, then, with the aid of a fixed-wing aircraft and men on the ground, they somehow drove the main bulk of the kangaroos out through the opening and then closed it up behind them. They had apparently vanished after that.

'A never-ending problem up here,' Jerry added.

'You know,' Neville said, 'this is where all those greenies have got it wrong. They don't come out here and see the 'roos like we do.' He snorted. 'There's no 'roos around town.'

The hard man at Roma bared his teeth and laughed.

14

By Whatever Means

They reckoned it was a wonder drug. It was going to do everything. And it was wonderful. Results were outstanding. It might have killed 90 per cent of the dogs. The problem was it also killed 50 per cent of the cattlemen's dogs. So a lot of them said to hell with that and vowed never to use it again. And to this day they haven't.
– Howard Jensen, Lyndale station north of Roma, talking about the introduction of 1080 to south-west Queensland

Howard Jensen, nudging 60 summers, has spent his entire life on Lyndale station, a small run for these parts, just 2,832 ha, north of Roma. His land is good country. Sheep, cattle, and countless kangaroos seem to like it, anyway.

'Dad took the place up after the First World War,' Howard said as we sat in the kitchen of his homestead and his wife, Anne, left us to it. 'He fought in both the wars as a matter of fact. Dad was tough.

'I was born right here on the place. Some of my earliest memories are of shots going off in the night and that would be old Dad giving the dogs hell. Course they gave him hell, too.' He smiled reflectively. 'You could say Dad was fighting one war or another all his life.'

Rennie Jensen had died a few years before aged 91.

'Naturally, I worked here when I left school; that was in '47. Terrible lot of dingoes here then but the Barrier Fence was in pretty good shape really.

'At that time a lot of people also had additional netting fences on their places. [These were for the most part rabbit and marsupial 'community' boundary fences.] So there were fenced-off blocks. This meant that when a dog came through the Barrier Fence he hadn't got too much scope to move. They held a lot of "drives" in those days and they were pretty successful as a rule.

'But I guess it must've been about, oh, 25 to 30 years ago that a lot of station people started to put more faith in the Barrier Fence. Don't know why, they just did. As a result, they started to ignore the netting fences. They were, I suppose, living under a sense of false security.

'Anyway, like I said 1080 came in and that did the trick all right. But because a lot of cattlemen weren't using it, the dogs built up again.

'Well, it was about that time too that the Barrier Fence started to fall into disrepair. Just no maintenance at all or what there was amounted to very little. There have always been heaps of 'roos in the country and they were on the fence in huge numbers. Don't have to tell you what happens then, do I? No, I thought not.' He smiled easily, sipped his tea.

'So with the Barrier Fence not looked after the dogs came in. They were everywhere. But by now all those netting fences that had done such a bloody good job were buggered. Useless. We were in real big strife.

'Then the cattle industry boomed. This was the answer. Sell sheep. Get into cattle. No worries about dogs then. Which is what a lot of sheepmen did.

'But after they did the cattle market fell away badly. So with wool prices shooting up everyone wanted to get back into sheep. But, like I said, there were dogs everywhere and the Barrier Fence was worse than ever. So a lot of heavy pressure was put on the Government to do something about it and, as we all know, they did.'

Howard paused. He looked good in stockman's gear. Looked good for 59 too. Fit and hard. His father had probably looked much as his son did at that age. Good chance Howard would see 90, too.

But despite the overall success of the re-vamped Barrier Fence, Howard's troubles with dingoes did not abate. He believed these were dingoes that had not penetrated the Barrier Fence—so few were doing that now anyway—but rather dingoes that had been born and bred on the inside of it.

Troubles with dingoes on Lyndale? Between 1984 and 1987, Jensen's flock of around 4,000 to 4,500 sheep, despite good lambing percentages, did not increase. In fact it fell away due to dingoes killing older sheep. Jensen was convinced that local authorities were not aware of how many dingoes were roaming the inside of the fence. A reason for this, he thought, was that most graziers would much rather display a dingo 'scalp' on a fence or wherever than hand it in and claim the $10 bounty.

A good example of this was Robert Blain, who worked a lone cattle station 40 km inside the Barrier Fence. Prior to the Barrier Fence being given a superior face lift, he had in about five years trapped some 90 dingoes. Not once had he claimed a reward.

'Running cattle he didn't really have to bother with them,' Howard explained when I asked why he'd trapped them and not bothered to cash in. 'He just enjoyed catching them. Doesn't like dogs, apparently.'

By mid-1987, then, Howard Jensen was heartily sick of dingoes and all that that involved when they were on your property. The constant pressure of it was incredibly wearing, a weary sort of helplessness because it was a no-win situation. It just made too many demands of both him and his 25-year-old son, David. Up before dawn. Saddling a horse in icy-cold conditions. Out to the trap line. The frustrations when 'roos set off carefully placed traps. The hours and then still more long hours trying to pin down a particular dog. In this instance, read bitch for dog. She was killing large–scale. Say 300 lambs and a good number of adult sheep before she vanished.

'If you beat the crows to one of her kills, you'd find in nine or ten cases she'd killed for the sport. There would be no visible mark on the lamb, no broken skin. But it was dead. Open it up with your pocketknife and you'd see why. The back of the neck would be severely bruised where she'd grabbed it and then crushed it to death. Enormous power.

'Smart too. She raised one set of pups we knew of about a hundred yards from a permanent 1080 bait we had set up. Never touched it. Some dogs—the smart ones—will never touch a bait. That's possibly more so of a bitch with pups. She wants them to have only fresh meat. That's the general theory, anyhow.

'David actually saw them one morning when they were leaving the den. He got four before the others got away. Just four shots, too.' Evidently, his son's marksmanship pleased him. 'Didn't get her, though. She was born under a lucky star. Must've been. She left a toenail in one of my traps early on.'

Three pups and a cunning bitch still at large then. More than enough on Lyndale in mid-1987.

In mid-1987, Howard Jensen wasn't the only Queensland grazier up to his neck in dingoes. Far from it. *Canis familiaris dingo* was having itself a high old time south of Roma. Down in the Shires of Warroo and Balonne, dingoes, drifting steadily southwards from their more traditional regions, were creating all sort of headaches. In the St George district, for instance.

On 55,000 ha Thomby (owned by Hollowtree Enterprise) Keith Khan was working a trap line. He had trapped 43 in the past three years. Since last shearing time, they had lost 3,500 sheep. The daily grind of a 100 km drive checking and resetting traps would continue.

Greg Courtney, of Mourachne, had seen his flock reduced by 10 per cent. He believed one dingo was responsible. God help him should more dingoes get up to similar antics. (Courtney would turn to cattle.)

Ewart Sylvester, a grazier and President of a local 58-strong Feral Dog Group formed in early 1987, was of the opinion dingoes were breeding up in the Thomby Ranges and Yuleba Forest—locations not previously known for dingoes. Like others on the same sinking ship, Sylvester found dingo control both demanding and tiresome. So badly did he want to account for one dingo on his property that he went to the expense of hiring a helicopter. But $3,000 worth of flying time later and, as he reflected ruefully, they still hadn't seen the crafty culprit.

On a station called the Homestead only one dingo had been sighted in 54 years prior to the summer of 1986. Since then they had trapped five there.

On Lochnager, Ted Humphries had trapped 15 dingoes in 18 months. He found they were attacking sheep in the early mornings and late evenings.

On his run, Wanganui, Rod Avery had shot two dingoes but had seen at least four more. His brother, on an adjoining place, had been trying to outwit a dingo for months. At last success! He found her den. Killed six pups, one of which he placed back in the hollow log, its body well laced with strychnine. On her return, the bitch sniffed at the limp bundle that, when she left, had been so full of life. The strychnine did the job sure enough.

On Enfield station, which had been in his family since the start of the century, David Coward trapped 15 dingoes and had seen them kill as many as 17 in one mob. The problem, he said, had only been there for four years.

Dingoes inside the Barrier Fence? There are bloody heaps of them inside the Barrier Fence, mate!

Meanwhile, back in Balonne Shire, the Feral Dog Control Group had taken a positive step in dealing with the situation by hiring a full time dogger, Les Grant, who had gained wide experience trapping both dingoes and feral dogs in Western Australia. Grant's wages would be paid in full by the graziers themselves. The dogger was confident enough in his own ability to work on a contract basis, that is so much per animal: $300 per bitch; $200 per dog; $50 per pup.

Simultaneously, the Member for Roma, Russell Cooper, was urging graziers in his electorate to form syndicates or dingo destruction groups to deal with the present calamity of just too many dingoes inside the Barrier Fence. Such groups—four graziers, say—required an aggregate of 5,000 ha between them. No registration process would be required. At his office at 67 McDowall Street, Cooper was only too willing to meet with anyone keen to form such a group and discuss the benefits of doing so. The fact that the main benefit appears to have been the availability of dingo traps through the local Rural Lands Protection Board's depot at a 20 per cent discount would not have had worried graziers stampeding through his office door.

And what about Howard Jensen north of Roma? Well, he 'got out of sheep!' in the year in question. A man could only take so much, couldn't he? Later, however, the opportunity came up to purchase sheep at a ridiculously low price and—if only in a small way—he was a sheep man again. As a sheepman, he pointed out what many consider is a big mistake almost anywhere along the Border Fence where a major or secondary road goes through it. The open 'stock grid' system which, around Roma anyway, occurs at regular intervals.

A sheepdog, for instance, will cross a stock grid the first time it sees it, Howard Jensen reckons. How about a dingo? What do you suppose would happen should a dingo be pursuing a 'roo and the stock grid loomed up in front of the 'roo and it crossed it. Would a dingo stop just because he really wasn't supposed to be on the other supposedly 'clean' side of the Barrier Fence? Jensen followed that hypothetical question with a scornful snort. I could see his point, though, and it made a lot of sense.

Regarding 1080, Jensen considers that even today, a good number of years after its introduction, there is no substitute for it. Yes, it represents the best method of controlling dingoes especially if a sensible regulated campaign is carried out at regular intervals. By that, he means not random poisoning but hitting selected areas where dingoes are known to be. In this way a grazier knows precisely where it has been placed and can make sure his valuable working dogs stay well clear.

On Listowel Downs, 18,211 ha, carrying 18,000 sheep, and midway between Blackall and Adavale, Steve Picone shares Howard Jensen's sentiments perfectly regarding 1080: 'At Listowel Downs there has been only one sheep killing in the last 15 years. We immediately followed this up with a bait trail around the carcass and the dog was not sighted again.'

What makes Picone's statement so remarkable is that his station is actually a few kilometres outside the Barrier Fence. He is, however, realistic enough to know he is perhaps fortunate that this is the case because there are other stations in the area that have more than their share of dingoes from time to time.

Picone is President of the Blackwater Dingo Trust (18 stations are involved). It is typical of other such groups formed by anxious graziers knowing they have a real fight on their hands they just might not win. Certainly not by a knockout. A split decision, maybe.

Once a year, in July, and with each station contributing one-cent-per-head of stock to a special fund (the Blackall Council has been known to add a small amount too) a fixed-wing aircraft is hired. It dumps about three tonnes of bait into areas largely inaccessible.

Steve Picone, a darkly-tanned, well-spoken type, said: 'The Terrick Trust is run on similar lines to us. It is pretty much the same size. They merge with another trust out west. There's another trust at Adavale too. We all link more or less together. We poison first, then the Terrick Trust, and so on down the line. That way we can get maximum results. We concentrate on riverbeds, around dams and bores.

'Eventually we can draw a line from north of Blackall right out to the Channel Country (Windorah). It works out extremely well.'

We were yarning in the sun, a lovely spring morning, about eight o'clock. I put it to him what did he think about the possibility that 1080—as it was in some other countries—could be banned in Australia.

Steve's face actually dropped.

'Don't even think about the consequences. . .'

'But it might.'

'Yeah, I know.'

'Go on, so how would you feel.'

'In a word?'

'Sure.'

'Mortified, mate! Bloody mortified!'

He wouldn't be lonely there.

On Tenham, a 64,752 ha property south-east of Windorah, 42-year-old Brian Tully says bluntly: 'Use 1080 or get off the land!' By that, he means get out of sheep.

Tenham borders the Barrier Fence. In September 1989, patrolmen Neville and Scott Geiger, while checking out the fence on the Tullys' place, saw a lot of fresh dingo signs. They reported it to Brian Tully. Consequently baits were laid along the fenceline.

For Gay Tully it was a normal thing for her husband or some of the men to say, yeah, the dogs'd been active again. No matter how often she saw dead lambs, she always found the sight of their pitiful broken little bodies an upsetting experience. Like other station women in dingo country, the responsibility of raising motherless lambs often was hers. No matter. She did it willingly enough. She had done so this spring. Almost certainly she would do so the next time it came around.

The Tullys have three children: Megan (7); Amanda (5); Joseph (4). They also 'had' a pure-bred miniature fox terrier called Goldie. She was one of two family pets, both dogs, doted on. But Goldie, well, she was something very special. Megan in fact adored her.

Somehow both dogs ate poisoned bait. Both died. It was not a pretty sight.

'Goldie went berserk,' Gay said. 'Went rushing in circles as her whole nervous system was affected. She took an hour to die. It was heartbreaking. We all cried for a day.'

So how did these pets, never straying too far from home and a good distance from where the bait was placed out, end up dead?

A possible answer might be found in the following letter which appeared in the *Western Star* on 26 May 1987.

Animal baiting: A cruel practice

Sir,—I live approximately 10 miles from Roma and recently witnessed my miniature Fox Terrier dog die a most cruel, horrible, agonising death and I was unable to help him.

I called the vet but Spot (my Fox Terrier) was dying while I was telephoning. There was no time to get him to the vet, and it seems there is no antidote anyhow.

I believed from all the reports I have received so far that Spot was poisoned with a 1080 bait, originally laid with the permission of the relevant authority on a property a few miles from my home.

Spot was poisoned in my house yard, by a bait or part thereof which was probably dropped by a passing crow.

I have been told by informed sources that birds can carry a poisoned bait for many miles.

It does not harm the birds, but pity help the poor creatures that then may pick it up from where it is dropped.

The death of my dog hurt deeply as he was a friend and companion.

Having to watch him die so cruelly because of man is something I shall never forget. But my great fear is that at any time this could happen again; only next time it could be a town or on a property and be a child's pet or a child savaged by a pet that has taken such a poison which has been dropped in a similar manner.

Imagine the agony the animals in the bush are suffering because of this terrible poison made by mankind.

Man claims to be so superior to the rest of nature's living creatures and yet this is the cruelty we dish out.

—DAWN BAILEY, 'Wahroonga,' Blythdale, via Roma.

So how specifically does 1080 kill? It kills by causing damage to body cells which in turn manifests itself clinically in disturbances to the central nervous system and heart.

An information bulletin published by the Queensland Rural Land Protection Board, *Ecological Effects of 1080* (and other poisons) contained this particular extract:

> 'Several human cases of 1080 poisoning, some of which have recovered, have been studied overseas. Although humans show severe epileptiform convulsions, as well as cardiac effects, no pain has ever been reported. It is responsible to assume that a similar lack of pain would be experienced by other animals.'

I should imagine that both the Tullys and Dawn Bailey would seriously question the last part of the above paragraph.

On 16 July 1987 Lands Department Project Officer, Lee Allan, stated in the *Western Mail* that 'poisoning with 1080 was the most humane and effective form of controlling dingoes'.

Effective? No question. But humane? Absolutely not! Again, what would be the Tullys' and Dawn Bailey's verdict on the word 'humane'?

But doesn't all this come back to an earlier argument: something to do with what side of the fence you're standing on? Yes, I really think it does.

15

Roughly West Of Roma

*I didn't really believe they could pull down a full-grown 'roo until I actually
saw it happen. The 'roos were hopping away from water and suddenly,
right out of the blue, eight or nine dogs appeared. They went in fast—not
appearing to single out any 'roo in particular. As soon as a dog had a
'roo down and had drawn blood the others were on it, too. What we're
really talking about here is the law of the wild.*
– Bruce Scott, President of the Maranoa Graziers Association, recalling
dingoes on Kynuna station, west of Winton, Queensland, in 1964–65

On Carinya station
Carrying 5,000 sheep on 4,856 hectares
Plus rabbits, foxes, lizards
An unspecified number of 'roos and wallabies
And, yes, the odd dingo from time to time
Late morning
'The Barrier Fence skirts those hills.' The speaker was Don Compagnoni, a
solidly-built, 48-year-old of Swiss ancestry.

Following the line of his finger, I shaded my eyes against the high, bright
sun, to gaze north beyond a wide plain to hazy timbered ridges.

'That's Mount Ascot country you can see. It runs right back to the Barrier
Fence.' He broke off and turned to me. 'Heard of it?' No, I hadn't. 'The
Brumptons own it,' he continued. 'Famous old merino stud—one of the three
biggest in the State.' He shook his head admiringly. 'Lovely country.'

Later, I would learn that Mount Ascot covered some 6,000 hectares. During
the mid-1980s, when controversy raged like a bushfire out of control over the
rebuilding of the Barrier Fence, Errol Brumpton, the studmaster, had been
highly vocal in his support of it. One of a minority, he knew only too well
what it was like to be shouted down angrily at public meetings by those who
wanted no part of it. Particularly when it came to costing them hard cash.

While he regularly patrolled his section of the Barrier Fence, Brumpton was
unable to comprehend why anyone would be against it. Just didn't make sense.
Couldn't they see how absolutely vital it was for the State's economy? Without
it being there, he was convinced Queensland dingoes would eventually merge
with those residing in Victoria.

All too frequently, Brumpton and his men saw dingoes on the outside of the Barrier Fence. Sometimes they got through. One time they lost sheep to the value of $10,000. Others fared far worse of course. On Tambo station, to the north-west, they lost 2,000 sheep and more than two-thirds of their lambs in 1983.

Unexpectedly, Don said, 'How did you find Jerry?' There was an enigmatic expression playing about his ruddy-complexioned features. Maybe an amused twinkle in his eye, too.

'No bullshit,' I replied, not having to think of a reply.

'Fair comment.' Don chuckled.

'Wouldn't want to tangle with him, though.'

Don's chuckle turned into a resounding belly laugh. 'The right man for the job, you reckon?'

'Anybody say otherwise?'

'Not that I heard,' Don admitted, still amused. Vastly so.

As Chairman of the Mitchell Branch of the Maranoa Graziers Association (involving 65 stations), Don Compagnoni and Jerry Stanley had naturally come into contact. While they were on the same wave-band today where the Barrier Fence was concerned, it wasn't always the case. Hence Don's amusement.

A rather delicate situation had arisen in April 1987. Specifically April 2 when a short but loaded article appeared in *Queensland Country Life*.

Graziers say fence failure

Graziers inside the dingo barrier fence, faced with increasing sheep losses through wild dog attacks, have decided to take their own control measures.

One group in the Mitchell area feels the fence is such a failure it has instigated dingo 'drives' to try and make the concept of controlling the dogs work.

Spokesman for the group, Don Compagnoni, said since September, 1986, they had organised six drives and caught a total of 17 dogs.

A further 10 dogs had been trapped during that period.

'The drives have been very successful because of the co-operation we have had from townspeople and local cattlemen,' Mr Compagnoni said.

He especially praised Neville Joliffe for allowing the drive onto his property.

He believed the dogs were the worst he had seen in 20 years, due mainly to many being shut inside the fence when upgrading work was done.

'Graziers feel short changed at the moment because the fence is definitely letting dogs through.'

There were also problems with maintenance of the fence in the Amby, Mitchell and Mungallala areas where it was in bad repair with old, rotting netting which was no deterrent to the dogs.

—By *Donnie Jenkins* in Roma

Upon reading this piece, Jerry Stanley told me: 'I didn't just hit the roof—I went right through the bloody ceiling!' Soon after, Don Compagnoni picked up the telephone to discover one very irate Jerry Stanley was on the other end of the line. Finally, Jerry Stanley said, 'Listen, round up your neighbours and be on the fence at six o'clock in the morning. We'll see where these bloody dogs're getting through, mate!' Compagnoni, shaking his head as though shell-shocked, put down the telephone. Mate? He'd never had a less 'matey' telephone call in his life!

Next morning they met on the Barrier Fence, in the area the graziers were complaining about. Jerry Stanley stood tall and powerful, quietly seething. A powder-keg about to explode.

The inspection started. The Barrier Fence looked good. No, better than that. Tip-top shape. So it should be. Men had worked their guts out to make it so. None more than Jerry Stanley. Nevertheless, Jerry was a wee bit perturbed. Not that he let it show, mind. To a man, the graziers were acting as though they knew something he didn't. Smug was the word. How long had it been since the boys went through? Jerry wondered. Only days ago. Why those self-satisfied expressions then?

The answer came when several of the graziers diverted from the main line of the Barrier Fence to show the Project Officer what they were talking about. Hands on hips, Jerry saw what they meant. The fence they were pointing at was badly holed, all but falling down in places, a bullock, never mind a dingo, could have marched through without disturbing a single hair. So what did he, Stanley, think about that, eh?

Terrible, all right, Jerry Stanley agreed. A disgrace all right. But did they realise that this wasn't the Barrier Fence at all?

Faces dropped. It wasn't?

No, this was an old divisional section that went right back to the days of the old Dingo Boards.

Couldn't be?

Was so!

Faces slumped even more.

'We bypassed this when the new alignment went through,' Jerry Stanley told them. The words tasted as sweet as honey to him.

Apparently there were quite a few red faces over that one. None more so than that of Don Compagnoni. The inspection continued. Not a single hole was found.

A subsequent article in the *Western Star*—'Graziers happy with dingo fence repairs'—did wonders for Jerry Stanley's morale and was perhaps the start of a new working relationship between him and the Chairman of the Mitchell Branch of the Maranoa Graziers Association. In particular Jerry savoured the words of its President, Bruce Scott: 'All landowners on the fence should be equally happy with the work carried out by the RLPB over the last five years.'

To his great credit, Don Compagnoni can laugh about it all today. Moreover, he can tell the story against himself. He might like to see in print that Jerry Stanley considers him a 'top bloke'. In south-west Queensland they don't pay higher compliments.

The noonday sun on Carinya was fierce. In this country the wide-brimmed

Above Wild pigs are a menace all along the Qld-NSW section of the Dingo Fence

Top There's some rough country in the aptly-named Wallaroo Range

Left Steve Picone of Listowel Downs, President, Blackwater Dingo Trust

Above A brumby stallion on the run in south-west Queensland

Left Joe Geiger runs Hammond Downs station

Below Joe's sons Neville and Scott Geiger, boundary riders on Hammond Downs

Above left Philip Hughes is manager of Bulloo Downs station

Above right Simon Read is head stockman

Left This rabbit on Bulloo Downs fell prey to a goanna

Above Spring rains leave temporary ponds — outback South Australia
Below Spring wildflowers and the northern Flinders ranges of South Australia

hats are not for show. Down from the station's highest point, the rutted track continually jack-knifed. Don, keeping up an interesting running commentary ranging from wildlife to the different types of trees we encountered, was constantly working through the low gears. Mostly a slick downshift.

Breaking out of thick cover overrun with swamp wallabies, Don informed me that there was a bore directly ahead where he'd recently seen pigs wallowing. Today, however, they were not there. Later, perhaps, they would turn up.

But as said there were wallabies on show—the well-named 'pretty-face' among them, the female of which would win any marsupial beauty contest. Eagles soared aloft. Hawks likewise, black against the sun. Crows perched on the skeleton-like limbs of long-dead trees. Rabbits darted into holes. A frilled-necked lizard (actually a dragon) sunbaked on top of a fencepost. And this was the middle of the day. Traditionally siesta time in the wild. At night, then, the whole place would be buzzing. The hunters and the hunted. Same old story. On Carinya station.

To my query, Don said that the place had been taken up by his grandfather, who, until then, had lived in Sydney. Quite a cultural shock. Carinya was, I thought, a delightful place. Not too big. Craggy rock and grassy plateau. A profusion of trees. Among them:

Coolabah: hardest of all eucalypts, the tree of legendary fame in the outback. It was ideal for posts and rails. In times of drought its branches could be hacked down and fed to stock. They would not thrive and gain weight on it, but on the other hand, they would still be alive next rainfall.

Myall: hallmark of top country. Grows in black soil. That too could be utilised to feed stock on.

Sandalwood: Yeah, said Don, that was okay too to cut down when things were real crook. See that tree over there? That's a she-oak. Same thing applies there too.

And prickly pear: curse of the outback one time. Largely under control now. Still rated a pest, however. Even so, cattle ate its fruit when there was 'bugger all' else. Water was contained in its stem or trunk. Man could survive if he knew that. Most men didn't of course. Especially those who had perished in country rampant with the stuff.

Oh, that was a gidgee tree: real hard wood. Great, like coolabah, for posts and rails. Last forever. Wouldn't find a better firewood, either.

No, I hadn't made a mistake calling in at Carinya station.

On a high, grassy ledge of no great size, Don switched off the ignition. Nice up here, a minute breeze tempered the hammer-like blows of the sun. High 30s. October? With a gesture, Don said he'd seen two dogs chasing a pretty-face wallaby here. But for him coming along he was sure they'd have gotten it. Just loping they were. Could have run like that forever.

Problems with dingoes?

'Sure. But not too much when you compare it with how others around here have fared. Lucky, I guess. Having Mount Ascot between us and the fence makes the difference. They keep a sharp eye on it.'

Any dingoes on the place now that he knew of?

'We don't think so. But you can never be really sure of that. They get cunning as hell when they're on your place for some time. Damn sure they watch you at times. Know exactly what you're up to.'

The other half of 'we' was Don's 19-year-old son, John. Father and son worked the station together. It would be John's one day, just as it was Don's now. Family tradition providing you had sons.

'About a month ago,' Don said, 'I went out looking for a dog that we reckoned had been here for years. Maybe all his life. Dog like that you'll never bait. Just too smart by half to fall for that. Lots of dogs won't touch the stuff, either. They want fresh meat, not small lumps dried out by the sun. Oh, 1080 has its place, don't you worry about that. The thing is, it's not the entire answer. You must have that fence back there.' He jerked a thumb over his shoulder.

'Anyway, I caught up with him as he was feeding on a rabbit he must have just killed. He was so close—five, ten paces maybe—that he filled the 'scope.' One shot from a .222 Winchester and it was all over for a huge black and tan dingo that stood about one metre high at the shoulder. It was the biggest dingo Don had ever seen.

Mid-afternoon. At the homestead. Sitting in reclining chairs in an outside living area. No, it wasn't a bad sort of life.

Don's wife was just as friendly as he was. I had had morning tea with them, lunch, and now afternoon tea. 'Smoko' on a station, even if you didn't smoke.

'Thanks, June.' My teacup was refilled. The home-made cake was going down a treat. Everybody was feeding me. Perhaps I'd lost weight on this project?

Don was eating cake with similar relish. 'When're. . .catch. .ing. . .up with Br. .u. .ce?'

'Tomorrow, I expect.'

'Good bloke, Bruce. He's been the President of our association for. . .June, how long has Bruce been President?' June was in the kitchen. Don repeated the question. Much louder.

'About three years, I think,' she said, rejoining us.

'Yeah, about that,' Don said, nodding. 'Anyway, he'll fill you in on a few points.'

From where I was sitting, you could look out over the sun-parched earth to a windmill, to the yards, and to the shearing shed. They had been built to last. A cat dozed in the sun with, yes, one eye partly open. A spread-eagled dog panted so hard it might have just completed a hard mile. The sounds of birds were so constant from the shade trees that you soon forgot they were there.

Top place, Carinya station. Top people, too. Just ask Jerry Stanley but don't get him started on that newspaper report of 2 April 1987, and subsequent events.

Located near Muckadilla, and approximately midway between Roma and Mitchell, is Bruce Scott's run, Crochdantigh. It has been in the family since 1953 and is 4,047 ha in size.

The Roma-born man himself was docking and ear-marking lambs when I cornered him at the yards. Two stationhands—Paul and Bruce Harris—were working side by side with their tall, strongly-built boss. An eager-faced kelpie was close to hand, too. Joe was just busting a gut waiting to be asked to contribute something—anything—to what was going on. At the present time, however, his services were not in demand.

'Be finished here in, oh, about an hour, I expect,' Bruce said in well-modulated tones. No rough-as-guts bush school here. A flash boarding school, more like. Down country. 'All right with you?' It wasn't really a question; he was merely being polite. So I slung one R.M. Williams-clad leg over the topmost rail and sat there as one by one lambs had their tails sliced off and then faced the added indignity of having a tag stapled to an ear.

Crunch! Blood jetted over Bruce's white overalls. The lamb screamed.

Crunch! An ear was pierced. No blood. The lamb cried out in pain all the same.

Country life. Basic when Crochdantigh was first taken up in 1880. So what's new?

Presently the work was done. The stationhands had the job of taking the lambs wherever they had to go. Never seen a more pitiful bunch of woolly youngsters in my life. Subdued isn't a strong enough word. 'Distressed', and badly, sounds more on the right tack. Still, as Bruce pointed out, they'd be leaping around as though nothing had happened in two days. Which meant a tough 48 hours to contend with before then. Glad I wasn't a lamb on Crochdantigh!

A light breeze had picked up when we started to yarn. Bruce fondled Joe's head as he talked; Joe didn't mind in the least.

Bruce Scott talked well, each word clear. There was, I soon noticed, an air of authority about him. In the last big war, he'd have been a Captain, or, more likely, Major. Never in the ranks. Just wasn't the type. He was outback aristocracy and it was as unmistakable as the red blood on his overalls.

All of which explained why he held such a lofty position in the Maranoa. President of the Graziers Association. Powerful stuff. The spokesman for in excess of 500 graziers covering 10 to 15 per cent of the State. An organisation that could, collectively speaking, make things happen in far-away Brisbane.

Bruce Scott's real introduction to dingoes came in 1964–65 when he worked as a jackaroo on Kynuna station 177 km north-west of Winton.

At that time about 112 km of the Barrier Fence extended through the property and it continued in a northerly direction from there. Now defunct, the fence protected the station's sheep from the west, beyond the famed Diamantina River. Rough, broken lands alive with packs of dingoes that, when the mighty river flooded and swept aside the Barrier Fence as though it were nothing at all, quickly seized the initiative.

'It was a case of all hands on deck then,' Bruce recalled. 'You had to get it up again quickly or you were in serious trouble.' Over the years, Kynuna was often in serious trouble. With dingoes. 'The station had two boundary riders camped on the fence all the time so the fence at that time was in good condition. We ran sheep right up to it and on some days you could see dogs padding back and forth—eight, ten strong. Of course we lost calves but, all things considered, it was not too significant a loss.

'Out mustering cattle—on the other side of the fence of course—we'd often see dogs on cattle. There would be three or four of them worrying the cow and the rest would be on the calf. Sometimes other cattle came to their aid but mostly once they'd drawn blood it was over.

'The biggest impression it made on me was that without the Barrier Fence it would have been impossible to run sheep.'

As Bruce recalled his long-ago days on Kynuna the weather changed. The breeze had fallen away. The sky was darker, the humidity greater. Rain? Bruce shook his head, no, and said it hadn't done that there since May and wasn't about to now, either.

Memories of the nostalgic past faded, for this was Bruce Scott 24 years on, speaking in his capacity as President of the Maranoa Graziers Association: 'We rely on our 15 branches for resolutions coming forward as being the true feelings of the people in their area. Sometimes a motion in regards to the fence is for emotional rather than good reasons. I want us to reach the best decision and also the right decision.

'It's been divided about the Barrier Fence, no doubt about it. The further south you go from the fence the less they think they benefit from it. That is wrong, of course.

'If dingoes weren't stopped they will continually move southwards and what you're doing is spreading the burden of maintaining the fence across all those who are in the protected zone. Otherwise you're leaving it to those who have the problem now but in 20 years it could be all over the area.

'Without the Barrier Fence you just can't measure the economic loss to the sheep country. People close to the fence would be out of sheep; it's as simple as that. We would be marginal here. So slowly it would spread south...' Bruce Scott pondered thoughtfully on that statement. He knew that it could happen.

'Eventually?' I prodded him.

'Eventually?' He looked up from his distasteful reverie. 'Eventually there would be no sheep industry, or a much diminished industry. You could see people netting their own properties again. At huge expense! Take the long-term view that one barrier does work must mean it's a smaller cost in the long run to all of us.

'This is really a co-ordinated approach to the whole thing: the whole dingo problem. Certainly there are major problems. Always will be. We have to rely on good staff on the Barrier Fence for one thing. But at present it works well enough for us.

'At this point in time we are keen to get a co-ordinated increase in the bounty for scalps right across our area, because one of the old arguments is that the fence does not kill dogs, it merely divides them. A $10 bounty is not really incentive enough for young fellows like my workmen to go out at weekends and pursue a few dogs. Trap them. Shoot them. Whatever.

'Last weekend a couple of my blokes got a pig. That was worth $50. Three such pigs add up to $150. Several 'roos and that's about $60. So we believe that if there was a higher bounty it would minimise them in our area: that is, inside the Barrier Fence. I believe it would help enormously.'

Interestingly enough, the Maranoa Graziers Association and south-eastern delegates had at a graziers conference in Brisbane two years earlier passed a resolution calling for a dollar-for-dollar bounty of up to $50 per dingo to be offered by shire councils on behalf of the Rural Lands Protection Board.

Speaking at that gathering, Bruce Scott made the telling point that in 1976 the number of scalps presented for payment was 3,200. By 1986 that figure had leapt to 14,000. Did that not say something? He also stated that the only positive way of dealing with their ever-growing numbers was by shooting and trapping, particularly since the strength of 1080 poison had been significantly reduced.

Against the motion, however, was a powerful force: northern cattlemen and far-western sheepmen. In a close vote the motion to increase the bounty was defeated. The Annual Report of the Rural Lands Protection Board for 1987/88 contained this pertinent extract:

Trapping of dingoes was again successful, evidenced by the large number of dingo scalps (19,995) presented for payment. This figure represents the highest number of scalps received since 1969/70. It is of interest to note that, according to figures released by the Bureau of Statistics, Australia is headed for its second highest wool clip on record. The Bureau forecasted that 192 million sheep and lambs would be shorn in the year ending June 30, 1989, 3 per cent more than the 186 million shorn in 1987/88, and the largest number since 192.7 million in 1969/70.

So in the spring of 1989 the Maranoa Graziers Association were still determined to see an increase in the dingo bounty right across the State. They will again present their case in Brisbane. It will be with dignity. With Bruce Scott at the helm it could not be otherwise. The man is a 'class' act. Has style, and polish. Bounties will increase in Queensland. It might not be while Bruce Scott is still President of the Maranoa Graziers Association, however.

16

Both Sides Of The Fence

The sheepman is always crying 'Dingo!' and the cattleman says 'Where?'.
It makes it very hard.
– Barry Phillips, Barlin station, south-west Queensland

Twin brothers Ron and Barry Phillips run properties adjoining the Barrier Fence a short distance north of Mitchell. With Ron's place on the outside of the wire and Barry's on the inside of it they were, as Jerry Stanley put it, well worth a visit.

About 7.30 on a wondrous Saturday morning I put Mitchell behind me and more-or-less headed north on a route that, if I had stayed on it long enough, would have eventually taken me to the fringes of the Carnarvon Range. Local graziers reckon with some justification that free-range dingoes must be breeding in there: a spectacular wilderness area of deep gorges and well-timbered ridges.

After a short run, the highlight of which was seeing a medium-sized black pig trot with tail swinging across the road in front of me, I spotted what I'd been told by Ron Phillips to keep an eye open for: an improvised but effective mailbox with, above it, the word 'Currawong' written on a split board. The weathered board had obviously been there quite some time. So has Currawong, apparently.

But once through the gate, I was not actually on Currawong land. Once, yes. For this was Barlin, owned by Ron Phillips' brother, Barry; I shall make it all clear soon.

This was typical country for the region. Ample trees: acacias, wattle, mulga, gidgee, the odd Queensland bottle tree. Which reminds me. In Roma. On Wyndham Street, an avenue of established bottle trees, planted to perpetuate the memory of those local men who died in World War 1, lines each side of the street. A lovely touch; what a nice way to be remembered. Far better than cold headstones. Rather fancy a Norfolk pine myself. Certainly not a ragged clump of tea-tree.

A few healthy-looking 'roos were kicking about. Nearing the Maranoa River that was to be expected, for, from what Jerry Stanley had said, the porcupines were light on the ground beyond there and the 'roos most certainly weren't.

Then through the trees, on a sandy track, I saw the Barrier Fence looming up. A big solid gate. Beyond it—a long stone's throw—stood a low-slung dwelling. Currawong homestead. I drove off Barlin station, closed the gate, and then, as I spun on my heel, a loud chattering arrested my attention. Along the fence were the cause of it. Birds. Green budgerigars and gaily attired finches and some other equally diminutive species I was not familiar with. But what they all lacked in the size department, they more than made up for vocally. And so many! Indeed, the fence, from top to bottom, was choked with birds, tightly compressed like sardines in a can. Strange?

Listening to that incredible racket reminded me of seeing budgerigars on the Border Fence one afternoon with Lenny Dixon. They flew low over the roof of the Toyota: an enormous green flock, like thousands of sapphires hurled at the dazzling sun. They wheeled, they banked, they rose as one in incredibly close formation, as tight-knit as bats in the night.

But that memory lasted only momentarily, and, still puzzled as to why these had gathered here in such numbers, I decided to attempt to move close enough to photograph them. Photographs combining both wildlife and the Dingo Fence were of special value to me.

But not on foot, as animals and birds do not respond well to the human form. In the vehicle. A slow approach, then, when close enough, shoot with the 300 mm telephoto lens supported by the top of the half-open window, a method that had worked remarkably well. Always an added plus on this trip was the excellent light, which meant, when using the big lens, I could shoot at 1/500 or 1/250 of a second. This also compensated for any movement of the camera.

But these birds, unfortunately, were in no mood to be photographed. As I turned so that I had a clear view through the driver's window, they exploded into the air. A dazzling flash of colour, mostly green.

But one bird remained. A bird so much larger than those that had been there. But almost impossible for a casual glance to observe because of the way in which the rest of them had been so tightly packed around it.

There was no need for stealth. The kookaburra wasn't going anywhere; not with its head lodged securely in the upper netting. What had happened, I deduced, was this: travelling at high speed, its attention was momentarily diverted or it simply hadn't seen the wire, or completely misjudged its height, and flew straight at the fence. The sheer impact had forced the bird's head through a gap in the netting less than half its size, and then, once through, the wire had snapped back to its previous circumference. In effect, the kookaburra then had a tight noose around its neck. The impact had also been severe enough to break a wing.

There was a growing sadness in me as I contemplated how cruel and unjust life can be to either wildlife or the human race. We never know what the future holds, what dangers there might be around the next corner. Perhaps it is just as well.

While the kookaburra's eyes were wide open, they were dull. Perhaps more than any other species of bird the kookaburra is symbolic of the Australian bush. But surely the one I was now looking at with compassion wasn't that same laughing cavalier? That cheeky devil with a glint in his eye and a merry, prolonged chuckle to greet a brand new day? No, it couldn't possibly be.

Careful of its broken wing (worse than I'd first judged), I prised the wire around its neck wide enough so that, without hurting it any more, I was able to free the bird. Carefully, I placed it face down on the ground. It was limp, gasping. Chalk up one more victim to the Dingo Fence.

But I couldn't leave it there like that. Death might come in minutes; which is what I suspected, for its eyes were much duller now, losing proper focus. Hunting around, I found a suitable stick. Ended it with one well-directed blow to the back of the skull, hurled the cursed stick from me, wondering why in God's name the death of a bird had upset me so.

Turning away, I also wondered why the birds had gathered around the helpless kookaburra. To torment it? No, the combined sound they had made was not that of anger tinged with malicious undertones. They could have pecked it without interference had they wished. But no, apart from the broken wing, the kookaburra was unmarked. Had they then tried to comfort it... somehow knowing it was dying. Only Mother Nature knew the answer to that and, as always, she certainly wasn't about to enlighten me. Whatever the reason, that was and would remain the most poignant incident I experienced along the Dingo Fence.

Up close, there was nothing pretentious about the homestead. The 42-year-old who ran the place was pretty basic too. Standing a chunky 178 cm and wearing a short-sleeved sportshirt that revealed hairy forearms the size of miniature tree trunks, Ron Phillips thrust out a ham-like paw.

'Come on in,' he said with a friendly smile. 'You're nice an' early.'

Ron's wife, Ann, was equally pleasant. Yes, I'd love a cup of tea.

After a few minutes, I mentioned the kookaburra to Ron. He nodded matter-of-factly as he listened and said, yeah, birds were always getting hooked up in the wire—emus, and especially, plains turkeys. 'Nuthin' you can do about it,' he finished with a philosophical lift of meaty shoulders. He wasn't fat, you understand. It was all hard compressed muscle. Met guys like that before. They often have prodigious strength, real killers when it comes to arm wrestling.

It took a little while for Ron to relax and talk; he warned me that his brother was even more taciturn. Not to worry. The subject matter was pretty basic around here too.

It was in 1963, Ron explained, when his father, Bob, took over Currawong from his own father. The station of 14,164 ha was stocked only with cattle.

'Me and Barry were going to school in Mitchell then,' said Ron, 'and at weekends and during holidays we'd help out on the place.

'Dingoes were really thick here then; you'd see them every time you went out mustering. Cheeky buggers would just stand there looking at you sometimes. We did a lot of trapping over the winters and caught a lot, too. But it didn't seem to knock them back much, though.

'Anyway, we left school at 14 and worked for Dad. When he retired, we took over the place on a 50–50 basis.' He smiled a little ruefully. 'Don't know anything else but working here.

'Later on Barry got married—I was married by then and had three kids—and we decided it would be best to split up the place. The fence made an obvious boundary.' He paused. 'Don't get me wrong, we are still the best of mates. Always have been. It was, well, some things change when you get married, right?' He looked across the table at me and I nodded in agreement.

'So we flipped a coin to see who got what.' Outside the fence added up to 10,117 hectares, inside, a mere 3,237 hectares. 'Anyway, Barry called "heads" and down it came the way he picked. That explains why he's running sheep and I'm still coping with the dogs.' Barry and Linda Phillips would call their station 'Barlin'.

'Tell me about the dogs,' I said.

Two years previously, Barry had gone out to a bore requiring work. Near it, he had spotted a sickly-looking calf. There was good reason, he discovered, for its distressed condition. A dingo had been at it. A large part of its flank had been ripped away. The sickening wound was oozing dark blood and pus, stank to high heaven and was badly fly-blown. For a moment, Ron deliberated whether or not he should shoot it. Then, feeling great pity for the calf, he had taken it home with him. They had nursed it back to health and then released it.

'We see it from time to time,' Ron said. 'Oddly enough, there's still discharge coming from the wound. It's a fair bit smaller than other animals of a comparable age, too. Apart from that, it's fine.' He smiled reflectively. 'Glad I didn't shoot it.'

On another occasion, when he was still a teenager, he and his father had spotted a solitary dingo amidst a number of cows and calves. 'The crafty bastard was actually playing with the calves.' Ron went on, 'You know, trying to lure them away from the cows. Anyhow, Dad shot him and said, "Keep your eyes wide open, son, there's bound to be another one pretty handy," and sure enough, we had only driven a bit further on and there it was.' It was a bitch they spotted, peering anxiously over a bank as though trying to fathom out precisely what had happened to her mate. But that one, Barry said with deep-rooted regret, had got away.

'We still have problems with dogs,' Ron continued. 'Everyone does; some of course more than others. But you can't afford to ignore them. Not ever. They soon build up if you do that.'

He then told me there were stations upriver where they still lost a great number of calves, sometimes as high as one-third of the yearly birthrate. The river he meant was the Maranoa, one of the top wool-growing centres in the State.

'Those places are close to the Carnarvon Ranges and the dogs come down from there in droves. Hmmmm...pity young David wasn't here; you'd have found him interesting to talk to.' David was his 16-year-old son. At this time, he was mustering cattle on contract on nearby Forest Vale station.

'David's camped at an outstation on the place. They see dogs all the time; you get pretty close to them on a horse. Don't seem to take much notice of a horseman. They shot 45 dogs this year and, I think, about 60 odd pups.

That was in six weeks.' He fingered his jaw. 'Worth a few bob at ten bucks a scalp, eh?' After a long pause he continued. 'Still, it's not difficult to get pups once you know where the bitches have their dens. They tend to use the same areas each year. Hell, we're still getting pups where we did in '63.' He stood up abruptly. 'Listen, there's not much on today: I'll show you where we got some pups this year if you like.'

About an hour later, amidst semi-desert country, Ron came to a halt on a winding sandy track. Not far to go, he said, striding off into what I soon discovered was extremely dry bush. It was getting hot, too. Over 30 degrees.

'Wouldn't want to strike a match in here,' I pointed out intelligently.

'You're not wrong,' he said over his shoulder.

Presently we came to a small grove of blackboy trees. Distinct trails went every-which-way. Barry, with a gesture, said that dogs had made them. A little further on, he bent down and tapped the trunk of a large, hollowed-out log.

'Got seven pups in here last May. Last year it was five. We reckon the bitch had a couple more hid around here somewhere; they often shift camp. Two years ago, we got six litters of three in termite mounds—the bitches dig out holes underneath them and make a good-sized chamber. Snug sort of place, I expect.' He straightened and removed his hat from his head, to run the back of his hand across his perspiring forehead. 'Never get them all, though. The pups you miss put real pressure on the fence later on. April and May is really bad news. The young ones are a year old then and on their own; the bitch doesn't want anything to do with them any more. So they're looking for territories of their own. They pace up and down that fence for hours trying to find a way through it. Grass is greener on the other side sort of thing. And sometimes,' he grinned without humour, 'they do find a way through.'

Six months prior to my visit, Ron's brother, Barry, had been feeling almost smug about the fact that for 14 months he hadn't lost a single sheep to dingoes. The previous five years, however, had been something else. For each of those years, he had lost around 200 sheep and twice that number of lambs. Obviously, he could not continue indefinitely like that; the mere fact of trapping so much (he'd trapped 59 dingoes on his place and Ron's in one year alone) accounted for precious hours away from essential work on Barlin.

So something radical had to be done. Something essential was. The Mitchell Barrier Fence Feral Dog Group was formed and Barry was voted in charge of the organisation of shooting drives. This is an effective way of dealing with small numbers of dingoes that over a period have become difficult to kill. On occasions, and particularly with a 'rogue' dingo, it was the only way to deal with a single, rampaging animal capable of killing hundreds of sheep before it was run to earth or simply went elsewhere to create havoc. It was also in this same period—the mid-1980s—that fence maintenance was tightened up considerably.

Dingo numbers on the wrong side of the wire gradually diminished because of regular shooting forays and also because there were few places left unattended for any length of time where dingoes could get through.

One thing that delighted Barry was the fact that local people in and around Mitchell were only too pleased to assist when it came to shooting drives. Obviously they too realised the full significance of keeping dingoes well under control.

Towards the end of April 1989, Barry Phillips discovered that the menace all sheepmen fear had returned, to kill and kill again. With haste, he contacted his brother. The two acted almost immediately. Since it was too boggy along the fence to use a conventional four-wheel-drive vehicle they each mounted a Yamaha 175 cc trailbike and, on their respective sides of the Barrier Fence, set off to see if they could discover where a dingo or dingoes were penetrating it.

Soon, Ron spotted fresh dingo tracks. He stopped and, as his brother looked back over his shoulder a little further on, raised a hand for him to come back. Kneeling, Ron considered the paw mark. A big dog. It was near this very spot, he thought, where he had actually seen a dingo attempting to dig under the fence. He'd regretted a much too hasty shot. Setting a trap, however, was not a wrong move.

Meantime, Barry had dismounted and was carefully checking the lower wire. Trap in hand, Ron said that he would set it there, indicating a pad showing clear-cut evidence of recent use.

'Uh-uh', Barry said with a shake of his head. 'Right here would make more sense.' He was crouched, pointing a finger at a near-impossible-to-see gap in the wire. Just one strand of wire was broken. But that was enough for a determined dingo to push its head through, and, with even more determination, to squirm through. A closer look confirmed a few dark hairs trapped in the wire netting.

As expected there was a well-used trail near there, too. Barry thought that they might have been coming through longer than he'd earlier estimated. A month, say.

A trap was set, the flattened plate covered with a piece of paper, dirt sprinkled lightly upon that until nothing could be seen. It only needed a light pressure on the plate to activate the wide-spread jaws. Thunk! Trapped! Instantaneous pain. Blinding panic.

The hole was left untouched. The harsh revving sounds of the trailbikes churning through glutinous mud faded away. The Barrier Fence stood where it has for so long. And the bushlands were quiet.

Early next morning the brothers returned to where they had left the trap. It had been set off. No dingo, caught by a leg, stared at them with a mixture of fear and hatred.

Hands on hips, Barry stared in a disgusted fashion at numerous small prints all around the trap. 'Bloody rabbits!' he complained.

Following a few minutes of careful checking the ground for signs, Ron said, 'Looks like one dog came through last night.' He paused and then added heavily, 'Doesn't look like he went back, either.'

Traps were placed on both sides of the hole in the fence. One was set where a dingo had obviously relieved itself on a low bush. Then dog urine from a bottle was spread around the general vicinity. This came from Ron's cattledog, Oz. The idea, Ron explained, was that you left him on the chain overnight. Next morning you put him on a short lead and took him to where he normally had his morning pee. When he reached the bush in question and cocked his leg, you quickly thrust a tin attached to a length of wire under his penis. All this without the slightest trace of a smile.

'Works real good as a rule,' Ron said. 'But you'll still get some dogs that'll go right past a trap no matter how well or where you set it. They just seem to know instinctively that it's there.'

Overnight, a dingo came to the Barrier Fence. All appeared well, safe. He lowered himself to the ground and thrust his head through the small hole he'd used to leave Currawong several times recently. With a snake-like wriggle of his lean hips, he was through. He was a big animal, tending towards black across his back and powerfully developed shoulders. Once again, a few of his dark 'tell-tale' hairs were lodged securely in the wire. The instinctive urge to urinate, as much from necessity as to assert territorial rights, was a powerful force within him. He heeded the compulsion.

For the second morning in succession they checked the traps. None had been disturbed.

'Look at this, will you,' Ron said, shaking his head slowly from side to side, a mixture of frustration and no little admiration. The dingo's front paw marks indicated where he had stood whilst cocking his back leg—one each side of the concealed plate. This was one dog, both brothers thought, that wasn't going to fall victim to a trap. The hole in the fence was closed.

On Barlin a 'drive' was arranged. On that particular weekend, 45 men turned up. Fifteen were mounted on trailbikes, the rest, afoot, armed with 12-gauge shotguns and high-powered rifles. The shooters were spread out in a line, each man in sight of the other. Safety measures were strictly adhered to. One big, brindle dingo was killed.

A week later, Barry organised a second drive. Seventy-five men participated. A small tan-coloured bitch with traces of black on her back paid the ultimate price for trespass. Seen but not shot at was a big dingo with lots of black across his back and over his hulking shoulders.

In all, five drives were held on the property in the late autumn and early winter of 1989. The lone dog was sighted more than once. Each time, however, he had vanished like a puff of smoke on a windy day.

August. Lambing time on Barlin. It was vital, Barry knew, to protect his more than vulnerable flock. He decided to camp in the shearing shed, close to a little holding paddock where ewes would be held.

'We had some of the ewes belled,' Barry explained, 'so that if a dog got in there we'd hear him.' Barry's father was keeping him company in the shearing shed.

Two weeks went by. Ewes gave birth to sprightly youngsters that frolicked in the sun. It was difficult to comprehend that they would turn all too quickly into such docile animals with no real idea of how best to defend themselves.

Snug in his swag one night, Barry heard his father snoring. He wondered what the dingo was up to. One thing he could rely on. It would be back.

Restless now, he recalled with vivid clarity that time he'd been here in the shearing shed and suddenly there had been a frantic commotion from the closest paddock. Sheep, he knew of old, only carried on like that for one reason. But here?

Outside, the sheep were rushing in a confused circle. Two partly grown dingoes had linked forces to tackle one big ewe. One dingo had it by the nose, trying to haul it to the ground. But the ewe was big, strong, putting up resistance. Meantime, the other attacker was busily tearing at her flanks, yanking out steaming intestines. For once, Barry did not have a rifle handy. Instead, he chased off the dingoes. Later, he caught up with the stricken ewe and ended her misery.

Eventually sleep came to the owner of Barlin station.

Then one frosty morning, just on dawn, Barry suddenly awoke. Bells were ringing furiously. Ewes bleated in absolute terror.

'Barry!' his father hissed.

'Okay, I hear them.' Quickly, he pushed back the blankets. Minutes later he was outside, holding a .243 rifle. The light, reflecting off the frost-tipped grass, was better than he could have hoped for. Still bells were ringing insistently. Tensely, he moved quietly towards the milling ewes. There! Yes, a dog had a lamb down.

Barry's heart thudded. He raised his rifle. But the dingo sprang stiff-jointed into darker shadows. Had he spooked it? No. It ran but a short distance before grabbing another lamb by the scruff of its neck. The lamb called out in distress. Carrying it with ease, the dingo ran perhaps 40 paces before dropping it. The lamb did not cry out with anxiety when the dingo lowered its head. It screamed in pain.

The chilling sound knifed into Barry. Steeling himself, he raised the .243. With the 4× 'scope to his eye, and the dingo clearly defined, he knew with stomach-churning certainty that this was about the most vital shot he would ever make. If only he was better able to gain some sort of measured control over his too ragged breathing!

The rifle cracked like a stockman's bullwhip. For a breathless second, the dingo stood transfixed. Then, before Barry had reloaded, it had vanished.

Barry groaned aloud, his mind churning with self-recriminating thoughts. He'd had it bang to rights and somehow he had missed! Sick at heart, he trudged back to the shearing shed.

Six days went by. Barry and his father kept up their nightly vigil at the shearing shed. A full week after the attack, the dingo's tracks were observed in a nearby paddock. What happened there next proved a disaster. In one night the dingo killed 21 lambs. He had also bitten, but none fatally, a number of sheep.

Another week slipped by. No sign of the dingo, day or night.

It was perhaps the eighth night after the dingo's last attack that he returned.

Barry's watch read: 1.30. The dingo had bailed up sheep in a small stand of trees. As Barry approached them, the bawling of the frantic sheep reached a horrendous pitch.

Suddenly a single sheep was bolting out of the trees. Another rushed after it. Both could be easily seen on the moon-dappled ground. Lambs materialised. They ran aimlessly, separated from their mothers. Then the dingo burst into the open. Fittingly it appeared black in the uncertain light. The devil itself.

Instinctively, Barry had palmed close the bolt of his rifle. As he whipped it to his shoulder, the dingo was running after a lamb. But there was no chance of a shot at such a difficult target. The unequal contest came to a sudden end when the dingo pulled the lamb to the ground. They cartwheeled out of sight, the lamb kicking frantically, behind a low bush.

Still he was unable to shoot. The lamb's dry cry rattled in the back of its throat. Suddenly aware of danger—either pure instinct or man-smell—the dingo faded into the night.

In the October of my visit to Currawong and Barlin stations the dingo still roamed inside the Barrier Fence. He seemed to follow no set pattern, his movements were erratic, impossible to predict.

When I talked at length with Barry Phillips, it was the afternoon of the day I had earlier met his brother. It was baking hot, the flies were bad news. Barry, a dead ringer for his brother, was in the process of erecting an electric fence. When completed, it would enclose a fair bit of his frontal country. In doing so, it would curtail drastically the dingo's movements. Also, it would restrict the availability of water, a critical factor with summer fast approaching. So with limited access to water, and it needed to have that every day, morning and evening by preference, the chance that Barry Phillips had of seeing it again had to be good. All he wanted, and desperately, was one clear shot at it. He couldn't miss twice, could he?

The final act of this grim vendetta had yet to be played out when I drove away from Barlin station in south-west Queensland.

17

Patrolmen Out Of Tambo

*Dad was a dogger on Tambo station. I've been a bushman all my life—
mustering, fencing, you name it. This isn't a bad job. What you make
it, I guess. Jerry's okay, too. Doesn't take any bull, though.*
 – Charlie Russell, Patrolman, Barrier Fence,
while camped on Caranna station

Evening.

A very warm evening at that, too. Humidity way up, almost sticky, the wind
drifted from the north. But, oddly, storm clouds were gathering forces to the
south and west. Angry hordes. A sudden sprinkle of rain lost itself on the
powdery surface of sun-baked black soil that had probably forgotten what
the wet stuff tasted like. Good. Maybe.

Wearing sneakers, and a towel around my waist, I hunted in the cluttered
back of my wagon for a toilet bag. My two companions—Barrier Fence
Patrolmen, Charlie and Peter 'Skeeter' Russell—had already tidied themselves
up in the dam close to where we had set up camp for the night.

This had been a long, hot, and very dusty day. More so for me. I had trailed
their Mitsubishi Triton ute for hours along the Barrier Fence. No way of
avoiding swirling clouds of dust unless I dropped too far back. Which wasn't
the point of the exercise.

Ah, I found what I was searching for. Meantime, Skeeter had exchanged
a soiled shirt minus sleeves for a similar but much cleaner model. All the rage
in outback Queensland. Shirts with the sleeves ripped or cut off. Macho, I
guess. Providing you have the muscles to go with the bare-arm look. Clean
shorts went with a fresh shirt. But Skeeter's brown, oil-stained hat remained
the same.

'That rain's gonna friggin' come, you know,' Skeeter complained in a high-
pitched nasal drawl. He was tall and reed-slim. Still three years shy of the big
four-O.

'Yeah,' Charlie said, glancing at the sky. 'Just enough to be a bloody
nuisance.' Reckon Jerry Stanley would have said the same thing. Charlie was
older than his brother by seven years. Shorter too. But still above average height.
He had the muscles to go with the short-sleeved-shirt look. Maybe Skeeter
would get his when he turned 40.

'Don't fancy getting drenched,' Skeeter said, combing his fingers through lank wet hair.

'Well,' Charlie said, 'it won't be the first time or, I expect, the last time, either.'

Until a month before, they had camped in the shearers' quarters on Caranna. But for reasons unknown these had burned down. Hence roughing it.

Leaving them to it, I angled up a low bank to top the dam. Above it reared a windmill. Weary arms moved sluggishly in the tepid air. Distantly thunder rolled. A drum beat. The sound of an unseen regiment of foot soldiers about to close in on the enemy. Rain fell on the calm waters of the dam, creating spreading circles. Moments later, lightning zigzagged where the thunder had broken. It was nearly black in that direction, the storm seeming to move from west to south-east.

I moved to the water. Unperturbed by my approach, large numbers of galahs had gathered here to water, and, apparently, to preen themselves. They were spread out at the dam's edge so that each had an allocated space. There was much chattering. Soon be time to get into their treetop swags and dream the night away.

More thunder sounded. But further in the distance. Less threatening. Cautiously, I waded out to knee-deep water the colour of mud. In fact, I was standing in the slimy stuff up to my calves. Disturbed, it swirled to the surface, mud within mud. Disgusting! But it was wet. And warm. Unlike the birds, I did not have to drink it. Main thing, I felt cool for the first time since morning.

About seven o'clock we had quit Tambo. Not much to Tambo. One main street, few shops, hotel/motel. New motel complex going up, though. Never fail to get a bed there, I'll bet. A stopping place, at best. Chiefly notable for the large numbers of dead 'roos lying on, or alongside, the road.

Nevertheless, the two patrolmen seemed happy enough living there. In Tambo. Near the Barrier Fence. Off on a Monday with a heap of gear and enough tucker to last until Friday. A regular, five-day sweep through to Adavale, to the south-west. Hard country most of it. Some of it wasn't called the Wallaroo Range because it resembled a plain. Even those chunky devils had a hard time getting around there!

Yes, the same old fenceline. Same old punch-drunk wallaroos that would never learn that it didn't make any sense at all to keep bashing your head on wire netting. Only rarely did they and their brothers see people out there. The wildlife did not react as sensibly as the patrolmen did.

But it was far from pleasant to see them panic when a vehicle came into sight. To repeatedly try and get through the fence. Jagged-edged wire cuts. Cuts bleed, sometimes profusely.

Equally distressing was to see families separated by the high fenceline. On one side would be an emu chick. On the other its brothers and sisters and harassed looking mother. Still, a brood of six or seven young ones to contend with would make any mother ruffled. No way back, of course. How would it make out? Badly unless by chance it stumbled upon a hole in the wire.

Above Rabbiter Aub Ali

Left The contents of Aub's chiller

Below Old Quinyambie homestead — now a rabbiters camp

Modern Quinyambie station is air-conditioned and complete with satellite TV dish

Above Roxby Downs, Australia's newest town

Right Bryan Lock, Manager, South Australia Dog Fence; Donald Byrnes, Pastoral Inspector; and Louise Davidson, Secretary

Below Coober Pedy — 871 km north of Adelaide, 686 km south of Alice Springs

Above Mount Clarence station is mostly hard open country with few dingoes

Right Mick Dobbins patrols the Dog Fence on Mount Clarence

Below Ray Wardle and his sons Peter and Bill at Mount Clarence

Same story with 'roos. A grey-coated 'roo in particular. Not a female red 'roo but a grey kangaroo. Her young one was also separated from her because of the fence. At one point they touched noses. But mostly they were running side by side, frequently crashing sideways into the wire. Very unlikely if they ever snuggled up together on a cold night. Few if any miracles happen on the Dingo Fence. Doomed then. Too young to really make out on its own. Bad luck it was on the outside of the fence. In dingo country.

Pitiful really. Nothing that could be done about it, though. Which didn't mean you had to like it. Just a fact of life that the patrolmen saw every week they travelled the Barrier Fence.

So, right, it is not difficult to get through this wire. But it still requires a head-on charge, so to speak, rather than a sideways crashing motion. Much of it is rusty. Brittle. Too ancient by half. Even a medium-sized 'roo could go clean through it with a direct approach. I saw three of this size achieve it, all dark-coated wallaroos of medium-to-powerful build. They did so after the Mitsubishi went past them on the fenceline, darting back, and, spotting another vehicle looming up through the dust, turned, and went hard at the fence. So three new holes were there, less than a few minutes after the patrolmen had been through. Providing they were spotted next time they would remain open for a week—if not, longer. A lot can happen in seven days. Just ask a dingo about that in sheep country.

So much of the fenceline does need to be repaired. Like yesterday. It has been patched and then re-patched so many times in recent years it is a wonder it doesn't collapse under all the additional weight of extra wire.

Meanwhile, the pink-chested galahs were still at the dam as I bathed. Still carrying on like women gossiping over a fence. Not the Barrier Fence, obviously. Suddenly the soap slipped out of my hand and I groped under the surface and finally found it. Believe me, much more than soapy suds end up in such watering holes as this. Cow dung, for one thing.

There was a new arrival at the dam. An emu. Whatever it might have made of me was obviously of no consequence. Unlike the galahs, it made no fuss. Just lowered itself at the water's edge in a rather dignified manner. Squatting, it then reached out its long neck and sipped in a ladylike fashion. A delightful incident.

Back in camp, I too changed into clean gear. Felt wonderfully alive and toned-up. Felt even better when Charlie dipped his hand into a container and fished out an icy-cold beer. 'Get that into you.'

'Cheers!' I said, tearing open the metal cap. 'Storm's moved away.'

'Uh-huh,' Charlie said.

'Best part of the day, I reckon.' Skeeter was leaning against the ute, brown legs crossed at the ankles, still wearing his hat. Bushman, like his brother.

'Not wrong,' his brother said.

'So that was a pretty typical day?'

'Yeah.' Charlie drained his beer. 'Yeah...typical enough, I suppose... What'dya reckon, Skeeter...?'

'..Yeah, typical...' Skeeter gathered up two more beers.

Later, we ate mutton stew. Afterwards, we hunkered down near the fire and stared into the dancing flames as though by doing so we would learn all sorts of secrets. Later still, we drank billy tea. Talked a bit. Not much. But enough.

The brothers came from a large family, 14 all told. All but one were still alive and well.

'We're a very fortunate family, really,' Charlie said.

'Miss Mum, though,' Skeeter said sadly.

'We all do,' Charlie agreed solemnly.

A very close-knit family, I thought. Nice. So how did each of their wives react to the five-day-absence of their menfolk?

Charlie was married to Carol: 'Aw, she was used to me being away fencing before I took on this caper. No worries.'

Skeeter was married to Patsy: 'Oh, she found it hard for a while there but now there's no problems.'

Presently the patrolmen spread out their roomy swags and slipped between the sheets. Skeeter called it quits immediately, turning his back to the last of the firelight. But Charlie, propped up on an elbow, read a paperback novel until he too snuggled down in his blankets.

Until sleep claimed me, I thought for a little while about life on the Barrier Fence. Being a patrolman. No, it wasn't boring, couldn't be. On the move too much for that. And there was always Friday. Home to the wife, the missus, whatever. Always your mates at the boozer, the pub, whatever.

'What the hell've you been up to this week, Skeeter?'

'Buggered if I know, mate.'

'Ya fancy a beer?'

'Naw, I came in here for a bloody coke!'

Yes. Patrolmen Charlie and Peter 'Skeeter' Russell. Decent blokes. Doing a cracker job if the truth be known. Long days. Heat. Dust. Flies. Rain. At times bogged to the axles in glutinous mud. Too many holes in the fence to attend to. Not enough money to replace rusty netting. Same old story. Can't expect wonders. Better fix a hole than leave it for a dog to get through. Jerry Stanley? Top man! Just do your job and he's okay. She'll be sweet. No worries.

Charlie and Skeeter Russell. Bushmen. On the Barrier Fence. Out of Tambo. October 1989.

18

On The Windorah

In my wild erratic fancy visions come to me of Clancy
Gone a-droving 'down the Cooper' where the western drovers go;
As the stock are slowly stringing, Clancy rides behind them singing,
For the drover's life has pleasures that the townsfolk never know.
                                    – A.B. Paterson, 'Clancy of the Overflow'

The unsealed road from Blackall to Windorah, which I reached mid-morning after visiting Steve Picone at Listowel Downs, is some 260 to 270 km in length. It's referred to in disparaging terms by the locals. They are not wrong. (In comparison, the mostly dirt track that exists between Broken Hill and Smithville Depot is a delight to travel!) This one at times proved murder. Never, ever, have I seen such a rocky, rock-strewn, vehicle-shaking route. They were not smooth rocks. They were rocks with sharp cutting edges which, if you were travelling too fast, would tear open the rim of a brand new tyre as easily as peeling a banana. Nor were they rocks you could drive over with confidence for, even though I had good ground clearance for a conventional wagon, I still had to stop frequently and physically haul them out of the way. I was not impressed!

There was only one way to overcome it without mishap. So I drove at such a ridiculously slow speed the fuel gauge hardly moved. Obviously the way to conserve gas. But who wants to drive at 20 kilometres an hour?

Eventually I came to Emmet and Yaraka, where, in both cases, the one remaining horse shot through years ago. At Yaraka, I had to wait for at least 30 minutes because a train had stopped at the station and the endless carriages blocked the road. They were loaded with sheep, jammed in so tightly they were unable to move, in stinking heat, no water to drink. Standing without complaint in each other's excrement. What a life!

But it was a lovely early evening when at last I joined the Diamantina Development road about 6 km east of Windorah. With the Barrier Fence on my right, I went on into town, crossing Cooper Creek via a bridge. A reason to stop on the far side, park, and stroll back.

Cooper Creek. A river, really, being a continuation of the Barcoo and Thompson rivers to the north. But in dry times, which it is most times out west, you might feel inclined to question that status. You might even have wanted to do so now. For the water wasn't free-flowing; rather, it had collected in big, deep-looking pools with raised, sandy bars separating them.

There were two pelicans on Cooper Creek, big white sailboats with the sort of gigantic, scoop-like beak a professional fisherman might envy. A kingfisher flashed low over the water, its chestnut rump glinting in the sun. That would make it a red-backed kingfisher, the most common and widely distributed of the eight species of these fantastic birds found in Australia.

Windorah. A main street. Petrol station. Scattered houses. The Western Star Hotel. The local watering hole was painted green, for an impression of coolness, I expect—and with one thing on my mind I parked outside it.

I camped that night on the Cooper. Made a fire. Drank my tea black. Thought about drovers and cattle duffers (rustlers) and words from Banjo Paterson's 'Clancy of the Overflow'. On the Cooper was the right place for such thoughts.

On Hammond Downs station, Joe Geiger was presently carrying nearly 5,000 sheep and around 500 cattle on 28,328 hectares. Normally, there would be more sheep than this, nearly twice as many, but in the aftermath of last year's drought he hadn't fully restocked.

Now in his early-to-middle 50s, Joe was telling me this next morning as we drove away from the homestead he shares with his wife, Nancy, towards the station's western boundary, Cooper Creek. Fortunately, Joe doesn't have a dingo problem. Sure, the odd one turns up from time to time but, where he is concerned, the Barrier Fence is doing 'a great job!'

To my great surprise, I discovered that he doesn't use 1080. Doesn't like it. Didn't even want to talk about it. I was more than happy at this stage to go along with that. While I haven't been able to avoid it, 1080 is not my favourite topic of conversation, either!

Rather, we talked about, and observed, wildlife. He had over 50 brolga breeding on the station, one pair, which nested in the same area each year, had produced two chicks instead of the usual one. They were doing nicely, too.

Wild pigs came into the conversation. Great pig country around the Cooper. When the news had spread around that they weren't using 1080 here the pigs had more or less heaved a collective sigh of relief. Joe seemed rather fond of his pigs and couldn't wait to show me some. Firstly, a fair-sized boar right out in the open. We gave chase. The boar might have ended up right out of puff but, apart from being out of breath, was otherwise unharmed. We saw others too. Gave them the hurry up, too. No wonder Joe's Toyota looked as battered as it did if this was what he put it through regularly!

And we saw other birds apart from brolgas. Always birds in the Australian outback. But nothing dying here from the effects of 1080. Lovely change, that. On Hammond Downs station, near Windorah, south-west Queensland.

Two days later on a sultry, breathless sort of late afternoon, I cruised into Thargomindah, on the Bulloo River. After filling up with gas, I found a likely hotel-motel complex. Yeah, they had a room. Fifty bucks okay? Sure. All I wanted was a shower, clean gear, a beer, and a feed. All in that order.

Armed with the key to my room, I swung into a big yard behind the complex. Stopping, I swivelled my head and was just about to start to reverse right up to the door of the unit, the better to unload, when in my peripheral vision I saw, away to the west, a large red cloud. Within milliseconds it had mushroomed to double in size. Was racing towards town.

What a photograph! Grabbing my camera, I leaped outside.

Whoosh! A sheet of corrugated iron flashed over my head like a magic carpet. At shoulder height it could have easily decapitated me. Which is exactly what happened to some dead unlucky person when Cyclone Tracy tore Darwin apart on Christmas Day 1974.

With no real opportunity to take a shot (and that was the last thing on my mind now) I was engulfed in choking sand and dust. Peppered with small stones, river grit, debris. An upturned iron drum cannoned past me. Somehow, I was able to force the car door open, to dive inside, to close it behind me with even more difficulty. You could see nothing but red sand through the windows. You would not have been heard had you shouted at the top of your voice either inside or outside the vehicle. The station wagon itself shook and rocks, stones and whatever beat a constant tattoo on the roof, on the sides.

For at least ten minutes Thargomindah was hammered by a raging sand storm unlike anything I had ever witnessed before. I was too numbed by it all to be frightened. And then, as suddenly as it had arrived, it was gone. It left behind a thick film of reddish-grey dust. Later, one of the locals told me he had known it to rage like that—without a break—for three days. When you got a beer off the tap, it came out red. Three days?

Come morning, I set off for Bulloo Downs station, a huge chunk of cattle country outside the Barrier and Border fences. Now, watching my speed, I mulled over the sand storm. A good experience the way things had worked out. Made me realise how easily such forces of nature could undermine or bury fencing. Made me recall, too, Lenny Dixon telling me about such sand storms when he and Gay had gone out to Smithville Depot. Each summer they came, without fail. He told me of Gay's distress when everything in their house was covered with thick red dust. In bed sheets. In cupboards. Between plates stacked together. In food. In drinks. In everything. On everything. For weeks, not days, on end. Worst of all, the sight of young Kenny, then a baby, sitting in a dejected fashion in his tub of bathwater like 'a little red blob'. 'You know,' Lenny said, still feeling it after all these years, 'that damn near broke your heart. Y'know what I mean?' I didn't then, not really. Now I had a much better idea.

19

Dingo Country

Mostly they eat rabbits, lizards, grasshoppers and pigs. They just love pigs.
Especially young ones; they really hook into them!
– Philip Hughes, Bulloo Downs, talking about a dingo's food preferences

Crouching easily on his haunches, Philip Hughes used a sharp-pointed stick to draw a rough map in the dry red earth.

'Right, this is where we are now.' He meant Bulloo Downs homestead—centre of operations for a 10,878 square kilometre property carrying 22,000 head of shorthorn/cross-bred cattle. They still use stock horses here—about 100 of them, I was told. The stick drew a line.

'This is the track you take.' He gestured over his shoulder. 'Go past that windmill and you can't really miss it.' The stick shifted again. The slim, 34-year-old manager of the station seemed to be enjoying himself immensely. Still, ever since his primitive days man has derived enormous pleasure from sketching crude maps in the earth.

Philip made a big X.

'This is Willala Tank. Can't miss it if you stay on the track. It'll be on your left. Should be a few 'roos out feeding, I expect. Great spot to see dogs; they water at the tank. Tons of tucker for them too. In fact, I'd be frankly amazed if you didn't see some this evening.' He paused, made hand movements in front of his tanned face; flies retreated momentarily. 'The track carries on,' the stick made a wriggly line, 'to Booka Booka waterhole. Can't miss that, either. Old rabbiters' camp there. A real mess!' He pulled a face. 'That's as far as you need to go.'

'How far to Booka Booka?'

'Twenty miles, maybe. Okay?' I nodded as he straightened slowly, something like a snake uncoiling itself after a winter-long hibernation. Understandable enough. Philip Hughes stood a good 1.98 metres in bare feet and that's up there with Marshal Matt Dillon.

'Listen, you're more than welcome to camp here tonight if you want,' he said. He meant the men's quarters. Currently they had a staff of around 14: head stockman, stockmen, horse tailer, general hands, cook, etc.

'Appreciate that,' I said, meaning it. 'But if it's okay with you I'd like to camp out near the tank.'

'Up to you,' he replied easily. 'One thing, don't forget to call in before you take off, okay?' I nodded and assured him he could count on it. This is a sound precaution anywhere in the outback and possibly applies even more when you're travelling alone. You let people know what you're up to, where you are, where you're bound for, and when you arrive. It's awfully big country out there, and, in times of emergency, terribly lonely. Ignore those basic safeguards and you just might end up feeding the crows.

With a smile, Philip turned on his heel. He walked loose-limbed towards the homestead. He was wearing a brown hat, dark blue shirt, brown jeans, and riding boots. He might have just stepped out of the glossy pages of an R.M. Williams catalogue advertising outback clothing. Only thing missing was his horse.

His wife, Adele, was over near the gate. She was saying something to one of their two young sons. She turned, smiled, and waved a hand as I drove away; I returned the salute.

Following Philip's directions proved simple enough. There was even a signpost on the other side of a river-crossing to indicate I was heading in the right direction. In a few places, I engaged four-wheel-drive. The Subaru revelled in loose sand.

A glance at my Omega wristwatch told me it was 2.30. Too early to go all the way to the tank. Later would make more sense. So I pulled off the track and killed the engine. Not that traffic was a real problem here, you understand.

No trouble to light a fire. Dry, stunted growth and dead branches made sure of that. The billy was boiling in extra-quick time.

Sipping weak black tea, I thought about the area I was heading to, the fact that I should see dingoes. A good thought. Indeed, there was no shortage of dingoes almost anywhere on Bulloo Downs. Driving into the station earlier in the day (from Thargomindah), I had seen two tan-coloured ones near the road. Soon after, I'd stopped to talk with a roadman. He lived in Thargomindah and had been coming there a week or so. He saw 'dogs' every time he crossed station land, coming in and going out. In the words of Simon Read, the slim, good-looking 28-year-old head stockman, there were 'heaps of them on Bulloo Downs'.

Dingoes apparently caused few problems on the place. True they might take the odd healthy calf but, apart from that, they were nothing to trouble yourself about. Somehow, they sort of went with the place, belonged. Many a cattleman thinks of dingoes that way. In fact, dingoes were of some benefit on Bulloo Downs because they kept wild pigs well under control.

Back in the 1970s when enormous amounts of 1080-poisoned-baits were dumped from fixed-winged aircraft over much of Queensland's wild dog country, dingoes on Bulloo Downs had fared particularly badly. Consequently the pig population boomed. That is, until the dingoes regained their former big numbers.

'Lots of the station is wonderful country for pigs,' Philip had explained. 'Ideal. Around the river [Bulloo] is especially good. Lots of feed, lots of water.

But there's hardly a pig to be seen there today. Without dogs the whole river country would be crawling with pigs. Yes, they're a great predator of the pig; no question about that.'

He then told me how dingoes worked pigs. He'd seen them doing it a number of times, either while mustering on horseback or while in a light aircraft checking on stock movement. One time, over near the Grey Range—the station's far western boundary—he had observed from the air six dingoes herding about the same number of pigs along. One dingo was up front, sort of leading the mob, the others had the pigs boxed in, a bunch of predatory drovers, say. Philip told the pilot to bank around. The dingoes ignored the low-flying plane. They played with the pigs for a short time and then, tiring of the game, picked off a couple of young ones from the back.

At 3.30 I was under way. Driving slowly, eyes watchful as they ranged on both sides of the track. Presently, I reached a large expanse of flat ground. Sun-burnished sandhills swept down to it on my right; the track skirted them. Well back to the left was a large, man-made hump. Willala Tank, no doubt. I switched off the ignition and, reaching for a pair of fieldglasses on the empty seat beside me, I got out to a warm, breathless sort of early evening.

Using the Nikon 7×35s, I swept across to the tank. A profusion of birds were flying back and forth to it. Below the tank, two 'roos were feeding. One of them moved a short distance to a large pool of water and drank. He was a magnificent animal, a big red buck.

Out in the sandhills were countless rabbits. Rabbits ducking out of sight under low growth, popping in and out of burrows. I had in fact been seeing them ever since I had started off again. Most were healthy enough, quite plump in some instances. Others were not so fortunate. A close-up view through a 300 mm telephoto lens revealed goblets of thick pus dribbling out of the corners of their blind or partly-sightless eyes. In most cases the eyelids were gummed over permanently.

And right now I was looking at a rabbit in that same terrible predicament. It was crouched, panting, under a low, tangled bush a short distance away. Death was certain. It would come because of a fatal, drawn-out virus or hopefully sooner by way of crunching jaws or tearing beak. The virus is called myxomatosis. And some people want to introduce the ghastly stuff into New Zealand!

Methodically, I swept back across the flat. The 'roos were moving away in slow, lazy bounds. No dingoes in sight. But after what I had been told, they had to be around here. Would turn up sooner or later. Had to. This after all was a dingo's paradise at Willala Tank.

There were birds of various kinds and a few brown and white cattle drinking at Booka Booka waterhole when I arrived there. The birds drank elegantly, with excellent table manners. The cattle, sad to say, slurped like rough, hillbilly peasants who didn't know any better.

No dingoes had been observed since leaving Willala Tank. I intended to return there about an hour before sundown. To kill time, I checked out the rabbiters' deserted camp. It was, as Philip had indicated, an eyesore. Rusting caravans, broken-down tents, heaps of rubbish better buried, and enough empty beer bottles and cans to make you wonder how they actually managed to hit anything. Still, there'd be so many rabbits about after dark that you'd most likely hit one by simply sticking a rifle out the window and hoping for the best as you pulled the trigger.

Presently, I started back. But this time I stopped before the tank came into sight. Armed with nothing more lethal than a telephoto lens and fieldglasses, I warily approached open ground. But even before I reached it a faint wind was nudging at my back.

Downwind, I saw the dingoes almost at once. They were on the far side of the tank, on the lower slopes. Almost certainly they had watered, or were about to. But now they were on the run, bound for the sandhills beyond the track. Four, five, six, I counted. They ran freely, powerfully, effortlessly. One big animal and the others smaller, but cut from the same cloth. Last May's pups, perhaps? They crossed the track close to where I had parked. Up into the sandhills they went, back legs kicking up sand, and vanished over the skyline.

Blast the wind, I thought sourly. But for that I might have taken them by surprise. Actually drinking.

It happened soon after, just beyond where their scuff marks in the sand indicated they had bounded across the track. A big golden-coloured dingo appeared out of a dip below the skyline. He checked himself a split-second before I instinctively braked. Obviously surprised, and possibly not hearing the vehicle because of a rising wind, he stared with wide open eyes at me.

He was, I judged, less than 40 metres away. Even then, I was distinctly aware that the wonderful scene before my eyes consisted of only three real colours: the deep blue of the sky, the glowing redness of the sand, highlighted with three-dimensional effect by the last of the day's sun, and the golden colour of the dingo itself. Had I been fortunate enough to take it, this, I later thought, would have been a wildlife photograph to treasure. But as it eventuated he whirled about and disappeared.

I was thrilled by what I had just witnessed: a splendid, wolf-like creature somehow surviving in a harsh land where almost every man's hand is raised in anger against it.

I made camp that evening where, earlier, I had built a fire. A sound choice with so much fuel about. In the fast-failing light I again put a sudden burst of flame to a small heap of kindling and broken branches. As usual the kindling exploded into flame; flames spread heat. Not that it was cold or even chilly; a lightweight woollen sweater sufficed. But the fire was for more than warmth and a means to heat water and food. Like early man had discovered, it was company too. The best of company.

Not yet ready to partake of my uninspiring fare, I hunted in my dusty supplies and found a can of Queensland's best: XXXX (Fourex). Despite being lukewarm, it was nonetheless agreeable.

Squatting, with my knees drawn up almost to my chin, I stared into the flames. I recalled with enormous pleasure seeing that big yellowish dog momentarily frozen on a background of glowing red sand. What a moment!

Pity there was only one can! The insistent crackling of the fire demanded more energy. Only too pleased to comply, I hunted up more gnarled branches and fed them to the hungry flames. The night closed in more.

Sometime in the early hours of the next morning, I awoke suddenly—found myself sitting up in my sleeping bag in the back of the Subaru. My heart was racing slightly. I felt apprehensive and wondered why. Both rear windows were wound down, the tailgate was raised. What could possibly harm me out here?

And then with relief I knew the answer. A long, drawn-out howl was coming from the direction of Willala Tank.

Fool, I thought, slipping out into the night.

The dingo wailed again. That too was a magical moment. Patiently, I waited to hear it again. But the night was nearly silent, just a light breeze shifting through the low grasses and working through the topmost branches of nearby trees. Reassuring sounds. A tiny heap of embers responded to the breeze. They glowed and then, like a cigarette being extinguished, died.

And yet the sound of the dingo remained in my too-active mind. It would, I realised, be very easy to attach sinister connotations to it; to associate it with dark tales of werewolves, ancestral spirits—or bunyips.

To some Sydney colonists such howling noises at night could be particularly unnerving. Sometimes they knew precisely what they implied. This is an abridged extract from a letter written in 1845 by Joseph Smith. It was included in *True Patriots All* by Geoffrey Ingleton and relates to 1790, at which time Smith was aged 15.

'About eight hundred prisoners died in six months at a place called Toongabbie or Constitution Hill. They used to have a large hole for the dead; once a day men were sent down to collect the corpses and throw them in without any ceremony or service. The native dogs used to come down at night and howl in packs, gnawing the poor dead bodies.'

Again the embers of my fire momentarily glowed. With a shiver, I realised how much cooler—no, colder—it was now and retreated to the warmth of my sleeping bag.

On a baking hot Saturday morning, I squatted down with Shirley Clifford at the pulse of Bulloo Downs station. As you will no doubt recall, it had been Paddy Barlow who had first brought her to my attention; who'd told me she was working on the property.

Shirley, was wearing a broad-brimmed hat, striped flannel shirt, jeans, and high-heeled boots. The gear went with the territory and on her they looked both good and natural.

As we talked, Tammy, her daughter, was playing in the sun with Philip Hughes' two young sons. Tammy, who was obviously enjoying herself, had to make the most of these infrequent visits (Shirley was there to pick up supplies and mail, and to fill a 44-gallon drum with petrol). For young Tammy there were no playmates at the outstation where she lived.

So how was life here? I asked Shirley. She said 'fair enough' and lit another cigarette. Nervous, I guess. Not of me. It was called 'life'. She added that Philip was great to work for: 'You wouldn't get a better boss.' Or a more understanding one, I thought.

'Oh, how's Paddy?' she asked, with feeling.

'Box of birds the last time I saw him.'

'That's Paddy. . .'

'Missing the "fence", though.'

'Yes,' she said, with a sad, reflective smile, 'I expect he is.' The smile was more than fleeting.

A little later Shirley was ready to leave and I sensed she would only really relax at the outstation. She called Tammy and her daughter, a pretty but naturally shy with strangers kid, came without hesitation.

With a roar, Shirley started up the engine of a Toyota flat-deck. With a smile and a wave, she drove off. Red dust lifted behind the four-wheel-drive. Mother and daughter. You and me against the world, kid! Mum 'running the bores'. A decent place to live, fair wage. Trapping a few dingoes? Too right at ten bucks a token. At an outstation on Bulloo Downs in the spring of '89.

Nearly noon now. According to Philip, a 'big' muster started on Monday; the men would be camping out over the expected two weeks it would take. They would be using horses. I didn't think Philip would mind that at all. But the extra-lanky one would need a tall horse otherwise his feet were going to be trailing on the ground.

So there was activity at the station. Stockmen sorting out their gear; stockman Shaun Core, with a saddle slung over a shoulder, angling across the red earth to the horse yard; head stockman, Simon Read, riding up on a trailbike from wherever he'd been. The youthful-looking Simon was tanned, dark-haired and good-looking enough to be considered the local version of Tom Cruise.

I yarned a short time with John Bird. The softly-spoken Aborigine was the horse tailer (wrangler) on the place. Bulloo Downs? Top station, was the reply. And that was it, really. This was a happy, contented outfit. It started of course with Philip Hughes and worked down from there.

I told John about the dingoes I had seen the day before at Booka Booka and about the other two I had observed near the water tank at dawn that morning. As Philip had said, that was the place to see 'em, all right. Should be coming on the muster with us, John reckoned. Dogs!

I mentioned a goanna I had spotted near my camp with a dead rabbit. With a flash of white teeth, John laughed and said they often went into the burrows after them and dragged 'em out by the nose or face. Tough on a rabbit. But then, so were eagles and dingoes and foxes and, worst of all, 1080 or myxomatosis.

Mid-afternoon. The track running mostly south-west from Bulloo Downs homestead to the Border Fence was no more than 160–193 km in length. But as it was alternately sandy and rocky—once terribly so—I drove with the utmost caution. This was once more really rough going. Any kind of breakdown, for whatever reason, would be enough to make a driver (certainly this one) leap out of the driver's seat, scream like a maniac, and then kick the guts out of one of the front tyres. You'd be surprised how much that helps. Better to do it on your own, though.

But it's true that I was in a mind to take it easy. I had ample time in which to reach Tibooburra. And there was much to see, to mull over, on Bulloo Downs.

When Burke and Wills, en route to what would be their supply depot on Cooper Creek, crossed the New South Wales-Queensland border in 1860 they would certainly have travelled across what is now the lower south-west part of Bulloo Downs.

In 1880 a cattle theft took place on the station. The duffers apparently mustered 500 head in the lower region of the run and with haste pushed on to Wilcannia. They followed the Darling River to the Murray at Wentworth, and from there they headed west. After selling the cattle, they vanished.

Cattle baron, Sid Kidman, would later make Bulloo Downs one of the hundred-plus stations he owned.

From the late 1890s to early 1900s rabbits virtually brought the run to a standstill.

A man and his wife were murdered there in the early 1960s. Months went by before they were reported missing. When they were, a long and extensive sweep of this part of the State was made by fixed-winged aircraft. When at last the missing couple's vehicle was spotted hidden in dense scrub, a ground party was sent out. It would have made a gruesome find.

In 1962 wild horses were in their thousands on the station. A muster was organised, using a fixed-wing aircraft, vehicles, and horsemen. A large number of the brumbies were rounded up and taken overland to Bourke. From there they were to go by rail to Sydney. Which is what happened. But they had been in bad enough condition to begin with—drought stressed—and since they were too unruly to be fed or watered they arrived at their destination in a terrible state. The ever-vigilant RSPCA heard about it. Newspaper reporters latched onto the story. They didn't use aircraft to muster brumbies on Bulloo Downs after that.

Yes, there was plenty to think about when driving across the Bulloo Downs country. Presently I came to the old brumby yards the horse tailer, John Bird, had told me about. There was, he had said, a fair sort of chance I would see wild horses in this area. So I was as keen-eyed as a hungry hawk from that point on. Turned out John was right about a 'fair chance' because I did spot five spirited animals difficult to get close to. Certainly they weren't station hacks.

Brumbies once ranged in their thousands over much of this part of Queensland, extending up to the Cooper and the Barcoo River. They were in fact spotted by a drover named McGillevery in 1871 in that region. At the time he was taking a herd of cattle from the Gulf of Carpentaria to Adelaide.

A bush turnoff was before me—that is, the track either went ahead or took a sharp swing to the south. Good. This was consistent with my map of outback Queensland. In country like this, and no matter what can be gleaned from a map, it's enormously reassuring to find a signpost. But there was nothing. Just open country that stretched for ever.

Not that I was too concerned, you understand: I had food, water, plenty of gas. Philip Hughes was expecting me to call once I reached my destination, just to say, yes, I'd reached there okay. No, it's just that a signpost or even an arrow and, say, 'Wompah Gate' painted on an old petrol drum would have made all the difference.

Again I checked my map, spreading it out on the bonnet. Straight ahead would eventually take me, via a number of stations, into South Australia— Moomba or, say, Innamincka. Heaps of dogs around Innamincka, I'd heard.

Maybe, I thought, the track to the left had been put in recently and the one I really wanted to take was, say, further on? Possible. When had the map been published? Didn't say. Edition 1 was not very enlightening. But distances were in kilometres. Now that was reason enough to break out with hysterical relief.

Mailman Brian Wren, working out of Tibooburra, would know this country well, made deliveries to stations such as Santos, Epsilon, and Orientos. Not much chance of seeing him turn up here on a late Saturday afternoon.

But I had lingered long enough: to the left, south, it was. Providing I had made the right choice, Wompah Gate was 40 km from this point. The map of Outback Queensland said so.

This was hard, open country I came to: a high plain. Wildlife was light on the ground, and in the air come to that. But there were lizards from time to time dead keen on playing a one-sided version of 'chicken'. One-sided meaning there was no way I would run them down. Oh, and there was one species of bird—the Australian pratincole—that was abundant. I later read that they favoured open bare spaces where on long thin legs they pursued insects on the ground, which matched perfectly with this country.

I was mulling over my time in south-west Queensland when suddenly I observed high wire running east to west. The Border Fence. With Wompah Gate closed behind me, I paused and looked along the fence in both directions. Immaculate. A fox appeared to the east before ducking off into low scrub. Hadn't seen a single fox in Queensland. Dingoes and 1080 were giving them heaps. Pity; I like foxes.

Yes, a memorable trip was behind me; one more lay ahead. Right then, on what was a lovely evening, I looked back to that hard stony land I had just crossed and let my imagination run riot. In my mind's eye, I visualised the land baked hard by an everlasting sun. Water drying up. Eventually gone. Hot winds sweeping from the west or north, bringing choking dust or sand. Animals appearing on the low skyline, moving south, drought stressed, and badly. Brumbies, 'roos, wild pigs, emus, rabbits, dingoes, too. All gaunt, some living skeletons, already dead on their feet but too game and too stubborn to admit it just yet.

They would, in time, come to a formidable barrier maintained by men. The biggest of the red kangaroos, but not smaller wallabies, had the ability to clear this height. But they seldom did, even when fully fit. Made more sense to try and smash a way, headlong, clean through it. Even a dingo could have clambered over it. Trouble is, no one ever told them that they had it in them to climb. So they never did get the hang of it. Which is just as well where the sheep industry is concerned. The point is, a full-grown alsatian, especially one trained as a police dog, could climb the Border Fence. A dingo is no less agile. But they don't climb for some unknown reason and that's enough of that.

So the Border Fence then, as on previous occasions, would represent the end of the line. Sure, some, a few, would make it through. But even for those that did make it to the other side there would be no relief. Drought in south-west Queensland didn't suddenly end at the Border Fence. No, it extended well into the Western Division of New South Wales, and, in a particularly dry period, well beyond there, too.

It was possible that some animals would survive. Find water concealed in the rocks, known by those who first came to this mostly dry landscape.

Most of them would die here, one by one until nothing but carrion remained. Food for the scavenging birds. Somehow, they could always find water, mostly south of the Border Fence. But this was the spring of '89, and I drove on to Wompah Depot and, after calling in there to see Geoff Smith, on to Tibooburra.

Later, of course, South Australia's Dog Fence beckoned. It seems in order to begin that section at Quinyambie station where I had been with Paddy Barlow just a few months previously.

PART FOUR

SOUTH AUSTRALIA – THE DOG FENCE

NORTHERN TERRITORY

3a

WESTERN
AUSTRALIA

SOUTH AUSTRALIA

•Oodnadatta

Lake Eyre

Innamincka •

7

8 •
Coober Pedy
Lake Eyre South

1

9
Marree
10

3

5a

2

Roxby Downs

5

6

Munkartie
Lake Frome

11

•Tarcoola

Woomera

4

Nullarbor
•

Lake Torrens

NEW
SOUTH
WALES

Fowlers Bay

Ceduna

•Port Augusta

Key for Stations
1 Anna Creek
2 Billakalina
3 Commonwealth Hill
3a Cordillo Downs
4 Frome Downs
5 Lyndhurst
5a Millers Creek
6 Moolawatana
7 Moomba
8 Mt Clarence
9 Muloorina
10 Murnpeowie
11 Quinyambie

•ADELAIDE

MAP 3 THE SOUTH AUSTRALIA DOG FENCE

20

Not Exactly The Border Fence

The general opinion of the New South Wales Board of the South Australian system is that it is (1) unfair, (2) unwise, (3) impractical.
– Report of the Wild Dog Barrier Fence Working Party, 1980

Quinyambie station
South Australia
July 1989
On a lovely winter's afternoon, the red kangaroos were flowing like the wind through sunburnt Mitchell grass; a big buck, all rippling muscles and easy grace, was about to break away from the mob.

As I explained earlier, he was apparently dead-set on making a bee-line for nearby New South Wales. A sensible move on the surface. Red kangaroos enjoy a more laid-back lifestyle there, especially those inhabiting Sturt National Park. Because of what eventuated, he might have been intent on running full tilt into the tautly-strung Border Fence instead of taking a more measured leap and clearing it.

Which is about when Paddy Barlow, driving the Toyota, informed me with a short gesture that the 'Dog Fence' was ahead. Close to where the Dingo Fence of two States merged, Paddy downshifted smoothly and cruised to a halt. If it was not exactly a historical moment, for me at least it was significant.

'That's Mulyungarie,' Paddy said, indicating the other side of the Dog Fence. He proved he hadn't forgotten where his smokes were. 'Pretty big place.' With a brisk shake, he defused a lighted match.

'Sheep?'

'Uh-huh. They run cattle too.' He nodded along the Dog Fence. 'The wire's old here.' He fingered his chin thoughtfully. 'Might even be the original netting.'

'Could it last that long?' I asked dubiously.

'My oath it could! Materials were made to last then.' Again he indicated the Dog Fence with a short flick of his head. 'Feel like a run along it for a few miles?' Already I was aware of a mischievous glint in his eye, as though he were about to play a schoolboy-like prank on his best mate. Like stuffing a small goanna down the front of his shorts or putting a bit of dog turd in his lunchbox.

'You're the driver,' I reminded him.

'True. But I seem to recall you're footing the bill.'

I really didn't need reminding how much a day that was working out at. 'Make my day!' I grated, pointing a stiffened finger at his chest. There was no reaction whatsoever from Paddy. Maybe the *Dirty Harry* movies hadn't got to Broken Hill? After a long pause I said, 'Sure, why not?' And I too nodded my head in a westerly direction.

Paddy grinned. 'Good. Now you'll really see what a good section of the "fence" is like.' That, I gathered, was the reason for his impish expression, the punch line, as it were.

More 'roos appeared on Quinyambie. They were in timber, darkly silhouetted. No mistaking their agitation as they followed our progress. Daytime 'roo shooters?

By now, I was starting to see why Paddy had wanted to bring me along Mulyungarie's northern boundary. Holes. Under the Dog Fence. But how, I wondered, had he known they were there? After all, he hadn't been here in quite some time. I put it to him.

'Always count on a few holes along here,' I was told. 'Like I said, the netting's old; you only have to look at it to see that. Never seen as many holes as this, though. Real bad.' The Toyota lurched in and out of a sandy depression. 'You know how they operate there?' He meant in South Australia and I said, yes, I did. 'So you'll know the responsibility for upkeep of the fence is the runholder's lot. Poor bastard. But you'll find out all about that once you get there.' He did a nifty gear change. 'By the way, when are you heading there?'

'Depends on how long I take in Queensland, Paddy. Late October, early November.'

'That late, huh?'

'Can't do it in five minutes, you know.' Perhaps a little indignantly.

'Course you can't. But you might be leaving it a wee bit late, that's all I was getting at.'

'Rain, you mean?'

'Got it in one. Nothing unusual to get heavy rains in November. Lot of country this fence goes through is awfully prone to flooding. You get stuck out there and that's your lot for months.'

'That bad?'

'No, worse!'

The Toyota lurched to a halt when I asked Paddy to 'Hold on'. Big hole here and I wanted a closer look. Hmmm...two dingoes could have prised through this gap simultaneously had one been clever enough to use a shoe-horn.

Kneeling alongside me, Paddy said, 'Oh dear!' His tone was prim, like that of a spinster who has no intentions of being otherwise.

'Sure isn't New South Wales,' I said.

'Just as bloody well,' Paddy snorted, most unladylike, 'or I'd be after my old job back.'

I gave him a penetrating look. 'But that's what you'd really like, Paddy. Isn't it?'

'What?' He was all wide-eyed innocence.

'To be back on the Border Fence again?' I made a sweeping, throwing gesture in the direction of New South Wales.

Lifting his shoulders as though they were a heavy weight, Paddy didn't reply. But I was too perceptive not to miss the flicker of regret or sense of loss that came to pale eyes that have stared at too many suns and faraway distances.

Alan Sinclair Barlow. Otherwise known as 'Paddy' Barlow. On the Border Fence. Where they would remember him, mostly with affection.

Footnote. Paddy Barlow was right about the section of Mulyungarie's fenceline I saw as being the original netting. It dates to 1904.

All told James Morgan—whose family's link with the station goes back to 1887—has the responsibility of 110 km of the Dog Fence. With dingo-infested Quinyambie beyond that ageing fenceline, pressure from dingoes is often intense. To combat that, Morgan has in the past had men camped out on the Dog Fence. In more recent times, however, he has had trouble finding men prepared to do so. The conditions are not easy and the job is not exactly overpaid.

There is also the cost of replacing suspect netting. Severe floods recently badly damaged about 6 km of the Dog Fence to a point, perhaps long overdue, where there was no option but to replace it.

In Adelaide, Bryan Lock, Manager of the Dog Fence, told me that to replace that particular netting cost around $30,000: 'They are endeavouring to do the best they can within their resources. That is, to repair, replace, and maintain the fence. We understand the situation and we are deeply sympathetic towards it.'

21

What Price A Crocodile Dundee Hat?

*Rabbits are a tremendous resource for production and export because they
are a multi-billion dollar market overseas.*
– Robin Swift, Managing Director, Bold Ridge Exports, Victoria, May 1989

Quinyambie station
South Australia
July 1989
High noon
How can a six-strong team of shooters operate from one base-camp six nights
a week over virtually twelve months and still shoot enough rabbits to make
it a viable proposition?

   On the face of it such a notion sounds about as likely as a tall tale from
back o'Bourke. I mean, there just aren't that many rabbits, are there? Oh, but
there are. And they can be found on Quinyambie station where Aub Ali heads
a team of hard-bitten professionals working a twelve-hour-shift in pairs starting
around five o'clock in the evening.

   The rabbiters' camp was mostly free of human activity when I arrived there.
Almost everyone but the man I had come to yarn with was still catching up
on their shut-eye. Incredibly (under the circumstances) there were even rabbits
in sight. They were scampering carelessly around low sandhills above which
a flight of corellas wheeled in perfect formation against an azure sky.

   Momentarily I paused, watching the rabbits at apparent play. Young stuff.
They were well beyond .22 calibre range. But no problem for a Col Pierce using
a triple-two. Not that you'd use that calibre on a rabbit. The thought occurred
to me that perhaps I should stroll over there and have a serious word with
those rabbits. Tell them what the story was around here. Living on Quinyambie
had its problems. The main one being premature death.

   These old buildings the professionals had set up camp in were once the nerve-
centre of Quinyambie station. Big cattle musters had been organised from here,
the boss and his stockmen discussing it in the sun, high-heeled boots caked
in red earth. Large gatherings would have also taken place here, people willingly
travelling enormous distances to attend. In the latter part of the last century
Sid Kidman had added the station to his already substantial cattle empire. No
doubt he had looked from his land across to New South Wales. It requires
little if any imagination to picture him slouched in the saddle, a thoughtful

expression on his face, shrewd eyes hungry for more land. Was there no end to how much land Kidman wanted to rule over? Apparently not. Ultimately the Cattle King would own 13 properties in what today is the far Western Division of New South Wales.

But all that was history now. This was called old Quinyambie. Fair enough, too. Everything standing was old. Over a century old. No one cared a damn any more. Deterioration was already taking place. But that process would be slow in such a dry atmosphere. Maybe in ten years it would appear very much the same. Maybe I'd check it out then. Maybe. But right now I was about to go see Aub Ali. 'I'll be up around midday,' he had said a day earlier. 'Come see me then.'

So I started towards a low-slung building. Yes, I thought, the overall setting somehow seemed right for a rough-as-guts rabbiters' camp miles from anywhere: a substantial power plant chugging away in the background, five big mobile chillers, blood-encrusted four-wheel-drive wagons, dogs dozing or scratching themselves, flies buzzing, and chickens (locked up overnight for obvious reasons) scratching ambitiously at the bare red earth.

Old Quinyambie. Piece of real history. Strong links with the old droving days. Reckon Sid Kidman would have squirmed in his resting place if he were to see it now. But then, nothing lasts for ever, does it?

Stooping under a low doorway (and I'm only 178 cm) I found Aub Ali in a rat's nest of a kitchen-cum-bunkroom. It wasn't dirty, you understand. Just messy. Few women could have tolerated it. But then, few if any of them are professional rabbit shooters.

'Cuppa?' Aub yawned mightily and then stretched.

Someone was snoring in one of the beds. I sat at a table. I could smell rabbit, a peculiar odour, unmistakable. Same thing applies in a possum hunters' camp. Only worse.

Aub placed an open packet of chocolate biscuits in front of me followed by a big chipped cup which might have been a touch cleaner. No matter. I'd drunk from dirtier cups and mugs than that. Never seemed to spoil the taste of the tea or coffee.

Sitting across from me, Aub savoured the first brew of his day. With an easy smile, he asked me what did I want to know?

Aub's grandfather came to this country from India and, like many of his race, worked as a camel teamster. Indeed, there were still feral camels on the station. Out west apparently. In low numbers.

Now in his 59th year, Aub Ali is lean and stringy. As tough and resilient as the hardy desert scrub. For five years, ending in 1968, he had worked on the Border Fence, based at Munkartie Cottage (since pulled down). It had been a good life but only, he pointed out, because his wife and four children were with him. Without them, the loneliness would, he believed, have been a killer.

Then in 1969 the State Government had increased the bounty on dingo scalps from four to six dollars, bringing it in line with the bounty in the other States. To Aub that seemed a great opportunity to cash in big. So with his equally adjustable wife, Helen, he had taken off to beyond Cameron Corner. Up towards Innamincka. Country where they once ran sheep but pulled out of that game for the very best of reasons. Killer dogs. Thousands of them.

'Oh, we were about 75 miles out from the Corner, I reckon. Never seen so many dawgs in my life. Went to the right place, no worries about that.' Aub selected another biscuit. 'We poisoned 52 one night. Not bad at six bucks each, eh? In nine months we took fifteen hundred. But then,' he shrugged a shoulder, 'they chopped the bonus to two bucks. Been that ever since.' His heavily seamed features registered disgust. 'Two bloody bucks! God, I pay my shooters a dollar seventy for a pair of bloody rabbits. Hell, you may as well not pay a bounty if that's all it's worth.' (The general view in South Australia at this time.)

'A token gesture?' I offered.

'Yeah, something like that.' He paused. 'Not worth the boys shooting a dog for that.'

'They see a few then?'

'See heaps. They often come up for a look when the boys're gutting. Foxes too.'

In the bunkroom someone broke wind indelicately. Moments later a still half-asleep figure stumbled outside. Busting for a leak, most likely.

Later, we strolled out into the sun. It was in the mid-20s, I judged. No humidity. You could smell the desert breathing. It was a good smell. Not at all like the stink of rabbit-impregnated clothing.

Aub was wearing a fur-lined leather hat. To him this was winter. 'We have an area 50 miles west of here and 40 miles to the north—that's right out to the Corner. That way,' he pivoted so he was facing south, 'we go for 28 miles.'

'A big hunk of territory.' I stated the obvious. Still, the sheer size of everything out here took some getting used to.

'An awful big piece of country.' It was nice that Aub agreed with me. 'Easy to get lost in. Especially at night.' Again he indicated south. 'Another team of shooters has the other half of the run.'

Other half?

Aub permitted himself a flicker of a smile and said, 'This place is around 5,000 square miles.'

'Never easy to fathom out just what that means, is it?'

'No,' he admitted. Then: 'Well, how does 114 miles long by at least 46 miles wide grab you?'

'With impact!'

Aub's smile was broad this time, a throaty chuckle went with it. As for me, I groped in my mind for a rough comparison of the size he had indicated. Right, the length converted to 183.42 km and that was, say, about the distance from the Sydney GPO to several kilometres north of Newcastle, while the width—74.01 km—extended well inland, deep into the Blue Mountains. By any reckoning this was a heap of country and explained why they were able to work year-round here. The numbers of rabbits helped, of course.

'Like I was saying before,' Aub said, breaking into my thoughts, 'the boys work in pairs: one on the light and the other shooting. They normally swap around; it can seem like a long night this time of the year. They gut every 20 minutes or so to keep them nice an' fresh—so they're virtually shooting and gutting non-stop.'

'No joy ride, y'mean?'

Aub shook his head vigorously. 'Absolutely not!' he fired back. 'Anyone who comes out here and expects an easy life is wasting their time.' Aub laughed. A brittle sound, like old bones rattling together. 'They only shoot pairs,' he went on. 'Adult rabbits, if you like.'

'Harvesting, huh?'

'Course!' he replied to an obvious question.

'We have one week off in five,' he continued without prompting. 'Live it up in the big smoke. . .' A smile meant he was only kidding. Home was Paddy Barlow's patch: Broken Hill.

We had reached a chiller. It was big, roomy enough to hold a small elephant. Aub swung open a door heavy and strong enough to contain a mass murderer. As expected it was chilly in there. And on the subject of mass murder there were rows and rows and still more rows of rabbits hanging upside down on racks, like a well-organised wardrobe.

'This one's full.' It was Aub's turn to state the obvious. Rabbits attired in brownish coats they no longer had any use for. Fluffy white tails. A surefire giveaway no matter the terrain. 'There'd be around 2,700 pairs in here.' Aub was matter-of-fact about it.

He shut up shop. Bolted the door. Swung an arm to include the other chillers. 'All up we'd have, say, 5,600 pairs on our hands right now.'

How often were they taken out? Which meant to Sydney Town. Human consumption. Fur for the local hat trade.

'Pretty regular this year. The shooting's about as good as you'll get.'

My mind was zipping along in overdrive. Simple mathematics said that so many pairs came to 11,200 rabbits. Eleven thousand? How many were there on Quinyambie?

Aub Ali said it in one word. Most succinctly. 'Millions!'

I was not about to argue with the man. No way! Considering those figures posed an interesting question. What represented a good night's shooting?

'Seven hundred pairs.'

I gave up. It was all on too large a scale for me to really comprehend.

Turning away from the chiller, Aub frowned and ran the back of a leathery hand across grey stubble. 'They were to be taken out yesterday, so there must be a hold-up somewhere along the line. Leave it much longer and we won't have any room to put them.'

'Better than the alternative.'

'True.'

'And you can always go bounty hunting at two bucks a pop.'

'Keep it in mind.' Aub gave me a rather odd look.

Taken all round this was a lucrative time to invest in a suitable vehicle with a 12-volt spotlight, a 'scoped .22 rifle and 'heaps' of ammo. Making much hay while sunny conditions prevailed was an enterprising Victorian businessman, Robin Swift. His Bold Ridge Exports company was exporting rabbit carcasses to Europe because local rabbit farmers were unable to keep up with the demand for such lean meat. Also, the fur went overseas for various items of clothing or, on the home front, was used in the manufacture of hats. Outback hats, snapped up by tourists. See them in Sydney every day.

A Crocodile Dundee hat to get to the point. Made famous by Paul Hogan in two *Crocodile Dundee* movies. If people overseas didn't know where Australia was before the first *Crocodile Dundee* epic, then they certainly did after its world-wide success. Adding to this his TV beer commercials and those for the tourist industry, Hogan almost single-handedly revitalised the Australian tourist industry. Men have been knighted for much less.

Apart from Hoges' natural charm, much of the success of his Crocodile Dundee creation was the colourful outfit he wore. His black hat, for instance. This, incidentally, inspired numerous Hogan-like clones to invade the outback wearing black hats with teeth-decorated hatbands. It looked just terrific in the movie. In real life? Forget it!

But to the bottom line. What's the point, if it were possible with a more potent strain of myxomatosis, of wiping out all the rabbits when such a market exists not only for the manufacture of hats but also in the rabbit-meat department?

Back to Robin Swift, who in the winter of 1989 had 28 shooters under contract in north-west New South Wales plains country. One of them was Wilcannia-based Lionel Turner. On an average night, he would account for 220 rabbits. Less running costs, they were worth $264 to him. Much better than standing in the over-loaded dole queue in Wilcannia and rubbing shoulders with dispirited Aborigines ready to splash out their regular government handout on gutrot wine.

Once a week, Turner hopped into his vehicle, loaded down with frozen rabbits, and gunned her down the Barrier Highway to Broken Hill. From there they were transported to Swift's abattoir—apparently the only one in the country—on the Mornington Peninsula on the south-eastern outskirts of Melbourne. From his entire band of merry professionals Swift was receiving 20,000 rabbits a week.

Meantime, graziers were only too aware of how dramatically rabbit numbers had increased. Reasons given for this were the heavy rains of earlier in the year which had revitalised vegetation, warmer weather (Greenhouse Effect?), and, significantly, a growing resistance to the same old myxomatosis strain introduced with outstanding success in the early 1950s when Australia's rabbit population was thought to number 6,000 million.

Many graziers were of the opinion, however, that there were as many rabbits now in the late 1980s as there had been in those dark days of nearly 40 years before. Not so according to the Bureau of Agriculture and Resource Economics which put the figure at 200 million. Which might be conservative. But for the sake of an argument, let's go along with their view.

Interestingly enough, the Australian Bureau of Statistics predicted in July 1989 that by the following June sheep in Australia would have reached an all-time high: 199.8 million (including lambs).

If both sets of figures are correct, or even close, then it's a toss-up which by mid-1990 there would be more of in the country. Sheep or rabbits.

Or is it? Consider if you will a few facts about one *Oryctolagus cuniculus*. In a favourable year, such as 1989 (and indeed 1990) a rabbit can breed up to 10 times a year. Your average doe can produce 25 to 30 young. True all will not reach maturity, but a rabbit is sexually mature at 9 to 12 months, with, in some cases, a doe producing young when she is much younger, at 5 to 6 months. Contrast this with a ewe which will not conceive until she is two years old and then at most can produce only two offspring each year.

In direct competition with sheep and native animals for grass, shrubs and weeds, a rabbit will outgraze either one. No contest. Given that eight rabbits eat as much as one sheep, and so increase the already enormous soil erosion in parts of the outback, the fears expressed by all those concerned with the sheep industry in 1989 were certainly well founded.

So the question is this: what price a *Crocodile Dundee* hat in 1990? Back to two sides of the coin again. Can't get away from that in the outback.

22

Straight From The Shoulder

*If the Dog Fence went down, the repercussions would be felt throughout
the rest of South Australia's sheep industry.*
– Bryan Lock, Manager, South Australia Dog Fence, November 1989

The administrative offices of the South Australia Dog Fence are found in
Wakefield House on 30 Wakefield Street, Adelaide. This section of the
Department of Lands is just one of a number dealing with various aspects
of the interior. Collectively they are known as the 'Outback Region'.

After taking the elevator to the 17th floor, and being confronted by spacious,
air-conditioned offices, it occurred to me that this was a world far removed
from sandy plain and craggy ridge. Yet here too the talk is constantly of the
most costly animal to ever undermine any nation's wool industry.

Bryan Lock is the Manager of the Dog Fence. He is a youthful 50. Not
lacking a sense of humour, his talk is direct, right to the point. Fools may
as well go speak with somebody else!

You soon realise that Lock, with a sheepman's faraway gaze, would much
prefer, if given a choice, to be back on the land where he has spent much of
his life. Back on Yarna station, in the rugged Gawler Ranges, say, which he
was managing in the early 1980s. But then hard times came. Even a new chum
could have read the signs, and none of them were any good for long-term
employment. Moreover, the time had come for their children's education to
be considered. Right, they would shift to town.

An ideal candidate with his extensive rural background, Bryan found
employment as an Inspector of Fences—a stepping-stone, as it were—to his
present position. Not that a collar and tie fitted too well, you understand. Apart
from his own personal code of behaviour, what gives Lock a decided 'edge'
in dealing with outback folk is that he can easily relate to their problems, be
it drought, the low cost of wool, the high cost of fencing materials, or the
constant trials and tribulations of trying to make a go of it where dingoes
regularly breach the Dog Fence.

Later, I would find that he is held in high esteem, and even in some instances
affection, on the frontline. On Mount Clarence, for instance, a 1,446-square-
kilometre sheep run near Coober Pedy, Peter Wardle summed it up nicely when
he said: 'Bryan's the best thing that's happened to us in a very long time.'

At the time of my visit, John Cook, Inspector of Fences, was in the field. His job is to patrol the Dog Fence four times a year. It is divided into three sections:

Eastern Section—from the New South Wales border to Roxby Downs.
Central Section—Roxby Downs to Tarcoola.
Western Section—Tarcoola to the Great Australian Bight.

Cook, however, is not responsible for a 355 km stretch of the fence in the Western Section. This is controlled by three Local Boards.

Bryan Lock explains: 'It wasn't practical for each of the wool growers in this area to individually maintain the fence, so they formed into local Dog Fence Boards. Each of these Boards then takes over responsibility on behalf of fence owners and, between them, they have one man that performs on a contract basis in maintaining the fence and it works out very well.'

These localised Boards were Fowlers Bay (32 ratepayers); Penong (106 ratepayers); and Pureba (236 ratepayers). At the present time, Lock said, John Norwood, of Ceduna, was in charge of looking after the Western Section length of the Dog Fence and doing a fine job.

But back to John Cook. Should he find damage to the fence (except in the section under local boards), he makes a written report and this ends up in the hands of the runholder in question. Herein lies a problem, a nasty one. It is the ever-escalating cost of repair, replacement of existing wire, and, of course, general maintenance of the fence. The Dog Fence Act states that not only is the maintenance of the fence the responsibility of the runholder whose property abuts it, but he must see that it is patrolled at least once each two weeks. A number of stations in South Australia combine forces in this instance to hire a man to patrol their fences on a regular run. Others normally give a stationhand the chore. Either way it is an extra cost, even with the government subsidy.

Bryan Lock: 'The Dog Fence Act goes back to 1946. It contains specific guidelines relating to the Dog Fence. Basically the reason for the Act is to specify a rateable area within which rates are collected for upkeep of the Fence. It is matched on a dollar-for-dollar basis by the State Government.'

For the record, the present rate was 61 cents per kilometre. For the financial year ending March 1989, this had raised $130,136 from pastoralists. With the State's subsidy this came to $260,272.

'Presently,' Lock continued, 'we pay a fence-owner $105 per kilometre each year for upkeep of the fence. We are of course well aware of the high cost of materials. The fact that they do not stand up as well as they used to is frustrating as well as putting an extra financial burden on the landowner.

'As an example of cost, what we pay out per kilometre would not cover the price of one 15-metre roll of netting wire. In terms of replacement, you're looking at, say, 30 rolls of wire per kilometre.

'It would be unlikely, I think, if that contribution would go any more than one-third towards upkeep of the fence.' At that point Bryan Lock broke off and, looking more than a little perturbed, he added, 'In fact, $105 per kilometre is in most cases a drop in the bucket as far as maintaining the fence is concerned.' Again he paused. 'The present rating system is, I personally feel, not the most equitable method of supporting the Dog Fence line. I feel that in South Australia the whole of the sheep industry should be making a contribution towards its upkeep.'

Which is precisely what Bill Edwards—Chairman, South Australia Dog Fence Board—said in presenting his paper at the Barrier Fence Adminstrators Conference at Thargomindah, Queensland, in August 1987.

> It is quite unrealistic to expect so few landholders to contribute to the upkeep of what is indisputably an inseparable part of the wool industry. It is the view of the Board and of industry representatives that it would not be unreasonable to expect financial contribution from all wool producers who directly or indirectly receive some measure of benefit from the protection the fence affords.
>
> Revenue increase generated by complete industry participation would enable the Board to plan future capital replacement of weaker fence sections and ensure that a satisfactory level of fence repair is maintained without increasing the burden of fence ownership.
>
> The Boad, in recognition of its responsibility to seek a more equitable method of funding, has instigated discussion on the subject with State Government and industry representatives; however, the Board is fully aware that the success of this or any system of funding improvement will ultimately depend on the level of co-operation and support given by the wool producers themselves.

It might pay to elaborate on that point. In South Australia there are an estimated 12,030 wool-producing properties within the Dog Fence. They fall into three distinct groups:

> *One:* the sheepman right on the fence. He pays Dog Fence rates, shoulders as best he can the heavy burden of fence ownership, and, when it occurs, bears the inevitable consequence when dingoes breach the fence.
> *Two:* the sheepman who is within the rateable area pays rates. His responsibility for the fence ends there.
> *Three:* the sheepman within the protected area but neither on the fenceline nor within the rateable area. To the consternation of the ratepayers, he pays nothing at all yet is well-protected from dingo attack at the expense of those on the frontline. To all intents and purposes he is living on the sheep's back.

Of the aforementioned 12,030 wool growers, it is significant that only 763 attract Dog Fence rates. Breaking that down even further, we find that 32 landowners (including those in the area supervised by the three Boards in the Western Section) bear the brunt of the cost. Even a dingo with a very low IQ would eventually reach the conclusion that something was not quite right there.

23

Wombat Territory

*If it were not for the presence of the wombat, the Local Board would
be capable of maintaining the Fence in dog-proof condition even though
the major section is now 78 years old.*
- Brian Johns, Chairman, Fowlers Bay Local Dog Fence Board, prior
to the installation of electric fencing

Much of the country in the far west of South Australia is semi-arid with an
annual rainfall of between 200–500 millimetres. It is the main range of the
southern hairy-nosed wombat which, apart from being slightly smaller, differs
little from the common wombat of south-eastern Australia.

Wherever they are found, wombats are constructed like miniature tanks,
meaning they are powerfully-built and travel low to the ground. While appearing
slow and ponderous they are, again like tanks, capable in an emergency of
a fine burst of speed, in their particular case up to 40 km per hour. Generally
speaking, however, they are not swift movers and, being nocturnal, spend most
daylight hours underground.

Wombats have short but sturdy legs and each paw is equipped with strong,
flattened claws. All four limbs are used to excavate a burrow. They are in fact
perfectly-designed digging machines which do not require spare parts. This
is taken full advantage of when numbers of them create an enormous maze
of warrens—much like rabbits—over a large area of, mostly, pastureland. Here
they emerge to feed at night on fodder of fibre-high content.

Naturally enough, this aspect of their behaviour did not endear them to
early settlers many of whom referred to them as 'badgers'. And got rid of them
in settled areas until their range was drastically curtailed.

Wombat damage on the Dog Fence in the far west was first noticed soon
after it was erected in 1905. In many ways it was a similar type of thing, although
the holes were deeper and wider, to that caused by foxes. An expected thing.
Simply fill in the hole. Forget it. Which was all well and good providing, of
course, there were not too many holes to contend with.

But for reasons which are still unclear, there was after the early 1960s a
massive increase in wombat numbers in the Fowlers Bay region. An explosion,
as it were. The Dog Fence, undermined by countless holes provided easy access
to sheep country for adventurous dingoes. The fence rider was openly
distraught. How could one man cope with this? He couldn't.

The problem of too many wombats on the fenceline continued. Teams of men with shovels proved a failure. So too did front-end loaders. Fill in one hole, and, overnight, a new one appeared in its place.

So drastic methods were brought into play. Shooting by spotlight. Trapping. Mesh-cage capture. Warrens were fumigated, then destroyed. But still the wombat population continued to expand. In desperation, the Local Board turned to various government departments to see if they could provide an answer. One by one the Department of Lands, CSIRO, the Vertebrate Pest Control Authority and the National Parks and Wildlife Service said, no, they could not offer a feasible solution.

The last-named department, however, was curious and interested enough in 1980 to commission a research scientist, P.J. Tiver, to make a report on wombats in the Fowlers Bay local Dog Fence Board's rateable area.

When it came through, Tiver's report was alarming. In the area in question—through which 90 km of the Dog Fence ran—there were 160,000 wombats. Over a 12-month period they had made a staggering 2,370 holes through the fence.

If the situation hadn't been considered critical before then it most certainly was now. And obviously something had to be done about it. But what? Hadn't every likely avenue been explored? Not quite, apparently.

In 1981 Brian Johns (Chairman, Fowlers Bay Local Dog Fence Board) and R.A. Everett (Chairman, Dog Fence Board) put their heads together, listened also to what everyone else had to contribute, and came up with the idea of an experimental electric fence as being a possible solution.

Bryan Lock: 'In all electric fence projects the underlying principle behind their success is the very basic rule of education through punishment. This is the code by which survival is achieved in the animal world: if it bites back leave it alone, and any animal that experiences the shock of making contact with an electric fence quickly learns to avoid future contact with it.'

At any rate, in 1981 sixteen kilometres of three-wire electric fencing were erected by ratepayers in the Fowlers Bay area on a voluntary basis 60 cm from, and running parallel to, the outside of the length of Dog Fence that had sustained the most damage from wombats over the past 12 months, that is, 624 holes. The power plant, located at the halfway mark, consisted of two solarex panels charging a 90 amp/hour wet cell battery through a voltage regulator, which, in turn, operated a Gallagher SB energiser.

During the first month of operation, the inside of the Dog Fence was subjected to the normal wombat attack. On the outside of the Dog Fence, however, wombats were confonted with a new fenceline. They would find the experience quite shocking.

To allow those wombats on the inside of the Dog Fence easier access to the electric fence, a number of 'invitation' holes were made. A joke in the worst possible taste, especially if you were a southern hairy-nosed wombat out to cause no-one any harm. The Board, in their wisdom, considered this a good move.

After four to six weeks, wombat damage to the Dog Fence fell away markedly. By October 1982, a year after the electric fence went into operation, the number of holes in the Dog Fence was as low as 42. A year later the figure was 14. A reduction of 97.7 per cent in just two years was the best possible news Johns and Everett, and of course everyone else concerned with the introduction of electric fencing to South Australia could have heard.

So the Wombat Fence, as it was now known, was judged a rousing success. Consequently it was upgraded to four wires and its length increased to 90 km, thus covering the entire section of the Dog Fence troubled by wombats. It is worth noting that as at January 1989, there had been no reports of dingoes penetrating through or under the electric wire, and, just as importantly, no evidence to suggest that kangaroos or emus had lost their lives through fence entanglement.

Footnote. Because of the great success of the Wombat Fence, electric fencing was extended in South Australia to provide total protection from damage by kangaroos and emus to some of the older sections of the Dog Fence. By 1984, one metre-high six-wire fences were in operation in the north west of the State and in the northern Flinders Ranges (Moolawatana station).

Between 1985 and 1987 more projects were under way. These included the virtual replacement of 120 km of the Dog Fence netting north of Ceduna, with 91 km of metre-high, seven-wire electric fence.

24

Outback

In the event of a breakdown or if lost—stay with your vehicle. You will be found more quickly. Lie underneath the car if shade is required. Remember radiator water, although containing impurities, is a valuable emergency water supply. Caution: Some vehicles' cooling systems contain chemical additives and in these cases the water should not be consumed.
– Flinders Ranges and Outback South Australia Visitor's Guide, 1990

Near Roxby Downs
Early evening
Overcast humid
On a winding sandy track

A sudden tight corner loomed up. Too fast! I went sliding sideways into it—out of control despite being in four-wheel-drive. The rear end started to fishtail. Not pleasant. But luck was with me, the rubber gripped in red sand, the back end straightened out. Relief! Which turned in an instant into near panic.

A thumping big 'roo, with a chest like a beer barrel with hair on, was positioned, motionless, right in front of me. No way could I avoid hitting him.

My mind screamed: Move, you bastard! Move!

But he remained there. Rigid. Like a museum job. If I were to hit him at this speed, that's about all he'd be good for. But in all honesty I was not over-concerned about him in the milli-moment of time this took. It was the front end of my vehicle I was concerned about. Sure, I had a 'roo bar. Which was dynamite when it came to nudging along dozy sheep or giving the brush-off to lightweight wallabies. But this was neither. This was a full-grown red kangaroo. That 'roo bar would end up under the bonnet somewhere if—

But at the last split-second of a split-second the 'roo sprang sideways off the track; the front, left-hand side of the 'roo bar actually scraped him, I believe. But when, still gasping in relief, I checked it I couldn't see a mark. Maybe I had imagined it.

This reminded me of another close call, which took place the day I was choking on Charlie and Skeeter Russells' dust on the Tambo-Adavale run in Queensland. At any rate, it happened near the Wallaroo Range. Significant. Wallaroos were directly involved.

Anyway, the boys had disturbed a number of the solidly-built breed with shaggy dark coats—rather ugly really. Some acted intelligently when the big

Left Almost anywhere along the
Fence you're likely to see pink-
chested galahs

Below The original Mount
Lyndhurst homestead, built in the
late 1860s

Above Bill and Hazel Mitchell of
Muloorina station

Right Neville Barnes of Mount
Lyndhurst

Below Some things never change

LINDY CHAMBERLAIN FENCE

DOG FENCE
NO BABIES PAST THIS POINT!
THIS GATE IS
TO BE CLOSED
AT ALL TIMES

Chairman Dog Fence Board

POISON
Laid on this property

DONNA

Mitsubishi powered up behind them and churned off into the low scrub. A few played the familiar game of silly buggers. Cracking their thick skulls on the fence. A single animal broke past the Mitsubishi and charged towards me. Quickly, hands working overtime on the steering wheel, I swung hard to the left, to open up even more of a space between my vehicle and the fence. But the wallaroo, in panic, which means it was not thinking too clearly, turned and came right at me. It was leaping off the ground—actually airborne—before I realised it. Up and over the bonnet so that, for a brief moment, all that could be seen through the dirty windscreen was one very dark-coated member of the 'hopping' family. A shattered windscreen—midway between Tambo and Adavale—would have been delightful. The same thing could of course apply to where I was now, in outback South Australia.

Still a little shaken over how close I had come to making contact with a big 'roo, I slipped into low gear. This route was the way to a number of stations: Purple Downs (I was on that run already, I think), Roxby Downs, Old Parakyila (which may have been deserted), and, 140 km away, my destination: Billa Kalina station. With dark clouds threatening rain, I drove with care. The intention was to camp out that night about, say, midway to the station homestead, leaving an easy enough run through in the morning where, at nine o'clock, they were expecting me.

Earlier, with several hours to kill, I had visited Roxby Downs, the township, not the station of the same name. It was more out of curiosity than anything else, it being Australia's newest town.

Roxby Downs was officially opened on 5 November 1988 by the Premier of South Australia, John Bannon. They mine uranium, copper and gold here. Mostly gold, I was told. Population at this time, and still mushrooming, was about 2,500. Men work long hours, usually 12-hour shifts, earn top money, live in good accommodation, and need to get out of the place now and then. Like desperately!

So everything is new in Roxby Downs: shops, hotels, manicured lawns, wide footpaths. Orderly. Even the low sandhills which encircle it appeared as though they were given a regular brush-down. It's all a little unreal stuck out there in the desert.

The Dog Fence is just a short distance to the north of the town. As a matter of interest, a 16 km rabbit fence, to protect native pines, has been erected around the town. So someone there must believe it has a future.

Before leaving I chugged back a beer. The bar was filled with miners of many nationalities. I said, 'How's it goin'?' to a swarthy bloke and he shook his head and shrugged. Maybe I wasn't speaking too clearly after half-a-glass of beer? A TV set was blaring, the pool tables were in use. Only a few women were there, typical of mining camps. No, there wasn't a friendly atmosphere here. Not where a stranger was concerned, anyhow. A closed shop sort of thing. You were only made welcome if you wore a hard hat.

But that was an hour ago. Yet another hairpin bend appeared at close range. No problem at all. But no sooner had I glided around it than floodwaters were lapping to the bottom of the number plate. Maybe I should have stayed in Roxby Downs.

With both forearms resting on the steering wheel, I gazed ahead. Rather bleakly, I expect: the landscape was as flat as the surface of an anvil. About as colourful, too. The track could not be seen anywhere. I reversed. Stopped. Considered my options.

Hmmmm...maybe it would get no deeper than this? And better still, perhaps further on, the floodwaters would cut out altogether? But what if they didn't? I asked myself dubiously. What, for instance, might happen if it were to rain?

You see, rain was not a rarity around here. Not in 1989, anyhow. In March, back at Roxby Downs, staff of the Olympic Dam had played good Samaritans by rescuing and then relocating 142 snakes and lizards, which, when forced to seek higher ground because of floods, had found comparative sanctuary on a 130-metre strip of elevated road. Apparently the snakes were so chuffed about this that they took a fast vote and agreed unanimously not to bite anyone.

Sitting there, I realised that, for the first time, the elements were against me. Nothing to complain about, right? This was Australia, after all. Land of extremes. Often violent. Couldn't really count on anything. Not in outback South Australia, that was for certain. So, yes, luck had been running my way. Not even a single puncture so far. But better not push Lady Luck too much; she was known as fickle. So common sense prevailed. I turned tail. Let's face it: there are more than enough clowns on outback roads at any given time of the year without me joining the same circus.

Dark now. Sky alight with a multitude of flashing lights. The Stuart Highway went on endlessly. Coober Pedy in the morning, Opal City. Too far to reach there tonight. Besides, I wanted to sleep in the vehicle, wake at dawn. So it was about time to think about calling it a day.

Back at a petrol station, I had rung Billa Kalina. Said I wouldn't be there, sorry. A different route was explained to me, less prone to flooding. Was it under water? Possibly, was the answer. Too chancy then.

On into the night, only the odd headlights stabbing the dark. My problem was time. It was well into November already. Up north tropical rains had already started. The Wet—suicide season. Very often the tail-end of those same rains spread down here. Outback South Australia is not appealing then. Another thing, I was running to a pretty tight timetable: I was expected to turn up at certain places at specific times.

The radio was playing a John Williamson song, 'Dingo', from his album *Warragul*. I turned up the volume; loved the man's voice, the simplicity of the words.

Dingoes on Billa Kalina, too. Back in 1948, Colin Greenfield, now in his 70s and retired in Adelaide, took over the lease of the station which had been in the family since 1938. In 1948, the country still hadn't recovered from the devastating effects of the 1944–45 drought. Locals reckoned there had never been a dry spell to equal that one.

So when Colin and his wife, Eunice, arrived there, things could hardly have been worse. There was no water on the place. Windmills didn't work; everything was buggered. It needed a hard and determined man to put things right. It needed rain, too.

Rain came with the next three years. On Billa Kalina, they went into fattening cattle in a big way. Did well, too. But it was a lonely life out there for a woman, and Eunice Greenfield did not see another white woman for over three years at one stage.

With the rains came dingoes. They preyed on stock. Usual thing—follow the cattle, cut out sickly animals, the odd calf, maybe its mother. No real worries, you understand. You could live with that. In less favourable times, the dingoes tended to drift away, using well-defined routes that generations of wild dogs had followed, back up towards the central deserts. Up around Lake Eyre and beyond there, too. They vanished into sandy reaches where only Aborigines and wild game knew where the soaks were, the odd waterhole hidden in the rocks.

But some dingoes remained year round on Billa Kalina, even close to the homestead. Oftentimes you could hear them at night. Fire a shot and they'd shut up. For a while.

Pity about Billa Kalina. I had enjoyed Colin's company a few days before in Adelaide; his son, Keith, who now ran the place, was most likely like his father.

Still the highway went on. A startled-eyed 'roo appeared in the headlights, and was then gone. Another but smaller version flashed past the 'roo bar. Close; a whisker in it, maybe. Better stop. With insects committing harakiri on the slimy yellow windscreen, I started to look for a place to stop.

Two days later. Stuart Highway. North of Coober Pedy. A lovely, early morning.

Right now I was nearing the northernmost extremity of the Dog Fence. Heading out to where Highway 27—on its way to Alice Springs—went through it clean as a whistle.

With Mount Clarence station now on both sides of the highway, I swung off it and parked. A huge road train hurtled towards me from the north. Cattle country where dingoes are mostly tolerated.

I knew about road trains, all right. They were the Kings of the Road, my friend, and there were no real pretenders to the throne. In short, they owned the road. Went over king-sized 'roos like they weren't there.

With an awesome roar, the cattle truck, hauling three separate wagons, each with three levels, came through the Dog Fence. With a sudden gush of hot air, ripe with the smell of cow dung, it was perhaps travelling at 130 km per hour.

Then, approaching from the other direction, Coober Pedy, was a smart coach. A flash of faces as it went by. At high speed too. Tourists, on their way to a Town like Alice. Mostly women. Made sense. They are more inquisitive than men. Smarter as a rule, too. Probably Americans looking for the 'Aussie' experience: 'Come on down; I'll throw another shrimp on the barbie.' Even better if you drank a 'Fosters' with it.

Ten to one they were the same American women I had seen yesterday in Coober Pedy. Shopping for opals, black opals; the US greenback nicely loaded their way. Very few men with them. Maybe they had killed off most of their husbands? More realistically, they had died from overwork. No place for losers, buddy! Trouble is, the mere fact of crossing the line first very often cost a man his health, and, ultimately, his life. In the United States.

Out over the stock grid and through the Dog Fence went the coach. Unless the driver had told them, none of those tourists would have known. But maybe the driver was clued-up. Did tell them a few well-known facts. . .

'Dingo? Say, Mary Beth, isn't that the same as a coyote?'

'I guess. . .'

'Did you catch *Evil Angels*?'

'Sure.'

'Didn't you just love Meryl Streep's 'Aussie' accent? Isn't that Sam Neill a real hunk?'

But seriously, are you really aware of the significance of the Dingo Fence? And have you any thoughts on the fact that you can drive right through what is supposed to be an unbroken barrier?

No. Fair enough. It's not your problem, right? But it's been a real bone of contention over here, let me tell you that. Back in June 1980, for instance, members of the previously-mentioned Wild Dog Working Party from Western Australia visited Wertaloona station, near the Gammon Ranges National Park, west of Lake Frome. Bob Wilson owned the place. His biggest gripe was about the stock grids that penetrated the Dog Fence and allowed dingoes unrestricted access to sheep country. On main roads in particular—such as this one on the Stuart Highway north of Coober Pedy—he believed they caused enormous problems. Defeated the purpose, really. Reckon he and Howard Jensen up there on Lyndale station near Roma would have got on real well together. No prizes for guessing what the main topic of conversation was!

But I really can't see anything changing, particularly on a major highway. A gate? Too dangerous to stop the flow of traffic. So perhaps appropriate signs could be erected at such spots:

Dingoes may enter at this point. Certain restrictions apply. No killing sheep!

They run 10,000 sheep and 500 cattle on 1,446 square kilometres on Mount Clarence station. A big run by any yardstick. But for all its size, Mount Clarence is actually dwarfed by another property on the Dog Fence. This is Commonwealth Hill, well to the south-west of here, where 70,000 sheep range over 10,567 square kilometres. It is, I believe, the largest sheep station in the world.

Some 200 km of the Dog Fence protects much of the station's western side. Dingoes thrive on the far side of the fence. It is impossible to run sheep there. It has been tried.

The Wardle brothers, Peter and Bill (both married), run Mount Clarence: their father, nudging 50, took the place on in 1983. Semi-retired now, Bill farms at Burra. A dogger-cum-stationhand, Mick Dobbins, 62, worked on the run too. I caught up with them at 'smoko' time.

Ray: 'The whole place was very rundown when we came here. Shocking really. Nothin' worked. The Dog Fence was the only thing in decent shape, 'cause the bloke who owned it before us was paid to upkeep it.

'There were, maybe, five or six dogs here we knew of. Every week we'd come across sheep with the livers eaten; funnily enough, it was always on their right sides. The problem was we didn't really know if they were dingoes or blacks' dogs getting stuck into the sheep. . .'

Peter: 'About three years ago we were baiting along the northern boundary— up where you were earlier—and we got a lovely red setter. It must've been dropped on the other side of the fence and picked up a bait while walking along it.'

Ray: 'We did the patrolling early on,' he gestured at his sons, 'and then Mick here,' a flick of the head at Mick, 'took over. Been doin' it ever since.'

Mick: 'Yeah, I've got 61 miles to look after. It starts at the Boundary with Mabel Creek; that's the next place south of here. I do it every two weeks. Normally it takes a day unless the 'roos are playin' up.'

Ray: 'Which they often are.' With a rueful smile.

Mick: 'I've got 40 traps out as a rule—attach 'em to heavy tyres 'cause dogs like to piss against tyres. Male dogs, that is. So mostly I catch dogs.'

Peter: 'Mick averages one a trip.'

Mick: 'Sometimes it's alive when I get there; sometimes not. I carry a twenty-two; that's enough.'

Peter: 'In summer there's a lot of dogs on the fence. They're trying to head south to better rainfall. We have trouble too when station dogs get on heat. We had two pure-bred dingoes hanging around here only recently. Shot them both. One over near the creek.' He meant a watercourse within easy range of a high-power rifle.

A short distance south of Coober Pedy, still on the Stuart Highway, is the turn-off to William Creek, on the Oodnadatta Track. The run through from here, straight across country, so to speak, is a notoriously risky one: flooding, bushfires, and sand drifts. Only a few years ago, in searing heat, a car carrying a family broke down. The father decided to seek help; his wife and children remained with the vehicle. Help arrived for the wife and young ones a day or so later. Too late to do anything for the husband, however.

At any rate, I was truly looking forward to this leg. Well-off-the-beaten-track type of stuff. The alternative to going this way didn't really bear thinking about. Back down the Highway to Woomera, then north to Roxby Downs, then, still heading north, on to the Oodnadatta Track, to finally reach Marree.

Normally I wouldn't have even thought for one second about retracing so many of my steps. Today, however, was different. Today was when a road works sign at the turn-off to William Creek spelled it out loud and clear: Road Closed.

Disappointed, I thought closed now but for how long? I knew where the best place to find out was.

In the Police Station in Coober Pedy, an officer was wagging a stern finger at an Aboriginal youth who stared at his feet while the local law read him the riot act over some (probably slight) misdemeanour.

'Watch yourself in future, right?' were the officer's parting words.

'Right, Boss.' The youth shuffled out through the door.

Fortunately, I was greeted with a warm smile and a cheery voice to go with it. Must help enormously being white in Coober Pedy. I was told that the road was due to be opened in the morning, first thing; he'd just had the word. Apparently only a short section at the far end on Anna Creek station had still to be cleared of sand. I was asked what I was driving; I told him.

'You'll get through in that okay.'

'Sure?'

'No worries,' he replied with confidence. 'It'll take you about three hours to get through; that's not pushing it.'

'I won't be.'

'Sensible.'

I thanked him and turned to the door.

'Call me when you get there; I'll still be on duty.' He pulled a wry face. 'Late shift.' I assured him that I would. 'If you don't ring we'll start looking for you day after tomorrow. Enough water?' I bobbed my head. 'Good, that's the main thing.'

Again I started to the door.

'Oh, one more thing. If you do break down remember to—'

'Stay with my vehicle?'

'Got it in one,' he smiled easily.

I walked out into the sun, feeling good, expansively so.

With a strong sense of adventure, I put the opal capital of the world behind me. Out through scattered mines, the hard, hillock-ridden landscape pock-marked with caves and shafts. Out through the Dog Fence too. Heading in an easterly direction. To the Oodnadatta Track.

Gradually the country changed until I was back in the desert again. Red sand. Back to rabbit country, too.

In dire need of a drink, I stopped. Outside, the heat was tangible. Had to be well over 40 degrees. Not summer yet, remember. No wonder underground motels and hotels are all the rage in Coober Pedy and miners burrow like rabbits to make their homes where it is so much cooler.

Recapping my flask, I gazed with interest around me: the track was hemmed in by low sandhills, most covered with low brush and scattered heaps of yellow melons. I was told they taste sour and that wildlife, with the exception of some birds, various parrots, leave them alone. There were no other tyre marks but mine on the track.

Smoke! Away to the north, a billowing dark cloud, climbing high. That meant only one thing in this country: bushfire.

Not without some apprehension I went on. By my watch, I should've been two-thirds of the way by now. But I had lingered to take photographs, to savour the sense of isolation. Nothing to fear even if I did break down. . .or was there?

The smoke came closer, or perhaps I was driving towards the source. Worse, when I checked behind, there was smoke there too, fanning out across the track so that visibility was restricted in that direction. But at least no flames were in sight. Just this ever-darkening cloud.

On a rise I stopped. So what, I asked myself, would I do if, suddenly, and it happens like that, I was caught in the middle of a bushfire? A sickening thought. On the same level, I suppose, as being grabbed by a croc or shark. Disturbs me just thinking about that kind of exit. One thought came to me: pray. Why not? Someone up there just might be tuned in to the same wave-band.

Feeling most unadventurous, I drove on slowly. Into even denser smoke. In fact, smoke seemed to be coming, but was not, from all directions. Here, too, a belt of scrub came right to the track on both sides. A sheet of flame could leap this track in a finger-snap of time. Anything in between was a goner. Charred meat or buckled metal.

And then—suddenly—the smoke started to thin until I was at last well clear of it. My relief was profound. You can't fight a bushfire and you can't do too much of a positive nature if a huge saltwater reptile or a grey nurse shark takes a sudden fancy to you, either. Dangerous country. Australia.

William Creek. Saturday afternoon. This was the kind of place you'd be pushed to get lost in. In fact, all that could be seen was a telephone kiosk, a black dog lying in the sun, a caravan, and the William Creek Hotel. All of which might explain why this just happens to be the smallest town in the State. By way of contrast, it also happens to be encircled by Anna Creek station. Maybe 30,027 square kilometres doesn't sound overly impressive until you realise that it's nearly half the size of Tasmania. Get lost there. No worries.

In case you're wondering, I did ring the police at Coober Pedy. 'Thanks for calling,' he said, meaning it. 'You'd be surprised just how many people say they'll get in touch with us once they've reached their destinations and don't bother to. Gives us all sorts of headaches,' he went on ruefully. 'Anyway, thanks again. Enjoy the rest of your trip.' I said I would.

25

Beyond Marree

Let me put it this way. The wild dogs I know wouldn't have done it. They wouldn't go near the tent. But a half-domesticated dog would...don't you worry about that.
– Paddy Barlow, discussing Australia's most celebrated human-dingo interaction, the Chamberlain case

Out beyond the sleepy old droving town of Marree, and then heading north towards Lake Eyre National Park, the Dog Fence cuts across a dirt road near Frome Creek and the big gate naturally brings motorists to a halt.

The fact that this was the Dog Fence was adamantly clear by the now familiar 'Dog Fence' sign. The red-lettered sign stating 1080 was laid on the property was of course a regular sight, too. But what I hadn't seen before was a metal, target-like cutout of a dingo. As expected, some armed clown had punched a couple of poorly-aimed bullet holes in the dingo, on which was written 'Donna'. Apparently the dingo was a bitch. Maybe somebody didn't like Donna very much? On the sign also were comments relating to the Chamberlain case.

Perhaps it was because Peter Chamberlain (Michael's brother) is such a good friend of mine that I really hadn't wanted to comment on the ten-year-old Chamberlain case. Would have considered it in bad taste had I done so. The Chamberlain family, I believe, have been put through the mill more than enough already and even at the time of writing the Northern Territory Government is still hedging about paying out adequate compensation for years of living hell.

Yet the fact of the matter is that wherever I went along the Dingo Fence the subject almost invariably cropped up. It was as though it were a general topic of conversation you brought up with strangers, just to get their views, and, if they differed from your own, it was enough excuse to ram your opinion down their throats. Hardly anyone was negative about the issue. They were either convinced of her innocence or they were not. Simple as that. The majority, sad to say, had been brainwashed by the press years before.

As already said, I had had no intentions of even mentioning the Chamberlain case and, were it not for those ugly words on the Dog Fence sign, I would not have. Still, as I closed the heavy gate behind me and once again found myself on the outside of the Dingo Fence, I knew this much was certain. The Chamberlain case, like the dingo, will never die out in the outback and both will remain a controversial talking point.

The Mitchell family own Muloorina station. Approximately half of it is on the outside of the Dog Fence and the other half, where sheep are considerably more safe, on the inside. All up that's 4,403 square kilometres.

They run about 2,000 Hereford cattle and 10,000 sheep; the merinos naturally on the inside of the wire. It wasn't always like this. Once they carried a few cattle. Ran sheep in a big way, up to 30,000 of them. Both sides of the fence, too. Once, that is.

Now that Bill Mitchell has retired and lives elsewhere, the station is looked after by his two sons, Malcolm, 36, and Trevor, 29. But it so happened on this dull and humid Sunday that Bill and Hazel Mitchell were visiting their family.

Muloorina, Bill explained, started off as a sheep station in the late 1880s. A family called Bosworth leased it and they employed Aboriginal shepherds. But like other big holdings in dingo country they faced eventual ruin and, instead of opting for cattle, which most others did in the same predicament, they abandoned the run.

Significantly to our story, it was also in the 1880s that the Birdsville Track was opened up. This became one of the most important stock routes in the country, linking Birdsville in south-west Queensland with Marree, a vital link on the Port Augusta/Ooodnadatta railway line.

But in times of drought the 'track' became impossible to use. Thousands of cattle perished. Men died. So the Government established a series of artesian bores, using donkeys and camels as a means of transporting building materials and supplies. Muloorina was one of a number of depots where, when not in use, the animals were kept.

And so with the 517 km route well watered, huge mobs of cattle, up to 10,000 strong, were driven down the Birdsville Track no matter how drought-stricken the land was. But in time the Government ceased to use Muloorina and the camels and donkeys, which had been kept there, were left to fend for themselves. No problem. The harsh, arid country presented few worries for such hardy and adaptable creatures as they.

In 1933 Elliot Price acquired the lease to Muloorina. Both camels and donkeys had multiplied to incredible numbers, leaving little choice but to shoot them. Ambitiously Elliot Price ran sheep.

It was in 1949 that Hazel Price, Elliot's daughter, while in Adelaide on holiday met a young man called Bill Mitchell. Bill's father was a businessman and what his 19-year-old son knew about the outback could have been written on the back of a postage stamp. Nevertheless, Bill fell in love with the girl from the bush and she with him.

And being in love, well, there wasn't anything he couldn't tackle. No river too wide to swim. No hill too high to climb. No horse too tough to ride. Speaking of riding horses, this is what he did when he went to work on Muloorina as a stationhand. If Bill didn't know a thing about dingoes at this stage, then his formal education started very quickly.

Dingoes were a fact of life on Muloorina. You had them for breakfast, lunch, and supper. And sometimes for quick snacks between meals. Dingoes! Bloody dingoes! On average the station lost 5,000 adult sheep to dingoes, and almost as many lambs. A year.

At any rate, Bill and Hazel were married. A classic case, Bill said with a rather sly sideways glance at his wife, of marrying the boss's daughter. But to go by the fond smile that flashed across Hazel's face when he uttered those words, then I doubt very much if she had ever regretted taking the city boy home with her.

Later, Bill would learn a great deal about dingoes from Tom Churches, a dogger there for 18 years. 'Tom was born on Lake Harry which was a part of the station,' Bill recalled. 'The place is a ruin now. He'd done nothin' but chase dogs all his life. He could track a dog for up to 20 miles. Never gave up. Always got it in the end. He was unreal.' Bill's admiration for the dogger was obvious.

Until 1979 there were three families living at Muloorina: Bill and Hazel (and their two sons), her folks, and Hazel's married sister. Enough manpower— but only just—to cope with dingoes.

But in that year a lot changed. Tom Churches was no longer there, Hazel's folks moved away, as did her married sister. To Bill's dismay, he was unable to find suitably experienced men. Those who wanted to toil the land, that is. And so in 1979 sheep were no longer run outside the Dog Fence on Muloorina.

'It had to happen in the end,' Bill admitted, 'and this only speeded up the process, I guess. So they beat us in the end.' He smiled broadly. 'But we gave the bastards a real good fight. Must've killed thousands.'

Sheep killing did not cease on Muloorina of course. Frequently dingoes got through the wire. But they were not always to blame for sheep killing. 'This particular dog was working out near Clayton Dam,' Bill said. 'We had a lot of wethers there. Over a couple of nights it killed 40 odd. So we put out a baited trap and got it a couple of days later. Turned out to be one of those black and white sheep dogs...'

'Border Collie?' I offered.

'Yeah, one of them.'

A vivid mental picture of Murray Ball's lovable creation in *Footrot Flats* flashed to my mind. But 'the dog' would never do that!

'That's not unusual,' Bill continued. 'Probably belonged to a black one time. Hmmmm...which way did you come?' I told him. 'Then you must've seen dogs hanging around blacks in town then?' I confirmed I had. 'Mangy lot as a rule. Most of them are half-wild. Always trouble with blacks' dogs around Coober Pedy.' Bill frowned heavily; the subject was a delicate one best not pursued further.

Muloorina, I was informed, receives around $11,000 a year from the Dog Fence Board to help cover maintenance of the fence. Bill considers they spend about twice that much over the year. Some of this money, he said, paid the wages of Eric Oldfield who patrolled the fence regularly. Sunday, Bill added, was a good day to catch him at home.

For a few minutes it was silent in the pleasant living room. I sipped at my second cup of tea. Presently I brought to their attention what had been written on the Dog Fence sign. Apparently it hadn't been there when they came in. It would be removed forthwith. Bill and Hazel held different views on the Chamberlain case.

Ready to leave now, Bill walked out with me to my vehicle and, without prompting, made a sweeping gesture. 'The dingo'll always be here. There's more of them now than there ever was. But if I were in cattle today, I don't think I'd be running around shooting dogs, either. I'd be like the rest of them. He's a part of the place, but,' and he shrugged philosophically, 'we've got to survive.' Survival. Name of the game for man or beast.

I found 56-year-old Eric Oldfield tinkering happily under the raised bonnet of an ancient, beat-up Land Rover. He wiped oil-slicked hands on a rag, then thumbed back a brown hat, lit a smoke, and settled down for a yarn. Nice sort, Eric.

On his three-day run, Eric Oldfield looked after the Dog Fence on two other stations apart from Muloorina—Mundownda and Callanna. He was paid $496 a trip, with each station contributing a third. He undertook it twice a month to comply with regulations. As he said, 'Not bad pocket money.'

And mere pocket money was an apt summing up. For Eric owns Marree sheep station, which surrounds the town. I was curious enough to ask him what size it was and he said 310 square kilometres.

'Yeah,' I said as though well-informed, 'they're all big out here.'

'That's not big,' Eric corrected me with a not unkindly smile.

'It's not?'

'Usual place out here is, oh, around 5,180 square kilometres. Mine's a dairy farm in comparison with that,' he added in a deprecatory manner.

Not a New Zealand dairy farm, I thought.

'Where you heading to from here?' No, he wasn't trying to get rid of me.

'Down the line. Mount Lyndhurst station and then'—I groped for the name and then it came—'Moolawatana.'

He nodded and cigarette ash dropped on his shirtfront. 'You'll see some good country past Mount Lyndhurst. The Flinders Ranges are worth seeing. Dogs in there too.' So I had heard. Apparently they believed in keeping a low profile.

'Decent road?'

'It is to Lyndhurst. Then you get on the start of the Strzelecki Track, you're off the bitumen then. You'll turn off—' I had produced my RAA map of the Northern Areas of South Australia '—here.' The spot was indicated with a blunt-nailed forefinger. 'You'll be okay if it doesn't rain.' He glanced upwards. 'Not much chance of that, though. Still, you never know out here.' He paused, and, dropping the butt of his smoke, crushed it out under a grinding boot heel. 'The feller than runs Moolawatana...'

'Sheehan.'

'Yeah, that's him. He's had heaps of trouble with dogs. Been in the paper a fair bit. His place backs against real dog country.'

Late afternoon: downtown Marree. The main street was deserted. No one was in the 1950s-style cafe where I had just purchased a soft drink. A couple of Aboriginal kids were playing over at the deserted railway station and I wandered over there for a look. They were all smiles and white teeth. I wondered what their father did for a living or whether he like so many of his unlucky race was on unemployment benefits and one of them said that he didn't live at home any more. They raced off then and, I suppose, were happy enough. Worse places to grow up than Marree.

I looked at the overgrown railway lines and at a couple of boarded-up carriages. No one rides the rail to Marree any more, either.

But despite it all the town continued to survive. Just. Not quite a ghost town, say. And yet on some cold winter's night, when chill desert winds rattle corrugated iron sheeting and ill-fitting windows, then you just might, providing you listen carefully enough, hear the pistol-like crack of a 10-foot stockwhip, the growing bellowing of cattle, and, soon after, the creak of saddle leather and the raised voices of dry-throated horsemen as they reach the cattle yards signalling the end of their long droving trip down the Birdsville Track.

26

Movin' On

Lots of dingoes have never seen the other side of the fence. Never even seen it. Wouldn't know what it was if you showed it to them.
– Neville Barnes of Mount Lyndhurst station, currently losing around 2,000 sheep each year to dingoes

Compared with William Creek, say, Lyndhurst comes as a shock to the system. There are more than two buildings here. It is in fact described in guide books as a 'small township'. By that, you must not expect too much. As Tina Turner sings, what you see is what you get. Small-town Australia. No pretensions.

So there's a hotel. The Lyndhurst Hotel, naturally. There is a big open area of cleared ground in front of it and on the other side of the road. A whole fleet of road trains could park there overnight and maybe they do at times. It's also a handy spot for dogs to fornicate. No, they were not dingoes. They are more discreet. Nor were they crossbreeds. Just a couple of enthusiastic mutts.

What else to Lyndhurst? A store, scattered homes. What is important about the place, however, is that it is the gateway to the Strzelecki Track.

With thoughts of daring cattle duffers (rustlers to those reared on pulp westerns), I climbed stiffly out of my transport and did what almost every other thirsty traveller does in this parched land of outback South Australia.

A couple of tough-looking stationhands were at the bar. They looked as if they'd been on a week's muster and hadn't seen running water. That was their battered ute outside. In the open back, a couple of hard-case dogs were guarding their possessions. They were also all agog, panting, as they watched what two townies got up to on a Sunday evening in Lyndhurst.

In the bar: 'G'day,' one of them greeted me. He was dark-haired. The voice was a dead-ringer for Bryan Brown's in *A Town like Alice*.

'How'd you be?' The other bloke was shorter, fairer. His voice was high-pitched like a girl's. Not in keeping with his rough-hewn features which might have been blasted out of granite.

The bartender seemed okay too as he asked what would I have and I replied 'Fosters'. Definitely not plastic-coated Roxby Downs.

The dark-haired one dug into the front pocket of his jeans and shoved change into a jukebox. Country and Western blared out. Fair enough. Lyndhurst was the right setting. Kenny Rodgers and Dolly Parton territory. Y'all come again, hear? Around here they would mean it. Most places they're just being polite.

But after a few words were exchanged, the stationmen returned to their private world. No matter; I'd be made welcome. My turn to feed the music box. Fleetwood Mac. Big Love. Maybe that was a mistake the way I'd been feeling about a certain lady recently.

At which time another traveller turned up. Red-faced. Sweating. In his mid-60s, I picked.

'How's it goin'?' I asked with a smile. He smiled back.

'Better for this, mate!' He flicked a fingernail against the side of the glass he'd just lowered. It made a dull thud. Cheap glass, obviously.

Turned out he was from Adelaide. Heading home. Easy run from here. He'd been cruising around for a couple of weeks on his own. Wife? Naw, she didn't want to come. Hated the outback. Too many flies. Too much dust. She'd much rather stay home and watch TV. Watched it all the time. The Morning Show on Channel Nine.

Brian Something-or-other. Didn't matter a bit, anyway, what his bloody name was. He stared moodily into his now empty glass, said the family cat got more attention than he did. Too late now to do anything about it. Browned off, all right. Poor bastard.

I bought him a beer. Asked the magic word: Dingoes!

My word, yes! He'd been seeing them almost every day. Even coming down the track from Innamincka today. Five, maybe six of them. Mostly they stood on the side of the track and watched him go by. Various colours too. Not all brown like you'd expect. But Moomba was the place to see them. They had a habit of gathering around the local tip. Got so bad they had to be thinned out at times; that was what he had heard, anyway.

I sipped on my second bottle. Drink out of a bottle at Lyndhurst. Like the hard-looking stationhands.

'Fancy another?' I shook my head, no, and thanked him all the same. Left him to his thoughts. Had a good idea he didn't want to go home. Hell of a thing no matter your age.

Dark now. I angled across to the Subaru. Since Mount Lyndhurst was only 37 km from town and 'right on the Track' according to Neville Barnes, I only drove a short way, perhaps half the trip, before stopping a short distance off the hard-packed earth road.

Bit cooler now. I dressed accordingly and set about building a fire. Later, having eaten, I sat in the glow of the flames and, as I had on Cooper Creek, thought about drovers and cattle duffers like, for instance, Harry Redford who in 1870 had with five similar-minded stockmen daringly lifted 1,000 prime bullocks off Bowen Downs station near the present town of Longreach.

Near Windorah the cattle had rushed and one of the stockmen was trampled to death. Two men had pulled out then, taking that as a bad omen. But Redford and the other two continued and eventually sold their stolen cattle in South Australia, thus opening up the Strzelecki Track. Redford's character would serve as the basis for Captain Starlight in Rolf Boldrewood's stirring novel *Robbery Under Arms*.

After Redford had travelled this route, the track was used for around a decade before drovers turned to a less dicey way of taking their cattle to Adelaide. This was via Cooper Creek, staying with it and its frequent waterholes until it joined the Birdsville Track north of Marree.

The billy was boiling on the Strzelecki Track. Last brew of the day. Stars twinkled. A 'one-dog' night coming up.

And then as I knelt to pour myself a drink into an enamel mug, a dingo howled distantly. Just once. I listened intently, head raised. Again it called out into the night. I don't really know why I was surprised. Mount Lyndhurst was on both sides of the road and I already knew how much trouble they had with dingoes. A fitting end, I thought, to an eventful day.

Mount Lyndhurst station. Thirty thousand sheep and a thousand head of cattle (they'd really miss a thousand head of cattle there) on some 33,670 square kilometres of mostly hard country.

Neville Barnes, 35, is the manager; the place is owned by an uncle. Neville is married to Pam. They have an 11-year-old son, Jason. Four stationhands work here. Firearms are carried most times. You shoot first and ask questions later when you spot a dog. The only good dingo here is a dead 'un.

The Dog Fence, to the north, is about 50 km away. It's patrolled every ten days. Neville and his men bait along it too. No let up on the dingo here. But by and large they had had a good year so far. Ten thousand lambs. In recent times they were losing half that number to dingoes.

That prompted a logical question as to whether or not the Dog Fence was doing its job. 'Most of the bastards haven't even seen the bloody fence, mate!'

Of great interest to me on Mount Lyndhurst was the fact that some of the original homestead was still standing. Neville reckoned it was around 120 years old. I pondered on that as I drove on. Providing that was right, and there was no good reason for it not to be, that would date it to 1869. So that being the case it would have been standing when in 1870, out of the vastness of the dreaded Strzelecki Desert, emerged three saddle-weary but triumphant cattle duffers, one of whom was to ride off into folklore.

Time to leave the track. How I would have loved to have had the time to press on. Up to Moomba. Innamincka. All the way to Cordillo Downs, a station of 10,360 square kilometres. They ran sheep there in the old days. Up to 120,000 of them. The shearing shed had 100 stands.

But they couldn't beat the dingo on Cordillo Downs. No way. So cattle eventually replaced sheep and later Sid Kidman stamped his name on the place. Today I am told it's still possible to see the remains of a wool-scouring plant— dating from 1885—near the station waterhole.

From this point, Moolawatana was 90 kilometres. A slow trip, I had been told. True enough. But it also proved a rewarding one. Taking my time, it took four hours. Yes, lovely country these northern Flinders Ranges on a very warm spring day: wildflowers, yellows and blues, covered rocky slopes, red river gums followed the path of watercourses.

And birds. Pink-chested galahs and white cockatoos and little corellas flocking to waterholes. A curious emu coming to say 'hello' while I boiled the billy. Eagles hunting. Kestrels not quite so common.

And always, away to the south, the central Flinders Ranges rising in ragged formation. Incidentally, they filmed *Robbery Under Arms* there in the mid-1950s. Peter Finch as Captain Starlight. A British production, Pinewood Studios, I think. Peter Finch all decked out in black; a sort of British western that just happened to be shot on location in Australia. More recently, a TV version, locally made, had Sam Neill playing the same part. Still haven't done the story real justice.

And I'd seen a dingo too. Didn't do a thing for me. Not when it was hanging in a tree on the side of the narrow sandy track on Mount Freeling Station. There, too, they believe that the only good dingo is a dead one.

Top Marree, main street, Saturday
afternoon

Above Eric Oldfield's Marree
station encircles the town

Left The trains don't run
any more

Above Moolawatana south of the Strzelecki Track is frontline country

Left It is constant war between graziers and dingoes

Below Beware camels, wombats and kangaroos — near Nullarbor Roadhouse, far western South Australia

27

Frontline Country

They're a magnificent-looking animal, they really are... Just as long as they stay north of the Dog Fence!
– Audrey Sheehan, Moolawatana station, northern Flinders Ranges, South Australia

As though deliberately positioned there to serve as a grim warning to other dingoes with untold mayhem on their mind, the two carcasses hung head down in macabre fashion on either side of the dirt track.

Moolawatana station. Frontline country.

'Barry got them about six weeks ago,' Mike Sheehan said matter-of-factly. He stopped the Subaru four-wheel-drive ute. 'Bastards were getting stuck into a sheep.' Barry's surname was Harder, the sole full-time help on the station's 1,113 square kilometres of sun-blasted terrain 54 km from the Strzelecki Track.

Dingoes have always been a major problem on Moolawatana. Mike is responsible for 115 km of the Dog Fence. It is considered 'rough country' in the main.

Beyond the fence is Frome Downs. According to Mike, the dogs were presently in 'plague proportions' on this 4,403 square kilometre cattle run and it wasn't unusual to see packs ten-to-fifteen strong padding along the Dog Fence.

(Later, I would call in at Frome Downs and talk with Bryan Nash, who worked there. He said that, yes, the dogs were thick all right. They were playing havoc with calves—ripping them badly about both neck and shoulders and God only knew what they were doing out in the sandhills country they hadn't been to lately!)

In November 1989, Mike Sheehan was 49 years old, a husky, bearded, no-nonsense type who, despite it all, still had the ability to see a certain grim humour about the dramatic impact dingoes have had on his life. Now as we pressed on to check out yet another windmill, he recalled how he had first come out there in 1954.

'Dad bought the place as an investment,' Mike said, his big, work-hardened hands resting lightly on the steering wheel, 'but he never lived here. Guess he liked the farm better [on the Eyre Peninsula]. Anyway, a string of managers came and went until I took on the place in '63. Oh, I didn't tell you that I worked here after leaving school.

'You wouldn't believe how many dogs there were on the place then. We even had one come on the veranda one time. Then they got stuck into a mob of sheep back of the woolshed—killed about 18, I think. Dingoes!' He was driving fast now, across country. The idea being that at speed you went over the endless corrugations instead of in and out of them with the expected jarring effect. Since the ride was mostly smooth, there had to be some sense to it.

'You know,' Mike said, 'I had bloody nightmares about dogs!'

On a bare, stony expanse of ground—big enough for your everyday farm—a windmill groaned as though its metal parts hadn't been oiled in years. It was hot and still. A pair of glossy-winged crows, like messengers of evil tidings, called harshly as they wheeled above. They alighted with uplifted wings a good distance away. Closer, a small percentage of the station's 8,000 sheep eyed us warily. Most had lambs at foot.

After making some adjustments to a pump, Mike, rubbing his hands on the ground, the better to remove oil, said she was okay now and started to the ute. 'Things are pretty good here these days,' he admitted. 'There aren't many dogs on the place—three at the most, we think. We've killed 18 so far this year; that's much less than in previous years.' He switched on the ignition key. The crows lifted lazily into the washed-out blue sky as Mike gunned away.

Most of the 18 dingoes Mike had mentioned were, he believed, killed soon after they had found a way through the fence. Stock losses had thereafter been kept to a minimum. Certainly he wasn't over-concerned about it.

'That's the way to do it. You get them real quick, before they get a taste for killing. If you leave them alone, well, they get the hang of the country. Know where to hide. Proper bastard to get onto them then. It might take a year to catch a particularly smart dog. It could kill heaps in that time, hundreds.'

Swinging the steering wheel hard, Mike linked up with a track, all sand, some of it loose. A sudden hairpin bend loomed up, the ute started to drift. With expertise—no braking of course—Mike corrected the sideways slewing motion.

Moments later, he gestured expansively. 'In this type of open country they're not too hard to run down on a trailbike.' Mike's machine was a gutsy Yamaha 200 cc, his weapon a Ruger .22 magnum handgun, which he carried holstered on his belt. Nice piece. Right now, there was a 'scoped Colt semi-automatic rifle in the cabin. Calibre .223, like they used in 'Nam. It was a dull, no-frills killing machine. Handgun and rifle added up to a real mean twosome. With his big hat and grey-streaked beard, Mike would have looked right at home in a sequel to *The Wild Bunch*—especially if toting all that hardwear.

Flocks of little corellas had gathered for an early evening drink when we reached the last tank for the day. A few rabbits scuttled off to hide. A hawk hung suspended on ever-present air currents high above the ground. In the distance, a few 'roos made off in no hurry. Nothing to fix here, either.

In due course we arrived back at the homestead. A big, roomy dwelling with wide verandas. Maybe too big for Mike and his wife now that their two children, Gerard and Jane, were at school in Adelaide.

'Beer'd go down well,' Mike said, ushering me into the kitchen, where Audrey was preparing a meal. Mike was in good humour as we sat down. Why not? Things were ticking along very nicely on Moolawatana these days. Which wasn't always the case. Take the early 1970s, for instance.

Mike and Audrey were newly married then. Mike: 'Dad died soon after we got married. That was a big enough blow on its own without the Federal and State Governments slapping death duties on us to the tune of'—it still rankled badly—'around $160,000! On top of that, there was an additional 40 grand to find for accountants' and solicitors' fees and various other,' the next word came out like a curse, 'parasites!' He did not elaborate precisely on who these 'freeloaders' were. Not good news, obviously.

After a deep glug of beer Mike continued: 'That was far from the end of it, though. Wool prices were down. Like rock-bloody-bottom down!' he snorted. 'Hell, you couldn't have given away a sheep if you'd wanted to! On top of that we were in the grip of a bad drought. And the final straw was,' he went on heavily, 'that the dogs were damn near eating us out of our home.' He shook his head reflectively, his manner suggesting that even after all these years he still found it difficult to comprehend that all this had happened in the space of such a short time.

Audrey, too, was looking pensive; the years slipping back too, the bad memories resurfacing. 'I remember one shearing time in particular,' she said. 'This was the period when we had the death duties to contend with. Mike,' she nodded at her husband, who appeared for the moment in quite another world, 'was so worried— '

'Worried!' he roared like an enraged bull. 'I'll say we were worried. We didn't have the money to pay them.' He stared almost moodily into his near empty glass. Some wounds never quite heal over.

'Like Mike said,' Audrey went on, unperturbed by her husband's interruption, 'the dogs were bad. They were killing sheep every day and there seemed no way of stopping them. Mike was so upset by it all he couldn't sleep properly for weeks. I remember him coming in here one day,' she made a sweeping gesture, 'and pacing up and down and round and around the table, saying that the dogs were going to be "the ruination of us".'

There was a heavy silence following her words and perhaps old ghosts, not disturbed for quite some time, rattled around in dark cupboards.

The way Mike Sheehan tells it, 1983 was far from a vintage year on Moolawatana, either. Extensive floodwaters undermined and then flattened large stretches of the Dog Fence. News of this was no doubt greeted with great joy by a section of the wild dog fraternity living on Frome Downs. And they too flooded unchecked onto Moolawatana. Large-scale killing began almost at once. Mike estimated that 1,000 pregnant adult ewes were killed. Cost? Around $40,000. This of course was not taking into account wool losses at shearing time, nor, for that matter, unborn lambs.

In due course the fence was repaired. Dingoes were either eliminated or shifted elsewhere. The Flinders Ranges were a likely choice. A dingo could hide itself for ever in those rocky strongholds should it want to.

The wine was rather flat on Moolawatana in 1987, too. This time 13 sections of the fence were put out of action by floodwaters. Again dingoes seized the opportunity and bloody forays were commonplace. Losses were again around 1,000 adult sheep. As for lambs?

Mike: 'In one paddock you might have, say, ten per cent lambs when you checked it out, in another it might be as high as ninety per cent. Now it doesn't take much to fathom out what's been going on with dogs in the ten per cent paddock does it? Course not. The dogs've been shaking the lambs to pieces like rats.'

On his second beer now, Mike was more expansive: 'I'm sure you've already been told that it's just fun and games to them. They rarely kill a sheep for a feed—much prefer a 'roo or rabbit for that. No, they just like to round up a mob of sheep and play silly buggers with them. The more panicky they become the better they seem to like it. If they push sheep too hard, there's always one or two that'll knock up and can't go any further and they'll lie down.' Mike waved an expressive hand in the air. 'Dogs'll invariably ignore them—no fun, you see. But should a big, strong wether or ram break away they'll be after it like a shot from a gun and they'll tear it apart, seen it happen.

'They're tremendously powerful in their jaws—one good grab at a sheep's flanks and the whole side could come away. Guts everywhere! Oh, they might eat a bit of liver but,' he lifted his shoulders eloquently, 'that's about it. That's how wild dogs in Africa hunt, they also disembowel their prey.'

Mike was firing on all cylinders now. A pet subject too. 'You get sheepmen in the south-west saying that dogs'll never get down there. Course they don't! We kill the bastards before they get a chance to!' There was no hint of a bushman's drawl now. Rather, he was biting off the ends of the words. Spitting them like well-aimed bullets. Blat! Blat! Blat!

'You hear talk from time to time that a dog wouldn't swim the Murray River if it got down there. That's bloody rubbish! Course they would if they wanted to; a bitch on heat on the other side and there'd be no stopping them. Hell, they can swim the Cooper all right, no worries. Yeah, they'd soon be down there if, say, all of us up here on the frontline turned to cattle overnight and said to hell with the dogs. They'd be there in good numbers inside two years.' He aimed a finger at my chest as if I ran a sheep property beyond the rateable area. 'Listen, I reckon every sheepman and every goat owner for that matter should pay towards the upkeep of the fence!' Mike Sheehan picked up an empty bottle of beer, and to add further impact to his words, struck the bottom quite hard on the table.

Not one of the other ratepayers who do contribute towards the maintenance of South Australia's Dog Fence would, I feel certain, disagree with those heartfelt sentiments.

Since my visit to South Australia in 1989, the state's wool and meat industry have agreed on some changes to the rating system in regard to the Dog Fence. In July 1990, some 4,000 landowners with holdings larger than 10 square kilometres received their financial statements for dog fence rates. The following now criteria applied:

A minimum of $45 to apply to holdings between 10 and 70 square kilometres.

Those of more than 70 square kilometres to pay at 65c per square kilometre and areas of all holdings to be calculated on a cumulative basis.

In clarifying this, Bill Edwards, in his capacity as Chairman of the Dog Fence Board, explained: 'This means that if a landholder has for example two properties, both over 40 square km, they will be levied at the 65c rate.

'Conversely, a person with three holdings of, say, 10 square km each will pay $45 a year.'

In addition to the changes in the rating system, on 30 September 1990 the $2 bounty on dingo scalps was dropped. Money set aside for such purposes would in future be used on research into more effective ways of controlling dingoes.

Selected Reading

Books

Basedow, H. *The Australian Aboriginal* F.W. Preece, Adelaide, 1925.

Breckwoldt, R.A. *A Very Elegant Animal The Dingo* Angus & Robertson, Sydney, 1988.

Bueler, L. *Wild Dogs of the World* Constable, London, 1924.

Carter, J. *In the Tracks of the Cattle* Angus & Robertson, Sydney, 1968.

Carter, J. and M. *The Complete Guide to Central Australia* Hodder & Stoughton, Sydney, 1989.

Cole, T. *Hell West And Crooked* Collins, Sydney, 1989.

The Complete Book of Australian Mammals The National Photographic Index of Australian Wildlife, Angus & Robertson, Sydney, 1983.

Dampier, W. *A Voyage to New Holland, in the year 1699* London (undated).

Davey, K. *Australian Lizards* Landsdowne Press, Melbourne, 1970.

Elkin, A.P. *Australian Aborigines: How to Understand Them* Angus & Robertson, Sydney, 1938.

Ewer, R.F. *The Carnivores* Weidenfeld & Nicholson, London, 1973.

Flood, J. *Archaeology of the Dreamtime* Collins, Sydney and London, 1983.

Gerritsen, J. *Tibooburra Corner Country* Tibooburra Press, Gympie, Queensland, 1981.

Hatfield, W. *Sheepmates* (14th edition) Angus & Robertson, 1946.

Holliday, I., and Hill, R. *A Field Guide to Australian Trees* Rigby, Adelaide, 1969.

Hudson, L. *Dingoes Don't Bark* Rigby, Adelaide, 1974.

Ingleton, G.C. *True Patriots All* Angus & Robertson, Sydney, 1952.

Moore, D.R. *Islanders and Aborigines at Cape York* Australian Institute of Aboriginal Studies, Canberra, 1978.

Mountford, C.P. *Nomads of the Australian Desert* Rigby, Adelaide, 1972.

Percival, D., and Westney, C. *Fence People* Hutchinson, Australia, 1989.

Riddle, M. *The Wild Dogs in Life and Legend* Howell Book House Inc., New York, 1979.

Slater, P. *A Field Guide to Australian Birds* (Vol. 1, 1970; Vol. 2, 1974) Rigby, Adelaide.

The Living World of Animals Reader's Digest Association, London, 1970.

The World's Wild Place: The Australian Outback Time-Life International (Nederlands), 1976.

Tindale, N.B. *Aboriginal Tribes of Australia* University of California Press, 1974.

Willey, K. *The Drovers* Macmillan Company of Australia, 1982.

Annual Reports, Articles, Papers

'Absentee landlords blamed for remaining dog problem' *Queensland Country Life* 7 July 1988.

'Australia: Along the Dingo Fence' *Time* 13 September 1988.

'Baits and barriers still not enough' *Queensland Country Life* 7 July 1988.

Barrier Fence Administrators Conference, Bulloo Shire Chambers, Thargomindah, Queensland, 26/27 August 1987.

Barlow, A.S. Problems associated with the operations of the New South Wales Border Fence. Paper presented at Thargomindah, 26/27 August 1987.

Broken Hill Tourist Information Guide (undated).

Carter, J. 'The longest fence in the world' *People* 26 April 1961.

Charnley, W. 'The dingo' *Walkabout* 1 June 1946.

Condon, R.W. The nature of the dingo problem in the Western Division of New South Wales. Paper presented at Thargomindah, 26/27 August 1987.

'Dingo baits most humane' *Western Star* 17 July 1987.

Dog Fence Act: 1946–1986.

'Dog fence breached: dingo threat spreads' *Stock Journal* 13 November 1980.

Dog Fence Administrators Conference, Arkaroola, South Australia, 1983.

'Dingoes force sheepman to reconsider his options' *Queensland Country Life* 22 July 1987.

'Dingoes rise to thwart the profits of sheepmen' *Queensland Country Life* 2 July 1987.

Donohue, J.T. *A Proposal for the Future Maintenance of the Dingo Barrier Fence in Southern Queensland* The Stock Routes and Rural Lands Protection Board, Brisbane, 1981.

Ecological Effects of 1080—an Information Bulletin Queensland Rural Lands Protection Board (undated).

Edwards, B. The South Australian Dog Fence background—operation—effectiveness. Paper presented at Thargomindah, 26/27 August 1987.

Everett, R.A. *The South Australian Dog Fence Scene* South Australian Dog Fence Board, November, 1983.

Flinders Ranges and Outback South Australia—Visitor's Guide, 1990. South Australia Regional Tourist Association.

'Foiling the rabbits, protecting the pines' The *Advertiser* 10 November 1989.

Grant, D.I. The Dingo Barrier Fence—Queensland. Paper presented at Arkaroola, South Australia, 1983.

Hogstrom, A.W. *The Vermin Barrier Fence System in Western Australia* Agriculture Protection Board of Western Australia (undated).

'In Australia: Along the Dingo Fence' *Time* 12 September 1988.

James, T.E. The Significance of the Dog Fence to South Australian pastoralists and the development of the Dog Fence since its inception. A student project towards Graduate Diploma in Agriculture, Roseworthy Agriculture College, South Australia, 1987.

Jenkins, D. 'Graziers say fence failure' *Queensland Country Life* 2 April 1987.

John, B. Wombat damage, electric fence—the answer. Paper presented at Arkaroola, South Australia, 1983.

'Keeping out the killer dingoes' The *News* 1 September 1987.

Lock, B.A. Electric fencing. An alternative dog control system. Paper presented at Thargomindah, 26/27 August 1987.

Long, J.L. *Introduced Birds and Mammals in Western Australia* Agriculture Protection Board of Western Australia, 1972.

Macintosh, N.W.G. 'The Origin of the Dingo' in Fox, M.M. (editor) *The Wild Canids*. Van Nostrand Reinhold, New York, 1975.

Macintosh, N.W.G. 'A 3000 Year Old Dingo from Shelter 6'. Proceedings Royal Society of Victoria, 1977.

Manufactured 1080 Dingo/Wild Dog Baits—Information Bulletin Queensland Rural Lands Protection Board.

Merrell, P.W. Dingo control inside the Barrier Fence. Paper presented at Thargomindah, Queensland, 26/27 August 1987.

'New dog control group to meet' The *Western Star* 24 July 1987.

Oliver, A.J. *Dingo Research* Agriculture Protection Board of Western Australia, April 1980.

'Patching holes in the dingo wrangle' *Stock Journal* 5 January 1989.

Pearson, D.A. Wild dog control in the Western Division of New South Wales. Paper presented at Thargomindah, Queensland, 26/27 August 1987.

Pearson, E. Fences and wild dog control in Western Australia. Paper presented at Thargomindah, Queensland, 26/27 August 1987.

Report of the Wild Dog Barrier Fence Working Party Agriculture Protection Board of Western Australia, 1980.

Reschke, W. 'Wild dogs and station men fight for supremacy' The *Sunday Mail* 21 June 1969.

Roma & Injune—Brochure Queensland Government Tourist Bureau (undated).

Roy, A. '3000 km fence can't keep dingoes out' The *Weekend Australian* September 1985.

Rural Lands Protection Board *Annual Reports: 1958–1989*.

'South Australian dingo bounty to be scrapped' The *Advertiser* 4 July 1990.

Stanley, J. Queensland and dingo barrier fence: present-day maintenance. Paper presented at Thargomindah, 26/27 August 1987.

Sturt National Park—Information Brochure National Parks & Wildlife Service (undated).

The History of Barrier Fences in Queensland—Information Bulletin Queensland Rural Lands Protection Board, 1986.

'The dingo' (extract from supplement in Rural Edition of the *Advertiser)* 1 August 1990.

'The rabbit killer who earns $264 a night' The *Daily Mirror* 15 December 1989.

Wild Dog Destruction Board (Broken Hill) *Annual Reports: 1974–1987*.

'2 million roos in kill quota' The *Australian* 29 August 1989.

Index

People

Places